9-19-14

D0060124

CAN AMERICAN CAPITALISM SURVIVE?

CAN AMERICAN CAPITALISM SURVIVE?

WHY GREED IS NOT GOOD, OPPORTUNITY IS NOT EQUAL, AND FAIRNESS WON'T MAKE US POOR

Steven Pearlstein

St. Martin's Press
New York

CAN AMERICAN CAPITALISM SURVIVE? Copyright © 2018 by Steven Pearlstein. All rights reserved. Printed in the United States of America. For information, address St. Martin's Press, 175 Fifth Avenue, New York, N.Y. 10010.

www.stmartins.com

Book design by Meryl Sussman Levavi

Portions of this book first appeared in columns and articles I have written for the *Washington Post*. That includes some of the discussion of "maximizing shareholder value" in chapter 1, which I later expanded for the Brookings Institution ("Social Capital, Corporate Purpose and the Revival of American Capitalism"). Thanks to the *Post* and to Brookings for allowing me to reuse that material.

Library of Congress Cataloging-in-Publication Data

Names: Pearlstein, Steven, author.
Title: Can American capitalism survive? : why greed is not good, opportunity is not equal, and fairness won't make us poor / Steven Pearlstein.
Description: First Edition. | New York : St. Martin's Press, [2018]
Identifiers: LCCN 2018026432| ISBN 9781250185983 (hardcover) | ISBN 9781250185990 (ebook)
Subjects: LCSH: Capitalism—United States—History— 21st century. | United States—Social policy—21st century. | Equality—United States—History—21st century.
Classification: LCC HB501 .P3823 2018 | DDC 330.973—dc23
LC record available at https://lccn.loc.gov/2018026432

Our books may be purchased in bulk for promotional, educational, or business use. Please contact your local bookseller or the Macmillan Corporate and Premium Sales Department at 1-800-221-7945, extension 5442, or by email at MacmillanSpecialMarkets@macmillan.com.

First Edition: September 2018

1 3 5 7 9 10 8 6 4 2

For Wendy
Who Made Everything Possible

Contents

CAN AMERICAN
CAPITALISM
SURVIVE?

Introduction

It was only 25 years ago that the world was celebrating the triumph of American capitalism. After a long cold war, communism had been vanquished and discredited, with China, Russia and Eastern Europe seemingly rushing to embrace the market system. America had widened its economic lead over European-style socialism while the once-unstoppable export machine, Japan Inc., had finally hit a wall. Developing countries such as India, Brazil and Russia were moving to embrace the "Washington consensus" of privatization, deregulation and free trade. Around the world, this embrace of market capitalism would lift more than a billion people from poverty.

In the years since, however, confidence in the superiority of the American system has badly eroded. A global financial crisis that started in Asia and spread to Russia and Latin America shattered the Washington consensus. Americans have lived through the bursting of two financial bubbles, struggled through two serious recessions and toiled through several decades in which almost all of the benefits of economic growth have been captured by the richest 10 percent of households. A series of accounting and financial scandals, a massive government bailout of the banking system, the inexorable rise in pay for corporate executives, bankers and hedge fund managers—all of these have generated widespread resentment and cynicism. While some have prospered, many others have been left behind.

A decade ago, 80 percent of Americans agreed with the statement that a free market economy is the best system. Today, it is 60 percent, lower than in China. One recent poll found that only 42 percent of millennials supported capitalism.[1] In another, a majority of millennials said they would rather live in a socialist country than a capitalist one.[2] Even champions of free markets tend to shy away from using the capitalism moniker.

"They're not rejecting the concept [of capitalism]," explained John Della Volpe, polling director at the Institute of Politics at Harvard's Kennedy School of Government. "The way in which capitalism is practiced today, in the minds of young people—that's what they are rejecting."[3]

Part of this disquiet has to do with the market system's inability to continue delivering a steadily rising standard of living to the average household, as it had for the previous half century. In the 15-year period from 1953 to 1968, the inflation-adjusted income of the median American family increased by 54 percent. In the 15-year period from 2001 to 2016, the increase was just 4 percent. No wonder that just 37 percent of Americans now believe they will do better financially than their parents, the driving idea behind the American Dream.[4]

But another part of our disquiet reflects a nagging suspicion that our economic system has run off the moral rails, offending our sense of fairness, eroding our sense of community, poisoning our politics and rewarding values that easily degenerate into greed and indifference. The qualities that once made America great—the optimism, the commitment to equality, the delicate balance between public and private, the sense that we're all in this together—no longer apply.

It has got to the point that we are no longer surprised when employees of a major bank sign up millions of customers for credit cards and insurance they didn't want or even know about, just to make their monthly numbers.

We are reluctantly reconciled to a system that lavishes $800 million in compensation a year—that's $250,000 an hour—on the head of a private equity firm simply for being clever about buying and selling companies with other people's money, while half of the employees of those companies still work for $25 an hour or less.

We are now barely shocked when a company tells long-time workers that their jobs are being sent overseas and that they will get a modest severance—but only if they train the foreign workers who will be taking their jobs.

We are both outraged and resigned when yet another corporation renounces its American citizenship just to avoid paying its fair share of taxes to the government that educates its workers, protects its property and builds the infrastructure by which it gets its products to market.

While we may have become desensitized to these individual stories, however, collectively they now color the way we think about American capitalism. In less than a generation, what was once considered the optimal system for organizing economic activity is now widely viewed, at home and abroad, as having betrayed its ideals and its purpose and forfeited its moral legitimacy.

* * *

To understand how we got to this point, we have to travel back to the mid-1970s. After decades of dominating U.S. and foreign markets, many of America's biggest and most successful corporations had become complacent and lost their competitive edge. They were less efficient, less innovative and less willing to take risks. Excessive government regulation had raised costs and sapped the dynamism of sectors such as transportation, communication, finance and energy, with government officials dictating which companies could compete, what services they could provide, what prices they could charge and what profits they could earn. Overzealous antitrust enforcement had prevented mergers among rivals that would have allowed them to achieve economies of scale. Unions had pushed wages and benefits to unsustainable levels, driving up prices and draining companies of the capital needed for investment and modernization. Loose interest-rate policy at the Federal Reserve and overspending by Congress had triggered double-digit inflation.

All that was happening at a time when European and Japanese exporters were beginning to make inroads into the American market. It began with shoes, clothing and toys, then spread to autos, steel, consumer electronics, computers and semiconductors, cameras, household appliances, chemicals and machine tools. Initially, the appeal of these foreign products was that they were cheaper, but before long these foreign firms began to offer better quality and styling as well. By the time American firms woke up to the competitive challenge, many were already playing catch-up. In a few industries, it was already too late.

With their costs rising and their market share declining, the large blue-chip companies that had dominated America's postwar economy suddenly found their profits badly squeezed—and their share prices falling. Although few remember it today, the Dow Jones index, reflecting the share prices of the 30 largest industrial companies, essentially ran in place for the ten years between 1972 and 1982, resulting in a lost decade for investors. Indeed, it was worse than that. When adjusted for inflation, the Dow lost half its value over that period.

By the mid-1980s, serious people were wondering if the days of American economic hegemony were quickly coming to an end. When Japan's Mitsubishi conglomerate purchased Rockefeller Center from the descendants of America's most celebrated business mogul in 1989, it seemed to many as if the American Century had come to a premature and inglorious end.

"The central task of the next quarter century is to regain American competitiveness," declared MIT economist Lester Thurow in a widely read jeremiad, *The Zero-Sum Solution*. Blue-ribbon panels were commissioned, studies were published, hearings held. In the corridors of government, at think tanks and business schools, on the covers of magazines, there was a sense of urgency about America's industrial decline and a determination to do something about it. And do something they did.

With support from both Republicans and a new generation of centrist Democrats, federal and state governments deregulated whole swaths of the economy, unleashing a burst of competition from upstart, low-cost rivals in airlines, trucking, freight rail, telephony, financial services and energy. Government spending was cut, along with taxes. Antitrust regulators declared that big was no longer bad, unleashing a flood of mergers and acquisitions. New trade treaties were negotiated that lowered tariffs while opening overseas markets for American products.

Across the manufacturing sector, inefficient plants were shuttered, production was reengineered, employees laid off and work shifted to non-union shops down South or

overseas. Companies that once employed their own security guards, ran their own cafeterias, operated their own
computer systems and delivered products with their own
fleet of trucks outsourced those "non-core" functions to
cheaper, non-unionized specialty firms. Over-indebted
companies used the bankruptcy courts to wash their hands
of pension and retiree health-care obligations and force
lenders to accept less than they were owed. Japanese management gurus were brought in to lower costs, improve
quality and create new corporate cultures.

Meanwhile, in the fast-growing technology sector, established giants selling mainframes and tape drives suddenly
found themselves out-innovated and out-maneuvered by entrepreneurial startups peddling minicomputers, disc drives
and personal computers that were smaller, cheaper, easier
to use and surprisingly powerful.

The transformation was messy, painful, contentious
and often unfair, generating large numbers of winners and
losers—exactly what the economist Joseph Schumpeter had
in mind when he identified "creative destruction" as the essential characteristic of capitalism. Along the way, the old
social contract between companies and their workers—and
more broadly between business and society—was tossed
aside. No longer could workers expect pensions, full-paid
health insurance, job security or even a Christmas bonus
from their employers. And no longer would business leaders feel the responsibility, or even the freedom, to put the
long-term interests of their country or their communities
ahead of the short-term interests of their shareholders.[5]
Chief executives found it useful to cultivate an aura of ruth-
lessness, winning sobriquets such as "Neutron Jack" and
"Chainsaw Al."

And it worked. By the mid-1990s, the hemorrhaging
stopped and corporate America was again enjoying robust

growth in sales, profits and stock prices. Chief executives and Wall Street dealmakers were lionized on magazine covers and on the front pages of newspapers, their dalliances chronicled in the gossip columns, their soaring pay packages a source of both fascination and controversy. Students at the best universities flocked to business schools, and from there to high-powered jobs on Wall Street or at management consulting firms. Individual investors began piling into the stock market through new tax-exempt retirement accounts and a dazzling array of new mutual funds.[6] For the first time, business books with titles like *In Search of Excellence, Reengineering the Corporation* and *Competing for the Future* regularly made it onto the bestseller lists.

America—and American capitalism—was back, stronger and more globally competitive than ever.

* * *

In June 1998, I tried to capture this turnaround with a long front-page story in the *Washington Post* that ran under the headline "Reinventing Xerox Corp."[7]

Xerox was something of an American icon, a home-grown company that sprang from American ingenuity, conquered the world and was run with old-fashioned American values. With the introduction of its 914 copier in 1959, which at the push of a button could turn out six plain-paper copies a minute, Xerox became a ubiquitous presence in every corporate office. Its sleek machines became the spot where gossip was exchanged and romances begun, while its name was turned into a verb. With a 97 percent global market share and 70 percent gross profit margins, Xerox shares topped the "Nifty Fifty" list of hot stocks during Wall Street's go-go years of the 1960s.

In many ways, Xerox was the model American corporation, cosseting its workforce with generous pay and benefit packages and lavishing its largess on its hometown of Rochester, New York, where entire families could be found on the Xerox payroll. Its sales force—proud, slick and high-commissioned—inspired countless imitators. At a corporate research laboratory in Palo Alto, California, Xerox scientists were encouraged to push back the frontiers of knowledge even if their innovations didn't seem to have much to do with xerography.

All that began to crumble, however, by the mid-1970s. The Federal Trade Commission launched an antitrust investigation that restrained the company's competitive impulses and ultimately forced Xerox to license its technology not only to American rivals, such as Kodak and IBM, but to Japanese firms such as Canon and Savin, which soon began flooding the market with low-cost alternatives. Around the world, meanwhile, once-loyal customers were growing frustrated with Xerox machines that were so poorly designed and manufactured that "Clear Paper Path" became a frequent butt of jokes from late-night talk show hosts and a metaphor for the decline in quality of American products.

Perhaps the biggest challenge, however, would come from the advent of the personal computer, which when hooked up to desktop printers threatened to make the Xerox machine a thing of the past. As it happened, much of the foundational work for the personal computer had actually been done at Xerox PARC, where the pathbreaking Alto personal computer system had been designed and built, mostly for internal use. Then, on a day in 1979 that is now the stuff of Silicon Valley legend, Steve Jobs and a team from Apple Computer arrived for a visit, part of a carefully negotiated arrangement in which Xerox made a $1 million investment in the young computer company in return for Apple's access to Xerox's computer technology. Jobs was so excited when he saw the mouse that was used to move a cursor around the computer screen, and the graphic interface that allowed the user to click on a function rather than type in commands, that he could barely contain himself. "Why aren't you doing anything with this?" he demanded of the Xerox engineers. "This is the greatest thing! This is revolutionary!"

Two years later, Xerox finally came out with a line of computers that was clunky and expensive and never caught on with users, and Xerox soon exited the market. Instead, it was the Apple Macintosh, with its Xerox-inspired menus and windows and sleek little mouse, that captured everyone's fancy when it was introduced in 1984. And the rest, as they say, is history.

"If Xerox had known what it had and had taken advantage of its real opportunities," Jobs would say years later, "it could have been as big as IBM plus Microsoft plus Xerox combined—the largest technology company in the world."[8]

Back in Rochester, however, Xerox executives remained in denial about the twin existential threats posed by lower-cost copiers from Japan and computer technology still in its infancy.

"The reality, which nobody wanted to admit back then, was that manufacturing was abysmal, research disconnected to products, corporate headquarters was bloated and smug and profits evaporating before our eyes," recalled Paul Allaire, at that time a top Xerox executive in Europe, who would go on to become chairman and chief executive.

Although the company's financial statements continued to tell a favorable story, that was largely a reflection of a one-time boost to earnings as corporate customers switched from leasing copiers to buying them. In reality, gross margins had declined from 70 percent to 10, and Xerox's share of the world copier market was hovering precariously around

10 percent. Then-chairman David Kearns told associates that unless something radical was done, Xerox would soon be forced out of the industry it had invented.

As Kearns remembered it, the turnaround began at one of his annual meetings with employees at the company's manufacturing center in Webster, New York. At the time, Xerox was ramping up production on a new low-cost copier, the 3300, which was supposed to be the answer to the Japanese competition. Unfortunately, the company hadn't really designed a low-cost machine—it had just simplified one of its old designs and then used a lot of cheap, shoddy parts to make it. Even at that, the $7,300 price tag was significantly above that of the competition, but well below a price that the commissioned sales force thought was worth its time. As the employees gathered under a tent in the parking lot, a line of idled rail cars sat nearby, each one packed with unsold 3300s.

"David, why didn't you ask us what we thought about this?" a union shop steward asked at the meeting. "We could have told you it was a piece of junk." At that moment of utter humiliation, Kearns recalled, he vowed to turn the company inside out to ensure it never happened again.

The renewal process proved anything but smooth, and at numerous points Kearns feared it would collapse under the weight of cynicism, poor execution and out-and-out resistance. While a new combination laser printer and copier boasted a new commitment to quality, it came to market too early, before much demand had developed. And an ill-timed foray into real estate and insurance eventually cost the company more than $1 billion. Plants were closed, pay cut and frozen, top executives fired and more than 40,000 jobs eliminated. Slowly but surely, however, Xerox was learning to do things faster, better and cheaper. For the typical corporate customer, the four-cent per copy cost was cut in half, and then in half again, along with the frequency of machine breakdowns.

To report the story, I had traveled to Aguascalientes, an industrial town north of Mexico City, to visit what had become the company's showcase production facility. Not only were labor rates in "Aguas" a fifth of what they were in the United States, but with its just-in-time inventory system, robots, laser-guided assembly and computerized production system, the plant there could produce 48 variations of the same copier on a single production line, using fewer man-hours and with fewer defects than other plants in Xerox's newly globalized supply chain. Ten percent of the 2,000 Mexican employees had engineering degrees, and they were responsible for making all design changes for all of Xerox's mid-range copiers.

Meanwhile, a joint venture with Fuji, Japan's photo giant, had allowed Xerox to get to market with a quality color copier in time to compete with one introduced by Canon. And following a seven-year, $400 million development effort, during which 3 million lines of computer code were written and more than 500 patents were filed, Xerox introduced a new line of high-volume digital copier-printers that were selling so fast that a second shift had to be added back in Webster. The new Document Centre 265 returned the luster to the Xerox brand, and sent its stock—which had floundered at $25 for the entire decade of the 1980s—to an all-time high above $160 a share.

* * *

Crucial to the revival at Xerox and other American corporations were three ideas used by political and business leaders to justify these dramatic changes in the relationship between companies and their customers, their workers, their investors and the rest of society.

Idea #1: The government was significantly responsible for the decline in American competitiveness. High taxes had discouraged investment and risk-taking by individuals and businesses, while overzealous regulation had driven up costs and snuffed out innovation. For Ronald Reagan and his heirs in the Republican Party, along with a supporting chorus of economists and business executives, it became economic gospel that cutting taxes and eliminating regulations would increase incentives to work and invest, and thereby increase the supply of goods and services produced by the economy. They called it supply side economics.

"Government's view of the economy could be summed up in a few short phrases," quipped Reagan in belittling the liberal approach to economic policy. "If it moves, tax it. If it keeps moving, regulate it. And if it stops moving, subsidize it."

Idea #2: The sole purpose of every business is to deliver the highest possible financial return to its investors. This was the only way to ensure that managers would take the tough actions—cutting costs, laying off workers, selling less profitable divisions—to ensure a company's survival in hypercompetitive global markets.

"There is only one social responsibility of business—to use its resources and engage in activities designed to increase its profits," conservative economist Milton Friedman wrote in 1970 in the *New York Times Magazine*. "Anything else," he declared, was "unadulterated socialism."

Idea #3: No matter how unfair it might seem to cut taxes for the wealthy, no matter how ruthless a com-

pany might have to be in its dealings with workers and consumers, no matter how unequal the distribution of income and wealth might become, we must ignore and dismiss such moral concerns as naïve and ultimately self-defeating. Such unpleasant outcomes were seen as the inevitable and unavoidable features of a free market system that had lifted much of humanity from the subsistence existence in which it had been trapped for millennia, generating the greatest prosperity for the greatest number. For that reason alone, free markets had to be accepted as fair and just. Let's label that view "market justice."

Beginning in the 1980s, these three ideas—supply side economics, maximizing shareholder value and market justice—were woven into the everyday rhetoric of economists, business leaders and conservative politicians, providing the economic, political and moral legitimacy for dismantling the welfare and regulatory state and jettisoning a complacent business culture. In time, they came to be reflected in a wide range of government policies, corporate strategies and business practices. And it was those policies, those strategies and those practices that, by the mid-1990s, had succeeded in restoring the competitiveness of the American economy.

However, when the competitiveness challenge had been overcome and the American economy was once again back on top, free market ideologues and those with vested economic interests continued to push these ideas to extremes never envisioned by those who first proposed them— pushed them so far, in fact, that they have now lost their validity and their legitimacy. What began as a useful corrective has, 25 years later, become a morally corrupting and

self-defeating economic dogma that threatens the future of
American capitalism. Almost everything people now find
distasteful about it can be traced to these three flawed ideas.

The mindless animosity toward all regulation, for example, has now provided a rationale for handing over the keys
to independent regulatory agencies to lobbyists and executives from the very industries they are supposed to regulate.
In a very real sense, the foxes have been put in charge of the
chicken coop, and their ambitions go well beyond "reforming" the agencies or "restoring a balance" between government and business. Their aim is to hollow out these agencies
from the inside—to maintain the fiction that the government is still protecting workers, consumers, investors and
the environment while, in reality, trusting markets to restrain predatory business behavior. These antiregulatory
zealots speak only of the cost of regulation but never the
benefits; of the jobs lost but never the lives saved; of efficiency but never fairness.

After gaining control of both the White House and Congress in 2016, Republicans moved aggressively to rescind
dozens of Obama-era regulations that would surely strike
most Americans as fair and reasonable. These include a rule
setting strict environmental standards for oil and gas drill-
ing in national parks and wildlife refuges, a rule barring federal student loans at for-profit colleges whose graduates
never get jobs and a rule requiring financial advisers to act
in the best interest of their customers. They include a rule
preventing mines from dumping debris into nearby rivers
and streams and a rule preventing cable and phone companies from collecting and selling information about the Internet sites visited by their customers. They even set out to
repeal a long-standing rule preventing restaurant owners
from taking waiters' tips for themselves.

So virulent is Republican opposition to regulation that

Don Blankenship, the former chief executive of Massey Energy—a man who spent a year in federal prison for conspiring to violate mine safety rules in connection with a 2010 mine explosion that killed 29 of his workers—used his conviction as a springboard for seeking the Republican nomination for the U.S. Senate in West Virginia. Rejecting the findings of a federal jury and a panel of mine safety experts, Blankenship blamed—you guessed it—government regulators for causing the explosion. He was defeated only after President Donald Trump and the party establishment mounted a last-minute campaign against him.

Supply side tax fantasies, meanwhile, have so warped the thinking of Republican politicians that many genuinely believe they can create jobs and raise wages for the struggling working class by lavishing a trillion dollars of tax relief on businesses and investors—the very businesses and investors who have spent the last 25 years eliminating working-class jobs and driving down working-class wages. The jihad against taxes has progressed to the point that any Republican politician who even contemplates raising any tax at any time is certain to be vilified by the conservative media and driven from office by an unforgiving and well-financed conservative mob. Even long-cherished conservative ideals such as balancing budgets and investing in infrastructure have been tossed overboard in the relentless pursuit of tax cuts, which are now the reflexive Republican solution to any problem.

A similar single-mindedness has taken hold in the private sector around maximizing shareholder value. For too many corporate executives and directors, that mantra has provided a pretext for bamboozling customers, squeezing employees, evading taxes and engaging in endless rounds of unproductive mergers and acquisitions. It has even provided a pretext for defrauding shareholders themselves. The executives at Enron, WorldCom, HealthSouth and Waste

Management who concocted elaborate schemes to inflate reported revenues or profits in the late 1990s rationalized their actions as necessary steps to prevent share prices from falling. It has become the end that justifies any business means.

The obligation to maximize shareholder value has also led business leaders to abandon their role as proud stewards of the American system. In today's business culture, it's hard to imagine them as stewards of anything other than their own bottom lines. But it wasn't always this way.

Working through national organizations such as the Committee for Economic Development, the Business Council and the Business Roundtable, the chief executives of America's major corporations during the decades right after World War II supported proposals to increase federal support for education and basic research, guarantee worker pensions, protect the environment, improve workplace safety and set a national goal of full employment. Although most of the chief executives were Republicans, business organizations took pains to be bipartisan and maintain close ties to politicians of both parties. Some of their motives were self-serving, such as reducing the lure of socialism or unionization, but there was also a genuine belief that companies had a duty to balance their own interests with those of society. As General Motors chairman Charlie Wilson famously put it at his confirmation hearing to be secretary of defense, "I always thought that what [was] good for the country was good for General Motors, and vice versa."

At the major business organizations today, that sense of collective social responsibility has given way to the grubby pursuit of narrow self-interest, irrespective of the consequences for the rest of society. While continuing to declare their bipartisanship, business groups such as the U.S. Chamber of Commerce, the Business Roundtable and the National

Federation of Independent Businesses have essentially become arms of the Republican Party. For the most part, these organizations are now missing in action on broad issues they once declared as priorities, such as climate change, health-care reform, immigration, infrastructure investment, education and balancing the budget, occasionally paying them lip service but expending no political capital on them.[9]

"Big business was a stabilizing force, a moderating influence in Washington," Steve Odland, president of the Committee for Economic Development and a former chief executive of Office Depot, told me several years ago. "They were the adults in the room." Nobody, including Odland, thinks business leaders play that role today.

And what of the third idea, market justice? For the most part, Americans are no longer willing to accept the glaring injustices created by the economic system simply because it provides them with a higher standard of living. For starters, many feel their standard of living is now falling, not rising. And even for those living better than ever, the American capitalism they experience feels more and more like a morally corrupt and corrupting system in which the prevailing ethic is every man for himself. Old-fashioned norms around loyalty, cooperation, honesty, equality, fairness and compassion no longer seem to apply in the economic sphere. As workers, as consumers and even as investors, they feel cheated, manipulated and disrespected.

I regularly ask undergraduates at George Mason University, where I teach, about their career aspirations and am struck by how few have any interest in working in a business (those who do invariably want to work for a startup run by a small group of idealists like themselves). It is the rare student who volunteers a desire to be rich—not because they wouldn't enjoy what the money could buy them, but because they wouldn't want to engage in the unsavory behavior they think necessary to attain it. To them, market justice sounds like a contradiction in terms.

* * *

Not quite two years after my story about Xerox was published in the *Post*, a colleague handed me a copy of a story that had just moved over the wires of the Associated Press. There was a mischievous smile on his face.

"SEC Investigates Xerox for Alleged Accounting Irregularities in Mexico Division," read the headline. The initial release from the company reported that a few rogue executives in Mexico had cooked the books to inflate sales in order to meet their quarterly targets. Subsequent investigation by the Securities and Exchange Commission, however, revealed that the accounting gamesmanship was endemic in Xerox operations across the globe, and reached right up to the top echelons at corporate headquarters. The goal, the SEC found, was to boost the company's stock price by consistently meeting and exceeding the expectation of Wall Street analysts. The company would later agree to pay a fine of $10 million for using aggressive accounting tactics to inflate its reported profits by $1.4 billion from 1997 through 2000. At the time, it was a record fine for an enforcement action. Xerox stock fell below $7 a share on the news. Two years later, six former executives, including the chief executive and financial officers, agreed to $22 million in fines and returned bonus payments to settle civil fraud charges. Xerox's longtime auditors, KPMG, also agreed to pay $22 million to settle charges that it had collaborated with the company to manipulate earnings.

The accounting scandal, however, was hardly Xerox's only problem. Competition from lower-cost Japanese copiers continued to cut deeply into sales, while Xerox's entry into the computer printer business flagged. As revenues fell and profits turned to losses, a new chief executive brought in from IBM was fired. A syndicate of banks threatened not to renew a $7 billion line of credit, without which the company would have had to file for bankruptcy protection. The company's new chief executive, Anne Mulcahy, was forced to fire more than half of the company's 96,000 workers, cut the research budget by 30 percent and sell half of Xerox's stake in its successful joint venture with Fuji to raise cash.

While Mulcahy managed to stabilize the company, the imperative to continually satisfy shareholders with quarterly earnings growth meant that Xerox was never able to invest sufficiently in technology or brand development to thrive again. And by late 2015, the company attracted the attention of a number of bottom-fishing investors, among them Carl Icahn, who had first made his name on Wall Street in 1980 by buying Trans World Airlines, then a storied airline, and selling it off in pieces. Icahn threatened to run his own slate of directors unless Xerox agreed to fire its top executives and explore "strategic options"—a Wall Street euphemism for selling the company and distributing the cash to shareholders. Caught between an unforgiving marketplace and unforgiving investors, Xerox bowed to the investors. In January 2018, Xerox announced it would sell what was left of its copier business to Fuji, distribute a one-time dividend of $2.5 billion to Icahn and other shareholders and cease to exist as an independent business.[10] The next day, a clever *New York Times* headline writer noted that the company whose name became a verb would now only be used in the "past tense."[11]

* * *

The old Xerox, the successful Xerox, the innovative Xerox—the Xerox that inspired loyalty and admiration—thrived in an America in which there was a high level of trust in each other and in our common institutions, in which we felt responsibility for each other and believed that we all would sink or swim together. In economics, that locus of characteristics is called "social capital." What the proponents of supply side economics, maximizing shareholder value and market justice overlook—why their formula no longer works, why their ideas are no longer valid—is that they have produced a kind of capitalism that corrodes social capital by undermining trust and discouraging socially cooperative behavior. That is the essential message of this book.

We all enjoy the benefits of social capital without thinking much about it. Social capital explains why our newspapers are still lying on the front lawn when we go to retrieve them in the morning, and why we take at face value the advice we get from doctors and lawyers and financial advisers. Because of social capital, we leave deposits with businesses we've never dealt with and work for days or even weeks in expectation of being paid later. Social capital explains why we hold doors for each other, and leave tips in restaurants we will never revisit and why we think nothing of withdrawing cash from the ATM with strangers standing behind us. In countries with high levels of social capital, people leave their front doors and bicycles unlocked, politely queue at bus stops and think nothing of letting their young children walk to school by themselves.

Social capital also provides the necessary grease for the increasingly complex machinery of capitalism, and for the increasingly contentious machinery of democracy. It gives us the confidence to take risks, make long-term investments and accept the inevitable dislocations caused by the gales of creative destruction. Social capital provides the support for formal institutions and unwritten rules and norms of behavior that foster cooperation and compromise—between management and labor, between businesses and their customers, between business and government and among people of different races, classes and political beliefs. Societies with more social capital are happier, healthier and wealthier. In societies without it, democratic capitalism struggles to survive.

Today, Americans see erosion of social capital in the declining trust they have in almost every institution in society.

We see it in lagging measures of worker engagement and the increase in the number of working-age males who have dropped out of the workforce.

We see it in the frequency of mass shootings, the decline in social contact with our neighbors and the appalling lack of civility on the Internet.

We see it in the way Americans sort themselves geographically—and virtually—into closed communities where everyone lives and thinks like they do.

We see it in a politics that has become polarized, partisan and paranoid.

We see it in a government where consensus is elusive, compromise is equated with treason and the aim of every newly elected Congress or administration is to undo everything done by its predecessor.

As a society, we are now caught in one of those self-reinforcing, downward spirals in which the erosion of social capital, government dysfunction, rising inequality and slowing rates of economic growth are all feeding off each other, with more of one leading to more of all the others. Such vicious cycles, by their nature, are very hard to stop. The rise of the Tea Party and the election of Donald Trump are both a consequence and a contributor to this dangerous dynamic.

The only way to break that cycle and replenish our stock of social capital is to do what Americans have done several times in our history, which is to embrace a different form of capitalism.

"Capitalism has always changed in order to survive and thrive," wrote Martin Wolf, the highly respected and uncompromisingly pro-market columnist for the *Financial Times*, in an essay published in the wake of the 2008 financial crisis. "It needs to change again."[12]

No less a figure than Laurence Fink, chairman of Black-Rock, the world's largest manager of other people's money, recently wrote to the chief executives of every public company in America to declare that an economy organized solely around the goal of making profits was no longer economically or politically viable. "Society is demanding that companies, both public and private, serve a social purpose," Fink admonished. "To prosper over time, every company must not only deliver financial performance, but also make a positive contribution to society."[13]

The starting point for this book is the recognition that our current prosperity is not sustainable because it is not producing the kind of society that most of us desire. While Donald Trump's election surely represented a rejection of the establishment elites, it was anything but an endorsement of leaving everything for the markets to decide. Those Americans waving pitchforks are not defenders of supply side economics, maximizing shareholder value or market justice—they are its victims.

Although this book is a critique of the free market ideas and conservative ideology that have recently shaped American capitalism, it also demands that liberal critics think harder about what is required for a just and prosperous society. Those who never miss an opportunity to complain about the level of inequality have rarely been willing to say what level, or what kinds, of inequality would be morally acceptable. Does it really offend our moral intuitions that billionaire hedge fund managers are pulling away from millionaire lawyers and doctors? Is it relative income and economic standing we really care about, or will gains in absolute income and mobility satisfy our concern? What if rising inequality in rich nations is part of a process by which billions of people in poor countries are lifted out of poverty—shouldn't we welcome that?

My aim in this book is to help rescue the public conversation about American capitalism from the easy and predictable moralizing of the pro-market right ("greed is good, redistribution is theft and concern about inequality is nothing but class envy") and the anti-market left ("all inequality is bad, the rich are just lucky and markets are morally corrupting"). Or, as Catholic University historian Jerry Muller has put it, to move beyond the unsatisfying choice between the "politics of privilege" and the "politics of resentment."[14] There is a rich and important conversation still to be had about what kind of society we want and what variety of capitalism would best achieve it. The reason our economic debate is in a rut is that it has become too much about means and not enough about ends—too much about tax rates and income shares and not enough about things like virtue, community and justice. It has become too much about rights and not enough about responsibility, too much about moral absolutes and not enough about striking the right balance among conflicting moral obligations.

What I bring to this discussion are the talents and habits of mind of a journalist who has been observing business, politics and the economy for more than four decades. I am not a social scientist, but I have drawn from a great deal of research by people who are, and I have tried to give a good account of their work and reconcile their often conflicting points of view. My hope is that you will find the analysis sound, the conclusions convincing and the observations consistent with what you have observed and experienced. But I will consider it a success if this book simply helps you to think about American capitalism in a new way, to see it in a different light and consider it from a different angle of view. In today's polarized and ideologically charged environment, that alone would be an accomplishment.

1

Is Greed Good?

In 2008, on the eve of the global financial crisis, Drexel University used the pomp and circumstances of its annual commencement ceremony to confer an honorary degree on one of Wall Street's most famous investors.

Carl Icahn had amassed a fortune estimated at $17 billion by buying large positions in companies he considered badly managed, then using his ownership position to force managers and directors to take whatever steps he deemed necessary—shutting plants, selling off divisions and assets, slashing worker pay and pensions, reducing investments, buying back shares—to boost the companies' stock prices and allow him to sell out at a handsome profit. The strategy was so effective that just the news that Icahn had taken an interest in a company could boost the stock price by 10 percent. His targets have included Trans World Airlines, U.S. Steel, Phillips Petroleum, Texaco, Time Warner, eBay, Yahoo!, Apple and, most recently, Xerox.

When he started in the mid-1980s, people like Icahn were referred to pejoratively as "corporate raiders," "greenmailers"

and "asset strippers," sneered at by the business press, crit-
icized by business school professors and shunned by the
business establishment. It should tell you how much our
sensibilities have changed that Icahn is now commonly referred to as an "activist investor," lionized on the cover of
Time magazine as a "Master of the Universe" and celebrated
with an honorary degree.[1]

"As a leading shareholder activist, Mr. Icahn believes his
efforts have unlocked billions of dollars in shareholder
value," Drexel's president declared in awarding him an honorary doctorate of business administration, awkwardly side-
stepping the question of what Drexel believed. To nobody's
surprise, there was no mention of the hardball tactics Icahn
used to unlock all that shareholder value and amass his personal fortune. Rather, the citation went on to praise Icahn's
generosity in giving away a portion of that fortune to benefit the sick and the homeless.

As the philosopher Charles Karelis has observed,
academic ceremonies like the one that played out in
Philadelphia—what was said as well as what was left out—
perfectly illustrate the moral paradox of free market capitalism.[2] The financier celebrated that morning had played an
outsized role in an economic system that had conferred on
every member of that day's graduating class a standard of
living well beyond the reach of those still trapped in societies
where free market capitalism does not exist. Yet despite those
incalculable benefits, we are reluctant to praise the self-
interested traits and aggressive tactics that have been vital to
the success of that system. If such traits and tactics are not
vices, we don't exactly view them as virtues, either.

Among the first to note this moral paradox between
what he called "private vices and publick benefits" was Bernard Mandeville. Born in the Netherlands in 1680, Mande-

ville studied medicine and philosophy at Leiden before moving to England, where he found both popularity and controversy as a writer. Mandeville's most famous work was *The Fable of the Bees*, which told of a flourishing hive of bees that, though relentless and sometimes dishonest in their individual pursuit of self-interest, had achieved a level of collective comfort and pleasure in which "the very poor liv'd better than the rich before." The industrious bees, however, were not content merely to enjoy their luxurious new paradise— they begged the gods for a more selfless virtue. So Jove grants them their wish to rid themselves of all their selfish vices, and almost immediately the bees discover that they are no longer driven to compete with each other. Their prosperity disappears, apathy sets in and the hive is left vulnerable to a devastating attack. The few bees that survive take refuge in the hollow of a tree where their newfound virtue and thrift condemn them to a simple, impoverished existence.

Mandeville said his intent was to "shew the Impossibility of enjoying all the most elegant Comforts of Life that are to be met with in an industrious, wealthy and powerful Nation, and at the same time be bless'd with all the Virtue and Innocense that can be wish'd for in a Golden Age." Three hundred years later, this dilemma still confounds. We are still looking for a way to reconcile our moral distaste for the ruthless pursuit of self-interest with our admiration and appreciation of the benefits it generates.

Amorality on Wall Street

Nothing captures this ambivalence about capitalism better than Wall Street, which for many has come to represent all that is right and all that is wrong with the free market economy. And no firm has come to epitomize the Wall Street ethic more than Goldman Sachs. In the years leading up to the recent financial crisis in 2008, Goldman was the most respected and profitable of the Wall Street investment banks. Two of its chief executives had served as secretary of the Treasury. Its bankers and traders were thought to be the smartest and toughest on Wall Street. So coveted was a seat at Goldman's table that, at one point, more than half of the graduating seniors at some of the country's most prestigious colleges signed up to be interviewed by a Goldman recruiter.

By April 2010, however, seven of Goldman's top executives found themselves testifying before the Senate Permanent Subcommittee on Investigations, which had spent two years poring through the firm's internal documents to determine what role Goldman had played in the financial crisis.

In the years leading up to the crisis, Goldman had made billions of dollars packaging residential and commercial mortgages into bond-like financial instruments and selling them to hedge funds, pension funds, insurance companies and other sophisticated investors—a process known as "securitization." When investor demand for these securities began to outstrip the available pool of mortgages that could be packaged, Goldman led the way in creating "synthetic" securities whose value tracked that of the real thing—in effect, allowing more people to invest in the mortgage market than there were actual mortgages for them to buy. And when investors wanted to protect themselves against the risk that these securities might someday fail to deliver on their promised cash flow, Goldman made it possible for them to hedge their bets with an instrument that amounted to an insurance contract known as a "credit default swap."

All of these activities put Goldman at the center of what came to be known as the "shadow banking system" that, by the first decade of the twenty-first century, had become larger than the traditional banking system. The shadow banking system flooded the economy with cheap credit, inflated real estate prices and sent Wall Street profits and bonuses to levels never before imagined. By 2007, however, there were some who were beginning to realize that many of the original loans should never have been made, that the prices of the securities and the real estate that backed them were unsustainable and that the credit bubble was about to burst.

One such skeptic was a hedge fund manager named John Paulson, who began looking for a way to profit from the market's inevitable collapse. Paulson called Goldman and asked if the bank would be willing to create a security backed by a basket of particularly risky subprime loans so that he could buy credit default swaps tied to that security—swaps that would generate handsome profits if, as expected, those securities failed to pay off. Paulson was a big Goldman client, so the bank was not only willing to accommodate his request but even allowed his associates to recommend specific mortgages for the package.

Until the 1980s, investment banks would compete to demonstrate to clients how trustworthy they were, and in that earlier era, the Goldman name was the gold standard. As the firm's legendary senior partner Gus Levy famously put it, Goldman meant to be "long-term greedy," never cutting corners to earn a quick buck and always putting clients' interests before the interests of the firm. When a blue-chip firm like Goldman put its name on a securities offering, it was a signal to investors that the partners at Goldman were giving it their own seal of approval. It wasn't necessarily a sure bet—nothing in finance is—but you could rest assured that it was an honest bet.

By 2007, however, the time horizon for Goldman's greediness had significantly shortened. Goldman was now willing to create for one client a security that was designed to fail, and then peddle it to other clients who were unaware of its provenance. The old presumption that an investment bank staked its reputation on the securities it underwrote had become a quaint anachronism.

Goldman's duplicity, however, went far beyond that one security. For by that time Goldman, too, had concluded that the real estate market was about to crash and began quietly scrambling to reduce its own housing risk. Even as it was moving to protect its own portfolio, however, Goldman's bankers were continuing to underwrite and sell new securities that its executives knew were backed by some of the dodgiest mortgages from some of the dodgiest lenders.

In January 2007, Fabrice Tourre, a Goldman vice president, wrote an email to a friend that would later be unearthed by Senate investigators: "The whole [edifice] is about to collapse any time now. . . . The only potential survivor, the Fabulous Fab, . . . standing in the middle of all these complex, highly leveraged exotic trades he created without necessarily understanding all the implications of these monstrosities!!!"[3]

At the Senate hearing, incredulous senators, Republican and Democrat, demanded to know why Goldman executives had sold securities to valued clients that even their own employees had characterized as "crap." The men from Goldman, however, were equally incredulous, failing to see why anyone would think there was anything wrong with what they did. Their answers were defensive, nitpicky and legalistic, and no purpose would be served by quoting them here. But if you will allow me a little license, here is a concise rendition of what they meant to say:

Senators, we operate in complex markets with other knowledgeable and sophisticated traders who spend all day trying to do to us what we do to them. What you find so strange or distasteful is, in fact, how the game is played.

In our world, in order for there to be a transaction, people must disagree about the value of the thing they are trading. The buyer thinks the price will go up, the seller thinks it will go down. Only one of them can turn out to be right. Finance is largely a zero-sum game—for every winner there is a loser.

As the middleman in these transactions, what Goldman or any of its 35,000 employees happens to think about a security is irrelevant. It's not for us to judge whether they are "good" or "bad"—it's for the market to do that. And the way the market does it is by determining the price. At $100, a bond might be a bad investment, but if you pay $10 for it, it could be quite good. If our sophisticated clients want to take housing risk, or oil price risk, or interest rate risk—or if they want to hedge those risks— our job is to help them do that by finding somebody to take the other side of the bet, or by taking it ourselves.

As underwriters, market makers and buyers and sellers of credit insurance, we are constantly on the other side of transactions from our customers. In doing that, we are merely cogs in a marvelous system that efficiently allocates the world's investment capital at the lowest price to those who can put it to the highest and best use, making us all better off. Within that context—a context well understood by our customers, our competitors and our regulators—we did nothing wrong and we have nothing to be ashamed of.

To those watching the exchange, it was as if the politicians and the financiers were from different planets. The senators imagined they were living in a world of right and wrong, good and bad, in which bankers owed a duty of honesty and loyalty to their customers and to the public that obligated them not to peddle securities they knew to be suspect. The men from Goldman, by contrast, came from an amoral world of hypercompetitive trading desks in which customers were "counterparties" and there was no right or wrong, only winners and losers.

"We live in different contexts," Goldman chief executive Lloyd Blankfein told committee chairman Carl Levin, who at the outset of the hearing had chastised the bankers for their "unbridled greed."[4] For hours, as almost everyone on Wall Street sat glued to their screens watching the drama play out, the two sides continued to talk past each other until an exasperated Levin finally gave up and gaveled the hearing to a close.

Over the next five years, the Justice Department and the Securities and Exchange Commission would extract record fines of $5.6 billion from Goldman, along with a grudging acknowledgment that it had knowingly misled its customers. Similar settlements, amounting to almost $200 billion, were reached with all the major banks. Yet through it all, Wall Street has continued to reject accusations that it did anything wrong, or that its practices and culture are fundamentally unethical or immoral.

"Not feeling too guilty about this," Tourre emailed his girlfriend in January 2007. "The real purpose of my job is to make capital markets more efficient . . . so there is a humble, noble, and ethical reason for my job." But then, after inserting a smiling emoji, he added, "Amazing how good I am [at] convincing myself!!!"[5]

Tourre, who reportedly earned annual bonuses as high as $2 million during his decade at Goldman, would later be convicted of six counts of civil fraud and fined $825,000. As the only Wall Street executive brought to justice in the wake of the 2008 crash, the young Frenchman became a symbol— some would say a scapegoat—of the financial crisis. After leaving Goldman, Tourre took up graduate studies in economics at the University of Chicago, where he was scheduled to teach an undergraduate honors seminar. Once word of his appointment leaked out, however, embarrassed university officials dropped him as the instructor.

The Hijacking of Adam Smith

That Fabrice Tourre chose to retreat to the University of Chicago was only fitting. Since the days of Nobel laureates Milton Friedman, George Stigler and Gary Becker, Chicago has become the Vatican for an economic ideology based on a holy trinity of self-interest, rational expectations and efficient markets. In time, this ideology came to be widely embraced on Wall Street and in the business community, providing an intellectual justification not just for lower taxes, less regulation and free trade, but also hostile corporate takeovers, outsized executive compensation and a dramatic rewriting of the social contract between business and society.

The man held out as the patron saint of this ideology was the eighteenth-century Scottish philosopher Adam Smith. In his most famous work, *An Inquiry into the Nature and Causes of the Wealth of Nations*, Smith demonstrated that our "disposition to truck, barter and exchange," driven by self-interest, had allowed millions of farmers, artisans and laborers to escape grinding poverty.

"It is not from the benevolence of the butcher, the brewer, or the baker, that we expect our dinner, but from their regard to their own interest," he wrote in one of the most famous passages in all of economics. "We address ourselves not to their humanity but to their self-love, and never talk to them of our own necessities but of their advantages."

Smith's great insight was that as each of us goes about selfishly enhancing our own wealth, we unintentionally but

magically—in his words, "as if led by an invisible hand"—
wind up enhancing the wealth of everyone else.

In pointing out the social utility of selfishness and self-
regard, Smith was well aware of Bernard Mandeville's fable
of the bees. He was also drawing on more than a century of
thinking by Enlightenment thinkers who rejected the traditional Catholic notion that wealth could only be acquired
through evil and exploitation.[6]

"It is as impossible for society to be formed and lasting
without self-interest as it would be to produce children without carnal desire or to think of eating without appetite,"
Voltaire wrote. "It is quite true that God might have created
beings solely concerned with the good of others. In that case
merchants would have gone to the Indies out of charity
and the mason would have cut stone to give pleasure to his
neighbor. But God has ordained things differently. Let us not
condemn the instinct."[7]

Looking back on centuries of war driven by religious
zealotry, Voltaire saw in our commercial tendencies a better
foundation for peace and social order. And it was Smith's
great friend and mentor David Hume who wrote of the civi-
lizing effect of wealth in an essay celebrating luxury.[8]

Today, Mandeville, Voltaire and Hume are remembered
only by students of philosophy, but Smith's "invisible hand"
has become the defining metaphor around which a gospel
of free markets has been constructed. If self-interest is the
instinct that animates free markets, and free markets produce the most peace and wealth for the greatest number,
then free markets must logically be the most moral of systems
for organizing our economic affairs. In such a context, there's
no need for the bankers from Goldman to worry about
whether any particular action or activity is right or wrong
because every self-interested trade ultimately serves this
higher social and moral purpose. And from there it is only

a short leap to the view that if some self-interest is good, more of it would be even better.

"The point is, ladies and gentlemen, that greed, for lack of a better word, is good," declares Gordon Gekko, the fictionalized fund manager in Oliver Stone's hit movie *Wall Street.* "Greed is right, greed works. Greed clarifies, cuts through, and captures the essence of the evolutionary spirit. Greed, in all of its forms: greed for life, for money, for love, for knowledge has marked the upward surge of mankind."

Director Stone, of course, meant to condemn greed, not to praise it, and Gekko is the villain of his morality play, a ruthless cad willing to do whatever it takes to make money—dismember companies, lay off thousands of workers, ruin families and screw other investors by spreading false rumors and trading on stolen inside information. But as professors of economics and philosophy regularly demonstrate to their students, it is easier to criticize greed than to distinguish it from more productive forms of self-interest. The classroom discussion follows a predictable pattern.

To the student who suggests that greed is wanting more than you need, the professor asks if it is greedy to want a BMW instead of a Ford Focus.

To those who speculate that greed is wanting more than you could ever spend, the professor will ask if billionaire Mark Zuckerberg is greedy because he still gets up and goes to work every day, aiming to make more.

To those who would define greed as wanting something that hurts someone else, the professor asks if it would be greedy for you to abandon an employer who took a chance on you by hiring and training you when you were fresh out of school, just because a competitor had offered an extra dollar an hour in pay.

While we can acknowledge that greed is devilishly hard to define, that doesn't mean that we shouldn't try, or that we must accept any level of selfishness as morally benign. I would suggest that greed comes in two varieties, one that is personally debilitating, the other socially.

The first type we associate with King Midas, who desperately wished for the golden touch but wound up using it to turn his own daughter into gold. This greed is a hunger for acquisition so excessive that it becomes a sickness or compulsion that prevents us from enjoying what we already have.

The other greed is an acquisitive selfishness so extreme that the harm it causes to others outweighs the benefit to ourselves. This greed leads to wasteful consumption and misallocation of scarce resources. It is the type of greed that requires a brutish indifference to the plight of others and offers a pretext for illegal or ruthless behavior. It is the greed that so undermines the faith, trust and confidence we have in each other that it leaves all of us less satisfied, economically and morally.

This latter is not just my characterization of greed. It is the one offered in 1759 by Adam Smith himself, in his earlier but oft-overlooked work *The Theory of Moral Sentiments*.

"How selfish soever man may be supposed," Smith writes in the opening sentence, "there are evidently some principles in his nature, which interest him in the fortune of others, and render their happiness necessary to him, though he derives nothing from it except the pleasure of seeing it."

As Smith sees it, it is not riches we seek but happiness, and the surest route to happiness is to have gained the respect and good opinion of others. Smith imagines that our behavior is driven by an imaginary interaction with what he calls the "impartial spectator" looking over our shoulder. In a genuinely moral man, this conscience becomes so ingrained that we rein in our selfishness and ambition to gain the respect of others. Eventually, this restraint leads to an even higher pleasure—self-respect.

"Man naturally desires not only to be loved but to be lovely," he writes.[9]

Smith takes great pains in *Moral Sentiments* to document our natural tendency to admire those who are rich and wrongly attribute their success to a higher moral character, which the rich come to believe of themselves. And this, complains Smith, leads them to believe that they no longer have to act in a moral fashion: "The disposition to admire, and almost to worship, the rich and powerful, and to despise, or, at least, to neglect persons of poor and mean condition, though necessary to establish the distinction of ranks and the order of society, is at the same time the great and most universal cause of the corruption of our moral sentiments."[10]

Unlike the classical or Christian moralists, Adam Smith did not believe that the enthusiastic pursuit of personal wealth by itself was corrupting. Indeed, for Smith, success in commerce required the development of such laudable characteristics as economy, industry, prudence and honesty. As he saw it, the desire for "luxury" and the desire for "virtue" could be reinforcing—but only if self-interest were tempered by a concern for the well-being of others.

"How disagreeable does he appear to be," he wrote, "whose hard and obdurate heart feels for himself only, but is altogether insensible to the happiness or misery of others."[11]

Nor is Smith's notion of a competitive market one that operates on Goldman Sachs's principle of "buyer beware."

"In the race for wealth, and honours, and preferments, he may run as hard as he can and strain every nerve and every muscle, in order to outstrip all his competitors," Smith wrote. "But if he should jostle, or throw down any of them, the indulgence of the spectators is entirely at an end. It is a violation of fair play."[12]

It is not just fair play that Smith requires, however. He

also demands a fair distribution of economic rewards. The rich, he writes, "consume little more than the poor, and in spite of their natural selfishness and rapacity, they divide with the poor the produce of all their improvements. They are led by an invisible hand to make nearly the same distribution of the necessities of life which would have been made had the earth been divided into equal portions among all its inhabitants."[13]

This, in fact, is Adam Smith's first use of the phrase "invisible hand," written more than a decade before the more famous passage in *The Wealth of Nations*. Rather than serving as justification for selfishness, however, this invisible hand is a metaphor for what he considered a natural instinct to share the fruits of communal labor. For Smith, it is a matter of simple "equity" that "they who feed, clothe and lodge the whole body of the people, should have such a share of the produce of their own labor as to be themselves tolerably well fed, clothed, and lodged."[14]

I am hardly the first to try to rescue Smith from being portrayed as the cartoon cheerleader for selfishness and greed.[15] Smith was a brilliant and insightful philosopher with a subtle and nuanced appreciation of individual motivation and collective behavior. For Smith, man was never the self-regarding individualist conjured up by today's free market purists, but a sentient, social animal whose motivations are complex and whose wealth and happiness depend on the wealth and happiness of others.

The real Adam Smith understood that the wealth of nations requires that our selfishness must be restrained by our moral sentiments—sentiments that are so natural and instinctive that, in his words, they "cannot be the object of reason, but of immediate sense and feeling."[16] This insight would be largely ignored by the classical and neoclassical economists who built on Smith's work. A century later, however, that insight would surface again in the pioneering work of an English naturalist and geologist.

Why Nice Guys Finish First

If Adam Smith's invisible hand seems to provide the theoretical basis for a market system motivated by selfishness, Charles Darwin's theory of natural selection appears to invest it with a scientific imprimatur.

To the early social Darwinists, the ruthless, unrelenting competition for food, water, shelter and sexual partners that was responsible for the evolution of primates into humans also provided the template for the ruthless and unrelenting competition that plays out in the economic jungle of modern capitalism. Any effort by society to restrain that competition, they argued, or redirect rewards to those less talented, less ambitious and less successful would thwart the continued evolution of the species and the upward progress of civilization.

In time, social Darwinism's focus on "survival of the fittest"—their words, not Darwin's—would come to be embraced by racists, eugenicists and proponents of a "master race," and be widely discredited. But today you can still hear the unmistakable echoes of that philosophy in the critiques of income redistribution and the burden that it imposes on "job creators." You can hear it in the diatribes against "job-killing regulations" meant to protect workers and consumers from the predations of business. And you hear it in their complaints about an economic safety net that has become a "hammock" for the lazy and the indolent.

But just as Smith's invisible hand was hijacked by market fundamentalists who mischaracterized it or misunderstood it, so too have Darwin's insights about evolution and natural selection.

In *On the Origin of Species*, published in 1859, Darwin the-
orized that it was our instinct for self-preservation—our
"selfish gene" as the evolutionary biologist Richard Dawkins
would later call it—that drove human evolution. In the struggle to survive and reproduce in an environment characterized by ruthless competition for limited resources, those
with certain traits survived and reproduced in greater number. Over many generations, those useful traits were "naturally selected" and became embedded in the species.

But in his subsequent work, *The Descent of Man*, Darwin
made clear that selfish genes did not necessarily produce
selfish people. Quite the contrary, in fact. For among those
traits that were naturally selected were instincts for cooperation and altruism that enhanced the ability of humans not
only to survive, but to become the dominant species.

The most fundamental of such instincts was the selfless
sacrifice made by parents on behalf of their offspring and,
more broadly, of family members on behalf of each other.
Even beyond the bonds of kinship, however, strategic cooperation among unrelated individuals had made it possible
for certain tribes to prevail in conflict and competition with
others. Even within tribes, those who exhibited the reciprocal instinct to trust and be trusted tended to be more likely
to be chosen as collaborators and as sexual partners. It was
through such an evolutionary process that a "cooperative
gene"—one no less powerful or important than the selfish
one—became part of our nature.[17]

Here's Darwin: "There can be no doubt that a tribe including many members who, from possessing a high degree
of the spirit of patriotism, fidelity, obedience, courage and
sympathy, [and who] were always ready to give aid to each
other and to sacrifice themselves for the common good,
would be victorious over most other tribes; and this would
be natural selection."[18]

Like Smith, Darwin believed that these socially beneficial instincts manifest themselves in a deep-seated desire to
be loved and respected. Those who were seen to reciprocate
trust and cooperation were more likely to survive and prosper, while those who were greedy and selfish were shamed,
shunned and punished. And it was from those early instincts
that sprang the more elaborate moral, religious and legal
norms and codes that govern our behavior today.[19]

For most of our evolutionary history, writes David De-
Steno, an experimental psychologist at Northeastern University, "it was far more likely that what led to success was
strong social bonds—relationships that would encourage
people to cooperate and lend support to one another. . . .
But to establish and maintain relationships, people would
have had to be fair, honest, generous, diligent and loyal.
They would have had to be perceived as good partners. In
other words, they would have had to behave morally."[20]

Cooperative social behavior, of course, can be found in
other animal species—birds that fly in formation, elk that
roam in herds, ants that cooperate in colonies and bees in
hives. Monkeys and apes commonly trade grooming favors.
Antarctic penguins engage in an elaborate group hug to
keep chick eggs warm before they hatch.[21]

There is disagreement among evolutionary biologists as
to whether this instinct for social cooperation evolved only
at the individual level, or at the group level as well. While I
won't try to resolve that debate here, I find an experiment
by geneticist William Muir to be highly instructive.[22]

Chicken farmers had reasoned that they could increase
egg production by focusing their breeding on hens that laid
the most eggs. Unfortunately, it turned out that the most
productive hens were also the most aggressive, so that
when the top-laying hens were bred and placed in the
close quarters of the henhouse, many died from fighting.

In the end, the higher death rate from all that alpha aggression more than offset the positive effects of the higher fertility of those who survived.

So Muir tried a different strategy. Rather than selecting the most productive hens for breeding, he found the cages in which the hens collectively produced the greatest number of eggs. Then he bred the entire group, irrespective of individual fertility. Within six generations, the death rate fell from 67 percent to 8 percent, while total egg production more than doubled. From this and similar experiments, Muir concluded that "group selection" offered a more powerful explanation for the natural selection of cooperative traits.

Recent brain research reveals there is a chemical basis for cooperative and altruistic behavior. Scientists have found that when a person is confronted with a kindness or sign of trust from someone else, the brain releases a chemical known as oxytocin. The oxytocin, in turn, has the effect of making that person more likely to reciprocate with trust or kindness, setting up a virtuous cycle in which trust begets trust, altruism begets altruism and cooperation begets cooperation. Oxytocin levels are also found to correlate with levels of happiness.

Paul Zak, an economist and founding director of the Center for Neuroeconomics Studies at Claremont Graduate University, used a classic economic experiment to demonstrate the connection between trust and oxytocin, which he dubbed the "moral molecule."

In the "trust game," two people are each given $10 that they can walk away with at any time. Under the rules of the game, Player A is invited to give any of his $10 to an unknown Player B sitting in another room, with the stipulation that each dollar given to Player B would be matched by three additional dollars from sponsors of the game. At that point,

Player B must decide how much of the enhanced donation she will kick back to Player A.

If we are all selfish, greedy people who assume others to be as well, then the rational decision by Player A would be to make no donation and walk away with his $10 windfall. And if, for some reason, Player A were silly enough to donate anything to Player B, then the selfish, greedy Player B would keep it all, with no reciprocation.

In fact, that's not what happens. In Zak's experiments, 90 percent of the A players donate something—on average between $3 and $4 of the initial $10—with 95 percent of the B players reciprocating, most typically one dollar for each donated dollar. A players walked away from the game with an average of $14 and B players with $17. That's still not the maximally trusting and cooperative outcome, which would be for A players to donate their entire $10, and B players, now with pots of $40, to split them 50–50, allowing everyone to walk away with $20. But it's a long way from the selfish and untrusting strategy of take the money and run.

Although many others have run trust game experiments with similar results, Zak's contribution was to measure the level of oxytocin in the players' brains while the experiment was going on. He found a "dramatic and direct" correlation between the level of the A players' original donation, the change in the oxytocin levels in the brains of the B players, and the amount B players returned.[23]

What this and other research suggest is that, "as a species, we are far less self-interested—and on balance, generally far kinder and more cooperative—than the prevailing wisdom has ever acknowledged," Zak concluded. "The Golden Rule is a lesson the body already knows, and when we get it right, we feel the rewards immediately."[24]

What we can take away from the work of Darwin and his successors is that our "moral sense" has evolved from millions of years of adaptive behavior, providing a useful restraint on equally powerful instincts that incline us toward selfishness, ruthless predation and immediate gratification.[25] Because of this moral sensibility, we sympathize with those in need, and take pleasure in helping them. We are willing to trust others in the expectation that we will be trusted in return, and we feel warm and cuddly when they do. When they don't, we are outraged and take pleasure in punishing them. We feel shame when we ourselves act too selfishly and feel pride when we do not. And all of these instincts and sensibilities are now part of our physiological and emotional makeup. They are hardwired into our brains and our hearts.

"Our moral instincts evolved . . . to help us put Us ahead of Me," writes Joshua Greene in his book *Moral Tribes*. Greene cautions, however, that we must be careful not to push the evolutionary basis of morality too far. While we are programmed for sympathy and cooperation, they are not extended to everyone—only those in our own family, our own circle, our own tribe. "Universal cooperation is inconsistent with the principles governing evolution by natural selection," Greene writes. In genetic terms, cooperation evolved not as a mechanism to promote universal peace and harmony, but more narrowly as a successful strategy for Us to beat Them.[26]

But if that is true, then why do we routinely find selflessness, sympathy and cooperation with people who are distant or different from ourselves? Why do we send pennies to starving babies in Biafra or take in desperate refugees from Syria? And why, if our moral instincts are universal and innate, do different societies adopt such different moral codes?

The answer is that while our moral instincts evolved on a genetic foundation, they require cultural and social institutions to actually refine and communicate the values,

norms and practices—the dos and don'ts. Morality evolved
through a combination of genetics and culture.[27] To use a
high-tech analogy, biology and evolution provide the operating software of moral sensibility, but it is culture that provides most of the apps.

It is this genetic and cultural coevolution that explains
why *homo sapiens* prevailed over their stronger, brainier rivals, the Neanderthals, 30,000 years ago. And it is this coevolution that explains why we have been able to widen our
lead over all other species in the years since. Physiologically,
we have evolved very little from those early hunter-gatherers.
But thanks to our unique ability to communicate stories and
myths that, over time, provide the basis for social norms and
institutions, we have made dramatic progress in our ability
to extend sympathy, altruism, trust and cooperation beyond our immediate circle to large numbers of people we
do not know, and even to those with whom we sometimes
compete.[28]

Given the litany of modern-day lapses—from the Holo-
caust and the Rwandan genocide to the atrocities of radical
Islam and the current scapegoating of immigrants—it would
be ridiculous to claim that humans have evolved to the point
that we now treat everyone as we would want to be treated.
However, to the extent we have succeeded in extending the
Golden Rule to those unlike ourselves, we can thank reli-
gions, laws and cultures for carrying our moral instincts
beyond the demands of biological survival, thereby allowing humans to achieve higher levels of cooperation than
bees, ants, penguins and chimpanzees.

The human species that emerged from the jungles and
the savannas was a stubbornly social animal, with instincts
for both competition and cooperation. And for that reason,
an economic system that is based on the presumption that
people will, or should, act only on the basis of selfishness

is no more likely to succeed than one based on the utopian presumption that people will, or should, act only on the basis of altruism. Both are based on a false understanding of human nature.

The Curse of "Maximizing Shareholder Value"

There may be no more pernicious example of the way the ethic of "greed is good" has been woven into the fabric of modern life than the widespread embrace of the idea that companies must put shareholder interests above all others. Much of what we perceive to be wrong with American capitalism is a consequence of this misguided ideology, which has no basis in law, history or logic.[29]

The poster boy for maximizing shareholder value is Martin Shkreli, as Robert Reich recounts in his recent book *The Common Good*. Shkreli was a two-bit stock speculator who started his own hedge fund to short the stocks of biotech firms he suspected might be hyping their research results—then took to Internet chat rooms to try to talk down their share price. A shameless self-promoter, Shkreli launched his own drug company, Turing Pharmaceuticals, in early 2015 with the aim of buying up licenses for generic drugs that had little or no competition in the marketplace, and then jacking up the price for patients or insurance companies who had no other choice but to pay it. One such drug was Daraprim, which was the only treatment for a rare parasitic disease that also was used to treat some AIDS patients. Shkreli raised the price of Daraprim from $13.50 a pill to $750. When this news hit the front pages, the public was morally outraged. Shkreli, however, not only refused to apologize or roll it back, but said his only mistake had been not to raise the price even higher.

"No one wants to say it, no one's proud of it, but this is a capitalist society, a capitalist system and capitalist rules," Shkreli told investors at a health-care conference as the controversy mounted. "And my investors expect me to maximize profits, not to minimize them or go half or go 70 percent, but to go to 100 percent of the profit curve."[30]

Shkreli was soon hauled up before a congressional committee to explain his price-gouging tactics. At the hearing, he refused to answer questions, citing his constitutional right against self-incrimination. When the pharmaceutical industry tried to distance itself from his tactics, an unrepentant Shkreli took to the Internet to argue that he had done nothing that many other drug companies hadn't done, and went on to cite numerous examples, to the embarrassment of industry executives.

Through it all, not a single business organization or business leader stepped forward to defend Shkreli or the doctrine of maximizing returns to shareholders. Nor did any step forward to acknowledge any second thoughts about that doctrine, or make any attempt to distinguish between Turing's hardball business tactics and those of other companies. Shkreli's sin was that he had exposed the moral bankruptcy at the heart of American-style capitalism.

In truth, there are no state or federal laws that require that corporations be run to maximize profits or share prices. Corporations can be formed for any lawful purpose. The late Lynn Stout of the Cornell Law School searched for years for a corporate charter that even mentions maximizing profits or share price. She never found one.[31]

Nor does the law demand, as many believe, that executives and directors owe a special fiduciary duty to the shareholders who own the corporation. The director's fiduciary duty is owed simply to the corporation, which is owned by no one. Corporations, like individuals, "own" themselves.[32]

Even if the law had required that a corporation should be run for the benefit of its shareholders, it would still beg the question of exactly which shareholders the law had in mind. Is it the individual investor with a 401(k) account who buys stock in a safe, solidly performing company with the intention of holding it until retirement, or the hedge fund with the elaborate computerized trading algorithm that holds it for two seconds? Is it an individual or taxable entity that would prefer taking profits in capital gains, or a tax-exempt entity that would prefer dividends? Is the shareholder a loyal employee who wants to share in his company's success or the activist investor who wants that employee's compensation to be cut or his job outsourced to Bangladesh? You see the problem.

Given this vagueness and the lack of legal or historical support, why has "maximizing shareholder value"—an expression virtually unheard of before the 1980s—become a widely accepted norm of business behavior?

The economist Milton Friedman is often credited with first articulating the idea in a 1970 essay in which he argued that "there is one and only one social responsibility of business—to use its resources and engage in activities designed to increase its profits." Anything else, he argued, was not capitalism but "unadulterated socialism."[33]

In those days, Friedman's was a minority view not just among economists but also among corporate leaders. A little more than a decade later, the Business Roundtable, representing the nation's largest firms, issued a statement recognizing a broader purpose of the corporation: "Corporations have a responsibility, first of all, to make available to the public quality goods and services at fair prices, thereby earning a profit that attracts investment to continue and enhance the enterprise, provide jobs and build the economy."[34] The statement went on to talk about a "symbiotic relationship" between business and society.

By 1997, however, the Business Roundtable was singing from a different hymnal. "The principal objective of a business enterprise is to generate economic returns to its owners," the group declared in its statement on corporate responsibility. "If the CEO and the directors are not focused on shareholder value, it may be less likely the corporation will realize that value."[35]

The most likely explanation for this transformation involves three broad structural changes then bearing down on the U.S. economy: globalization, deregulation and rapid technological change. These three forces have conspired to rob what were once the dominant American corporations of the abundant profits they earned during the "golden era" of the 1950s and '60s—profits so abundant that they could spread the benefits around to all corporate stakeholders, without anyone wondering if they were being shortchanged.

It was only when competition from foreign suppliers or newly deregulated upstarts began to squeeze out those generous profits that these once-mighty corporations were forced to make difficult choices. In the early going, corporate executives found that it was easier to disappoint shareholders than customers, workers or even their communities. The result, during the 1970s, was a lost decade for investors.[36]

Beginning in the mid-1980s, however, a number of companies with lagging stock prices found themselves targets for unsolicited takeover offers launched by rival companies or corporate raiders such as Carl Icahn. Shareholders who had seen little movement in the stock price were only too willing to overrule naysaying executives and directors and accept the premium price being offered for their shares.

The bruising takeover battles of the 1980s transformed Wall Street, overturning the gentlemanly competition that had prevailed among the white-shoe law firms and investment houses and upsetting the old order. Making use of new "junk bonds"—bonds that carried higher risk but offered investors higher interest rates—to finance their shopping sprees, private equity funds began making bids for major companies, prompting counterbids and elaborate defensive strategies by management to fend off the "raiders." Speculators began piling into stocks of other companies in anticipation that they, too, would be takeover targets, some trading illegally on inside information. A bid for any one company in an industry instantly put every other company "in play."

Just as a hanging has a way of concentrating the mind, the threat of a hostile takeover—and with it, the loss of lucrative jobs and prestigious directorships—had a profound effect on the mind-set in corporate boardrooms and executive suites. The best defense against a takeover was a high stock price, and the best way to raise share prices was to increase profits. Almost overnight, executives and directors tossed aside their more complacent and paternalistic management style, and with it a host of old inhibitions against laying off workers, cutting wages and benefits, closing plants and taking on debt. Some, having once denounced hostile takeovers as unsporting and economically counterproductive, even made hostile bids themselves.

Spurred on by this new "market for corporate control," as it was called, the era of "managerial capitalism" soon gave way to the era of "shareholder capitalism," which continues to this day. Corporate executives who once arrogantly ignored the demands of Wall Street now profess they have no choice but to dance to its tune. In their private moments, they worry less about competitors than they do about activist investors.

   This mandate to maximize profits and share prices is now reinforced by an elaborate infrastructure that includes think tanks and executive training programs, court decisions, executive compensation schemes and Wall Street investors and analysts.

   To justify the idea that the stock price is a reliable measure of a company's economic value, conservative think tanks and university faculties continue to spin out elaborate theories about the efficiency of financial markets. An earlier generation of economists, led by British economist John Maynard Keynes, had looked at the stock market boom and bust that led to the Great Depression and concluded that share prices often reflected irrational herd behavior on the part of investors. But in the 1960s, a different theory began to take hold in intellectual strongholds such as the University of Chicago that quickly spread to other economics departments and business schools. The essence of the "efficient market hypothesis," first articulated by Eugene Fama, was that the current stock price reflects all the public and private information that could be known about a company, and therefore was a reliable gauge of the company's true economic value. For a generation of business school professors, it has been only a short logical leap from this assumption to a conclusion that the share price is the best metric around which to organize a company's strategy and measure its success.

   With the rise of behavioral economics, which has demonstrated the often-irrational behavior of economic actors, and the onset of two stock market bubbles, the efficient market hypothesis has become harder to defend with a straight face. Yale economist Robert Shiller—who, in an ironic twist, shared a 2013 Nobel with Fama—demonstrated the various and predictable ways in which financial markets are anything but rational.[37] But the efficient market hypothesis is still widely accepted by business schools, whose finance professors continue to indoctrinate their students with it. The shareholder-first ideology remains so entrenched that even business school deans who publicly reject it acknowledge privately that they have given up trying to convince their faculties to take a more balanced approach.[38]

Equally important in sustaining the shareholder focus are corporate lawyers, who now reflexively advise companies against actions that would predictably lower a company's stock price.

For many years, much of the case law coming out of the Delaware courts—where most big corporations have their legal home—was based around the "business judgment rule," which held that corporate directors have wide discretion in determining a firm's goals and strategies, even if their decisions have the effect of reducing profits or share prices.

But in 1986, the Delaware Court of Chancery ruled that directors of Revlon, the cosmetics company, had to put the interests of shareholders first and accept a takeover offer from the highest bidder. As Lynn Stout explained, and the Delaware courts subsequently confirmed, the *Revlon v. MacAndrews & Forbes Holdings* decision was a narrowly drawn exception to the business judgment rule, applying only when a company has decided to put itself up for sale. But it has been widely—and mistakenly—used ever since as a legal rationale for the primacy of shareholder interests and the legitimacy of share price maximization.[39]

Reinforcing this mistaken belief are the shareholder lawsuits that are now routinely filed against public companies by class action lawyers any time their stock price takes a sudden dive. Most of these are frivolous and, since the passage of reform legislation in 1995, most are dismissed. But even those that are dismissed generate cost and hassle, while the few that go to trial risk exposing the company to significant embarrassment, damages and legal fees. The result is that executives and directors are wary of taking any action that could adversely affect short-term share prices, even if it would benefit the company over the long term.

Surely the most extensive infrastructure supporting the shareholder-value ideology is to be found on Wall Street, where money managers and the analysts who give them advice remain stubbornly fixated on the quarterly profit performance in deciding which stocks to buy and sell. Companies that refuse to give advance estimates of their next-quarter profits find that their stock is systematically shunned by money managers, while any that miss their earnings projections, even by small amounts, see their stock prices hammered.[40]

There is, of course, a good reason for this obsession with companies' quarterly results: pension and mutual fund managers are themselves judged by their investment results each quarter. Those who produce big increases in the value of their portfolios are showered with generous bonuses, while those with disappointing returns soon find themselves looking for another job.

In a now-infamous press interview in the summer of 2007, a year before the crash, former Citigroup chairman Charles Prince provided a window into the hold that Wall Street money managers have over corporate behavior. At the time, Citi's share price had lagged behind that of the other big banks, leading to speculation in the financial press that Prince would be fired if he didn't quickly find a way to catch up. In the interview with the *Financial Times*, Prince seemed to confirm that speculation. Asked why he was continuing to make loans for richly priced corporate takeovers despite evidence that the takeover boom was losing steam, he replied that he, or anyone else in his job, had no choice as long as other banks were making big profits from such loans.

"As long as the music is playing," Prince explained, "you've got to get up and dance."[41]

Of course, it is not only Wall Street money managers and bankers who are responsible for this fixation—many of us are also to blame. When those of us who put our savings into mutual funds decide to move to a new fund with a different manager because it had a better return last quarter or last year, we are sending a very clear signal that we want to maximize the value of our holdings. Those fund managers, in turn, send the same signal to the executives of the companies in which they have invested our money. The comic strip character Pogo had it right: "We have met the enemy and he is us."

It is not simply the threat of losing their jobs that causes corporate executives to focus on shareholder value, however. There are also plenty of carrots to be found in those generous—one might say gluttonous—pay packages whose value is closely tied to the performance of company stock.

The idea of loading up executives with stock and stock options also dates to the transition to shareholder capitalism. The academic critique of managerial capitalism was that the lagging performance of big corporations was a manifestation of what economists call an "agent-principal problem." In this case the "principals" were the shareholders and the misbehaving "agents" were the executives who were spending too much of their time and the shareholders' money trying to satisfy employees, customers and the community at large.

In what came to be one of the most widely cited academic papers of all time, business school professors Michael

Jensen of Harvard and William Meckling of the University of Rochester wrote in 1976 that the best way to align the interests of managers to those of the shareholders was to tie a substantial amount of the managers' compensation to the share price.[42] In a subsequent paper, Jensen went even further, arguing that the reason corporate executives acted more like "bureaucrats than value-maximizing entrepreneurs" was that they didn't get to keep enough of the extra value they created.[43]

With that academic foundation, and the enthusiastic support of executive compensation specialists, stock-based compensation took off. According to the Economic Policy Institute, the average chief executive of the country's 350 largest public companies now earns more than $15 million a year, or 271 times the pay of the typical worker in their companies. In 1965, that ratio was 20 to 1. As recently as 1985, it was only 59 to 1. CEO pay has grown faster than the sales and profits of the companies they run. It has grown faster than the pay of other highly skilled workers, those in the top one-tenth of 1 percent on the income scale.[44] But the ultimate irony is that it has even grown faster than the return to shareholders whose interests they claim to represent.

Roger Martin, the former dean of the Rotman School of Management at the University of Toronto, calculates that from 1932 until 1976—roughly speaking, the era of managerial capitalism, in which managers sought to balance the interest of shareholders with those of employees, customers and society at large—the total real compound annual return on the stocks of the S&P 500 was 7.6 percent. From 1976 until 2011—a period of shareholder capitalism—the comparable return has been 6.4 percent.[45] Meanwhile, the ratio of executive compensation to corporate profits has increased eightfold.

As Harvard's Rakesh Khurana has written, there is

something fundamentally corrupt—and corrupting—about
an arrangement in which corporate executives are no longer treated as trusted professional managers but as free
agents who have to be lavishly bribed by shareholders to
ensure their undivided loyalty over other stakeholders. In
such an environment, it is hardly surprising that Corporate
America has suffered a string of ethical scandals involving
misstated earnings, backdated options, overhyped business plans and market manipulation.[46]

In recent years, the most common—though perfectly
legal—form of market manipulation has been the stock buyback, where companies purchase millions of their own
shares on the open market. The buybacks increase demand
for a company's shares while reducing the supply, driving up
the stock price. Buybacks are seen as such an effective, tax-
advantaged way to boost short-term stock price that they are
invariably the first thing activist investors like Icahn now demand of their targets. And they have become so popular
that, over the last decade, the largest American corporations
have spent over half of their profits buying back their own
shares—in addition to the 35 percent distributed to shareholders in the form of dividends.[47]

One consequence of this undue focus on today's share
price is that corporate and investor time horizons have become shorter and shorter. The average holding period for
corporate stocks, which for decades was six years, is now
down to less than six months.[48] The average tenure of a corporate chief executive has fallen to less than five years.[49]

Given those realities, it should be no surprise that corporate executives are less willing to sacrifice short-term profits in order to make expensive investments in the new
equipment and new products that keep companies growing
and competitive over the long term.

A study by McKinsey & Co., the blue-chip consulting

firm, found alarming levels of short-termism in the corporate executive suite. According to the study, nearly 80 percent of top executives and directors reported feeling the most pressure to demonstrate a strong financial performance over a period of two years or less, with only 7 percent feeling pressure to deliver strong performance over a period of five years or more. It also found that a majority of chief financial officers would forgo an attractive investment project today if it would cause the company to even marginally miss its quarterly earnings target.[50]

More recently, McKinsey's research arm went back to compare the performance of the companies that took the short view with the dwindling number of companies that took the long-term view. It found that from 2001 to 2014 the revenue of companies with a long-term view grew, on average, 47 percent more, and their profits increased 36 percent more. The McKinsey researchers concluded that public companies would have generated an additional $1 trillion in economic output and added 5 million more jobs in the United States if all public companies had taken the long-term view over that 15-year period. That works out to the equivalent of a 0.8 percentage point difference in the annual rate of economic growth.[51]

Most significantly, the McKinsey study puts the lie to the idea that running a company to maximize short-term profits and share prices is what's best for shareholders. In fact, total return to shareholders—that is, dividends plus share appreciation—was systematically better among firms with a long-term focus, with a 50 percent greater chance that they would be among the top 10 percent of companies in terms of shareholder return.

Perhaps the most surprising aspect of *shareholder uber alles* is how at odds it is with every modern theory about managing people. David Langstaff, chief executive of Total

Administrative Servicing Corporation, a government con-
tracting firm, framed it this way:

"If you are the sole proprietor of a business, do you think
that you can motivate your employees for maximum performance by encouraging them simply to make more money
for you? For that is effectively what an enterprise is saying
when it states that its purpose is to maximize profit for its
investors."[52]

Recently, economists have been trying to figure out why
growth in worker productivity has been so disappointing
over the last several decades, a phenomenon Harvard's Lawrence Summers has dubbed "secular stagnation."[53] Do you
think, just maybe, that this stagnation might be related to
the fact that American workers have come to understand
that whatever financial benefit may result from working
harder or smarter is almost certain to be captured by shareholders and top executives and not themselves? Of course it
has been a factor, as anyone who has worked in or managed
an enterprise will tell you. Yet, if the chief executive of any
public company would dare to buck the prevailing ethic and
declare that, going forward, the company's success would
be shared broadly with all employees, he could be fairly certain that his share price would be hammered and he would
be skewered in the financial press.

Indeed, that is exactly what happened to Doug Parker,
chief executive of American Airlines, in the spring of 2017.
After years of pay and benefit cuts, American was finally sol-
vent again and Parker felt he had the financial headroom
to give raises to pilots and flight attendants who were complaining that they were being paid less than employees at
other airlines. Parker called the raises an "investment" in improved morale that would eventually lead to improved customer service and higher profits.

Wall Street, however, didn't see it that way. "This is frustrating," complained Citigroup analyst Kevin Crissey in a note to the bank's clients. "Labor is being paid first again. Shareholders get leftovers." A J.P. Morgan analyst worried aloud that the move "establishes a worrying precedent." On cue, American Airlines' shares ended the day down by more than 5 percent.[54]

Compare that negative reaction from Wall Street to the hosannas that greeted Seattle entrepreneur Dan Price when he announced, in the spring of 2015, that he would set a minimum $70,000 salary for all employees at his credit card processing firm, Gravity Payments. He even cut his own pay from $1.1 million to $70,000 to help pay for the raises. Price called the wage floor not only a good business practice but a "moral imperative." The story was picked up by hundreds of newspapers and TV stations around the world, and Price was invited to become the host of a new reality TV series and speak at the Aspen Ideas festival.

Not everyone celebrated the idea, however. Price's brother and partner filed what turned out to be a costly and unsuccessful lawsuit and a few higher-paid employees quit because their raises weren't as large. A handful of customers cut ties after complaining that the news had prompted their own employees to demand higher pay. Rush Limbaugh took to the airwaves to criticize Price for undermining capitalism.

"I hope this company is a case study in MBA programs on how socialism does not work, because it's gonna fail," fumed the millionaire radio host.

When Harvard Business School professor Michael Wheeler checked in two years later, however, he found Price's "socialism" to have been a smashing success. Customer-retention rates, revenues and profits were up substantially. Employee turnover was greatly reduced and the company was flooded with job applications from highly skilled candidates just dying to work there. Price's employees were so grateful they chipped in and bought him a Tesla. A number of other entrepreneurs have since followed suit.[55]

What was most surprising about Price's pay strategy was that people found it so surprising. The idea that companies have any obligation to their employees to provide a decent standard of living had long since fallen out of favor.

So, too, had the idea that companies owe any allegiance to the public. In the view of many directors of public corporations, the mandate to maximize shareholder value carries with it a fiduciary duty to oppose any government actions that might negatively impact company profits, irrespective of the benefit to the country. This fiduciary duty is now routinely used to justify multimillion-dollar lobbying and advertising campaigns against regulations designed to protect consumers, workers, the environment and small investors, which are invariably characterized as "job-killing, one-size-fits-all solutions" to problems that don't exist. And it's the rationale for engaging in elaborate schemes to avoid paying their fair share of taxes that the government relies on to guarantee the rule of law, educate their workforce and build the public infrastructure on which their business depends.

All of which brings us back to the Senate Permanent Subcommittee on Investigations. Three years after failing to get the men from Goldman to acknowledge the ethical lapses that led to the financial crisis, the panel was back at it, this time trying to get some of the country's top executives to see the connection between the $2 trillion in profits they had stashed overseas to avoid taxes and the federal budget crisis back home.

In May 2013, Chairman Levin summoned before the panel the top executives of Apple, Inc., arguably the country's most successful and respected company, and, at $6 billion per year, its largest corporate taxpayer. But with worldwide profits of $42 billion in 2012, Apple's federal tax payments were still well below the average effective tax rate for American corporations of 22 percent, due primarily to the fact that its overseas profits went largely untaxed by any country.

Opening the hearing, Levin laid out how the company's "crown jewels"—the intellectual property developed by Apple's American engineers that accounts for the lion's share of the profit earned from the sale of every iPhone, iPad and MacBook computer—had wound up in the hands of a wholly owned Irish subsidiary that had few employees and, for tax purposes, was a resident of no country. By Levin's calculation, this clever gambit had saved Apple $9 billion in taxes in 2012 alone.

What Apple had done was a clever twist on a tax-avoidance strategy widely used by global firms based in the United States. The aim is to rearrange the company's operations and internal accounting so a disproportionate share of worldwide expenses are booked in high-tax places like the United States, while a disproportionate share of worldwide revenues are booked by subsidiaries in low-tax jurisdictions. To accomplish this, parent companies strike one-sided arrangements with overseas subsidiaries to buy and sell things at artificially high or low prices.

In Apple's case, the company had arranged for its Irish subsidiary to use untaxed profits to buy, at a sweetheart price, the patent rights associated with all products sold outside North America. And then by cleverly arbitraging the different criteria used by Ireland and the United States to determine what profits are subject to tax, Apple arranged things so the income from the transferred patents was subject to tax by neither country.[56]

Apparently it was all legal, as long as you accepted the company's assertions that the overseas subsidiaries were set up for legitimate business reasons other than avoiding taxes, and that the terms of the deal between subsidiary and parent company were similar to those that might be struck in an arm's-length transaction. Stephen Shay, a professor of tax law at Harvard Law School and a former Treasury official, told the committee that in Apple's case, such assumptions "strained credulity."

But Tim Cook, Apple's chief executive, was determined to give no quarter to the Senate committee when asked to explain this convoluted effort to shift profits overseas. "We not only comply with the laws, we comply with the spirit of the laws," Cook told the senators with a straight face. "We do not depend on tax gimmicks."[57]

A week later, Google's executive chairman, Eric Schmidt, was in London trying to assuage an even more outraged British public after a parliamentary committee revealed that the search giant had paid £3.4 million in taxes in 2012 on British sales of £3.2 billion. Like Apple, Google had avoided British taxes by shifting its intellectual property through a series of tax-avoidance arrangements known as a "double Irish" and "Dutch sandwich." As Schmidt explained to the BBC, Google had a "fiduciary responsibility to our shareholders" to pay no more taxes than legally required.[58] As recently as 2016, Google reported moving nearly $19 billion a year in profits through a Bermuda shell company, saving $3.7 billion in U.S. taxes.[59]

Just as the executives from Goldman had denied they had any duty of loyalty and honesty to their trading partners or the financial system, the executives from Apple and Google had come to believe that they owed no duty of loyalty and honesty to their country or fellow taxpayers. In a competitive marketplace, their only role was to maximize the income of their shareholders while staying, however barely, on the right side of the law. The invisible hand would magically take care of everything else.

As Harvard's Khurana has lamented, today's corporate executive "is someone who does not feel constrained by norms arising from social values such as fairness or equity, or by allegiance to social institutions such as nations, firms or even jobs. Such individuals lack any sense of moral responsibility. . . . [They] thrive in amoral environments in which ideas such as duty and reciprocity seem alien or are ridiculed as old-fashioned and naïve."[60]

This corporate amorality certainly doesn't sit well with the public. The most recent Gallup survey found that people's trust in, and respect for, big corporations has been on a long, slow decline in recent decades—only Congress and health-maintenance organizations are lower.[61] And when you think of chief executives who have managed to win public admiration, the ones who most readily come to mind are Jeff Bezos, the founder of Amazon, and the late Steve Jobs, founder of Apple—executives who, together, have created more wealth for shareholders than any two people on the planet by largely ignoring shareholder value and putting customers at the top of their priority list.

That customer-first conception of corporate purpose was certainly the one favored by Peter Drucker, the late management guru. "There is only one valid definition of a business purpose: to create a customer," he famously wrote.[62] And as Roger Martin demonstrates in his book *Fixing the Game*, there is plenty of data to suggest that companies that put customers first consistently produce higher profits and shareholder returns than those that claim to put shareholders first. The reason, according to Martin, is that a customer focus minimizes the chance of undue risk-taking and maximizes the chance that a company will reinvest more of its profits in ways that create a larger pie from which everyone can benefit.[63]

A study by Jon Picoult of Watermark Consulting lends support to that conclusion. Picoult created two portfolios of stocks, one with the top ten companies in Forrester Research's Customer Experience Index, the other with the bottom ten companies, and ran the numbers for the years 2007–2012. The customer service leaders had a five-year return of 43 percent while the laggards lost 34 percent.[64]

These and other studies call into question the widely held assumption among executives and directors that companies that refuse to genuflect daily before the altar of shareholder value will be unable to compete in the global marketplace or attract sufficient numbers of investors. Nobody—and certainly not me—is arguing that companies don't sometimes have to make hard choices with painful consequences in order to remain globally competitive. Nor is anyone arguing that companies should not aim to earn healthy profits and provide shareholders with consistent, above-average returns. The problem is with the word "maximizing," which, in practice, seems to demand that every cent of economic surplus generated by a company's business be captured by shareholders.

What's the difference between providing shareholders a consistent, above-average return and maximizing shareholder value?

It's the difference between gradually globalizing your supply chains to remain competitive and shutting down factories with little notice and meager severance payments.

It's the difference between paying a reasonable tax on profits and renouncing U.S. corporate citizenship and moving the company headquarters to a tax haven.

It's the difference between standing up to piggy and pigheaded unions and crushing unions with illegal, bare-knuckle tactics that won't be punished until long after the union organizers have moved on.

It's the difference between giving bonuses to every employee at the end of a profitable year and giving lavish bonuses only to executives.

It's the difference between honoring pension commitments and cleverly running the company through the bankruptcy process to foist them onto the federal government.

It's the difference between having enough people to speak to customers when they call and routinely leaving them on hold for an hour.

It's the difference between maintaining a healthy balance sheet and loading the company up with debt to pay for dividends and buy back shares.

A common retort from corporate chief executives is that maximizing shareholder value isn't a license for ruthless predation. In the real world, they explain, there's no way to maximize shareholder value without doing what is necessary to attract and retain great employees, provide great products and services to customers and support efficient governments and healthy communities. In this way, markets provide a reliable check on socially irresponsible corporate behavior.

But if optimizing shareholder value implicitly requires firms to take good care of customers, employees and communities, as executives claim, then by the same logic optimizing customer satisfaction would require firms to take good care of employees, communities and shareholders— or that maximizing any particular value inevitably requires the same messy balancing of interests that executives of an earlier era sought to do. In that case, why not acknowledge the inevitability of having to make such tradeoffs rather than oversimplify the challenge in a way that shreds the social contract between business and society?

In a 2017 article, Harvard Business School professors Joseph Bower and Lynn Paine, describing themselves as "capitalists to the core," summed up the case against the shareholder-fixated corporation: "A better model would recognize the critical role of shareholders but also take seriously the idea that corporations are independent entities serving multiple purposes and endowed by law with the potential to endure over time."[65]

Having spoken with more than a few top executives over the years, I can tell you that many would be thrilled if they could focus more on maximizing the satisfaction of customers rather than that of shareholders and stock analysts. In private, they chafe under the quarterly earnings regime forced on them by asset managers and the financial press. They fear and loathe activist investors. And they are disheartened by the distrust and disrespect with which they are viewed by the public and even by their own employees. Yet few have dared to challenge the shareholder-first ideology in public.

To some extent, this is a classic collective-action problem. Although the executives, as a group, would be better off moving away from shareholder-value maximization, it is irrational for any one company to do so lest it be singled out and punished. They all have to do it collectively—which, in fact, was a big reason why organizations like the Business Roundtable and the Chamber of Commerce were formed. But rather than providing a vehicle for raising norms of corporate behavior, these organizations have now become apologists for lowering them.

There's no better example of this abdication of civic leadership than the tax bill passed in December 2017 that dramatically lowered corporate tax rates and ended U.S. taxation of overseas profits. For years, there had been a bipartisan consensus that the official corporate tax rate was too high and put U.S. companies at a disadvantage. And for years, the assumption was that when corporate tax reform was finally passed, it would pay for lower rates by eliminating hundreds of loopholes and tax preferences like those used by Apple and Google. In that way, the government could raise the same amount of revenue in a fairer way with less economic distortion.

But what emerged from the Republican Congress late in 2017 was short on reform—almost no loopholes or tax preferences were eliminated—and long on cuts, not only for corporations, but for rich households and large privately owned businesses and hedge funds. Not only will it exacerbate the problem of income inequality, but it is estimated to add $150 billion a year to a federal deficit that the business community has warned for years is about to spiral out of control. In the view of many tax experts, the tax proposal was morally offensive and economically reckless, and the right thing for business leaders to have done was to have insisted on a plan that was less regressive and more fiscally responsible. Instead, they pocketed a tax cut that far exceeded what businesses then earning record profits needed or deserved, and washed their hands of the consequences.

Companies that are run to simply maximize shareholder value make themselves free riders on an economic system whose past success has been due, in no small part, to the strength of our public institutions and a collective commitment to shared prosperity. They want all the benefits of such a system, but without engaging in the cooperative behavior and making the sacrifices necessary to sustain it. The moral outrage we feel about their business tactics and tax dodging and lavish pay is not class envy—it is a natural and healthy reaction designed to punish and deter antisocial behavior.

As a presidential candidate, Donald Trump tapped into

that outrage. What is ironic—and disappointing—is that now that he is in the White House, Trump has surrounded himself not with critics of maximizing shareholder value, but with its champions. Indeed, until he resigned over questions of self-dealing and conflicts of interest, that inner circle included an activist investor who once told a biographer, "I don't believe in the word *fair*. It's a human concept that became conventional wisdom."[66] The activist investor? Dr. Carl Icahn.

Doing Business on a Handshake

In any market economy, people have to decide whether to trust other people. Think of the farmer who agrees to exchange some of his June peas for another's August wheat, or the hunter who agrees to flush out the quail with the expectation that the other hunters will share the covey. These are examples of how the "trust problem" had to be overcome in a simple agrarian economy. And the need for trust has only grown exponentially as economies have become more complex and exchanges increasingly impersonal and conducted over longer distances and periods of time.

Even cheerleaders for free markets acknowledge that government is usually needed to overcome some of these trust problems, through the creation of property rights and development of the rule of law. But these externally imposed legal restraints can only take us so far. There could never be enough laws and regulations—or courts and jailers to enforce them—to ensure that people don't lie, cheat and steal in their economic interactions. That level of cooperative behavior is possible only if there is a foundation of mutual trust reinforced by a moral code that is broadly accepted and socially enforced.

As Lynn Stout, the Cornell law professor, once wrote,

most of us so routinely act in an unselfish and trusting manner that we no longer even notice it. "Newspapers are left in driveways when no one is about; brawny young men wait peacefully in line behind frail senior citizens; people use ATM machines without hiring armed guards; stores stock their shelves with valuable goods watched over by only a few sales clerks."[67] In other words, most of us do not behave like selfish, untrustworthy sociopaths. If we did, there would be fewer market exchanges and those that occurred would be more expensive because of the elaborate rules and enforcement that would be needed to prevent and deter stealing and cheating. Such enforcement regimes would also make the economy less able to adjust quickly to changing tastes and technologies, inhibiting the innovation and risk-taking essential to the success of a market economy.

Moreover, as we over-rely on these external restraints on our selfishness and greed, we run the risk that our internal restraints—our moral sensibilities—will atrophy. An experiment by a pair of economists illustrates the point.

While living in Israel, Uri Gneezy and Aldo Rustichini discovered that a chain of day-care centers was having trouble with parents showing up late to pick up their children. What would happen, they asked, if parents were fined each day they showed up late? The fines were set at $3, and imposed at only six of the ten centers in the chain, with the other four set aside as a control group. Within three weeks, late pickups had doubled at the centers that imposed fines. At centers with no fines, there was no change.

What happened, Gneezy and Rustichini reasoned, was that while fines provided a small financial disincentive for showing up late, they also changed the way the parents thought about the issue. Before the fines, parents felt a moral obligation not to be selfish and cause inconvenience for the staff and anxiety for their own children by arriving late. But once the fine was instituted, shame or guilt went away. They began to think of it in financial rather than moral terms, and became comfortable with the idea that, when necessary, they could now buy their way out of the obligation to be on time. This view persisted even after the fines were removed; the tardiness rate remained at the elevated rate.[68]

The lesson to be drawn from this study is simple and profound: to succeed, a modern market economy requires not only the hard work and innovation that flow from vigorous pursuit of self-interest, but also the trust and cooperation that flow from our moral instincts. A successful market economy cannot be amoral. It must rest on a solid moral foundation of fair dealing and social cooperation.

Back in 1958, political scientist Edward Banfield published his landmark study of a poor small town in southern Italy, whose lack of vitality he attributed to an almost universal lack of trust or concern for anyone beyond immediate kin. In *The Moral Basis of a Backward Society*, Banfield observed that a mafia-like clannishness—what he called "amoral familism"—prevented residents of the village from acting cooperatively to address common problems or pool common resources. The resulting isolation and poverty stood in contrast to the more prosperous villages in northern Italy, where trust and cooperation were the norm.[69]

Building on Banfield, sociologist James Coleman thirty years later introduced the concept of social capital—a catch-all for the norms, values, networks and institutions that lubricate the machinery of market exchange by nurturing trust and cooperation. The level of social capital, Coleman suggested, was no less important a determinant of a society's economic success than the better-known factors of physical and human capital.[70]

Among the examples of social capital Coleman cited was the wholesale diamond market in New York, where merchants delivered bags of stones worth hundreds of thousands of dollars to each other for inspection without any formal mechanisms to ensure that the diamonds were not stolen or replaced with less valuable stones. This level of trust was reinforced by strong family and ethnic ties: the market was dominated by Orthodox Jews who tended to intermarry, live in the same neighborhood in Brooklyn and attend the same synagogues. Coleman concluded that without those social ties and the moral code that sustains them, elaborate and expensive bonding and insurance mechanisms would have been necessary for the transactions to take place.[71]

In other words, norms of trustworthiness and collective responsibility don't just make life more pleasant and satisfying, although they certainly do that. They have a significant effect on economic output, efficiency and innovation.

The punch line here is that societies with more trust and cooperation and strong moral codes tend to be more prosperous, while greedy societies in which corruption is rife and people can't do business on a handshake tend to be poor.

For most of its history, the United States benefited from this virtuous cycle in which trust breeds prosperity and more prosperity breeds more trust. As far back as the 1830s, Tocqueville found that high levels of trust and social collaboration held in check the natural individualism of Americans that might otherwise have given way to "an exaggerated love of self which leads man to think of all things in terms of himself and prefer himself to all."[72] But in the last 30 years, those checks and that balance have badly eroded.[73]

Consider that when Americans are asked whether most people can be trusted, only 31 percent say yes, down from 46 percent in 1972.[74] Our prison population is exploding, and with it the number of police and private security guards.[75] There has been a steady increase in the volume of civil litigation and the number and pay of lawyers.[76] Americans are less likely than ever to bother voting, while the percentage of those who believe that the government can generally be trusted to do the right thing has fallen from 75 to 25.[77] Our lack of trust now extends to almost every institution: business, religion, the press, the courts, police, labor unions and doctors.[78] In this most philanthropic of countries, even the percentage of household income donated to charitable causes has declined.[79]

Is it just a coincidence that this broad decline in social capital occurred at the same time that there was an intellectual and political embrace of unfettered market competition, a turn toward shareholder primacy and a moral acquiescence to selfishness and greed? I somehow doubt it.

Rather, the story of the last three decades is one of a loosening of moral and ethical norms and a depletion of trust that has weakened our economy and left us worse off as a society. The delicate balance between selfish individualism and cooperative altruism—identified by both Adam Smith and Charles Darwin as the key to human progress—has been lost. This imbalance now manifests itself daily in our polarized and dysfunctional politics, a badly skewed economy and a social fabric that is torn and frayed. The sanctification of selfishness, self-interest and greed has been bad for our economy, bad for our politics and bad for our souls.

2

Not-So-Just Deserts

The moral case for market capitalism rests on two principles that strike us as fair and just.

The first is that markets are rooted in voluntary exchange—my tomatoes for your cauliflower, my money for that dress, my labor for your paycheck. People make such trades because they believe they will be better off than if they did not. And among the liberties to which we are all entitled, this freedom to engage in consensual exchange is high on the list.

The second principle is that people are entitled to own and keep what they produce.[1] Embedded in this notion of "just deserts," as it is called, is that what we earn should reflect not just the amount of time and effort we put into producing things, but the talent and ingenuity and risk-taking that we bring to that effort.

So if it is fair and right that people get to keep the fruits of their own labor, and it is fair and right that they be free to use these fruits to enter into a voluntary and mutually beneficial exchange, then it is logical that an economic system based on these two principles must also be fair. This is an essential component of what we might call "market justice," and it is on the basis of these principles that cheerleaders for free markets argue that any effort by government to interfere with those trades or alter the market's distribution of income and wealth would be akin to theft.

No one has given a clearer account of market justice than the late Harvard philosopher Robert Nozick. As a thought experiment, Nozick famously asks us to imagine a society in which the distribution of income was thought to be fair and just. Then, he asks, imagine that someone like Wilt Chamberlain—or LeBron James, to use a more contemporary example—comes along and offers basketball fans the chance to watch one of the most exciting players in the history of the sport. Millions of people are willing to exchange some of their hard-earned money for the privilege of seeing James play—so many that James becomes fabulously rich relative to everyone else. And, suddenly, the distribution of income becomes much less equal than it was before, when it was judged to be fair and just. Does justice demand, Nozick asks, that James be required to play for something less than what his fans are willing to pay him? Would it demand that he give back his new wealth once he had earned it?[2] Nozick argues not, and rests his case there.

Our moral intuitions, however, reach beyond such simple logic. No matter how voluntary the exchanges, the distribution of income that can result from them can offend our notions of fairness in other ways.

Does it seem right, for example, that rock musicians earn more in a month than high school music teachers might earn in an entire career? Is a hedge fund manager who spends his days speculating in arcane financial instruments really many thousands of times more valuable to society than a nurse? Should the owner of a chain of fast-food franchises live like a pasha while the children of his employees are forced to get by on food stamps?

Allowing such a skewed distribution also seems at odds with other moral intuitions we have—for example, that we are all of equal worth and that we are all entitled to the basic necessities of life. Or that we are all entitled to share equally in our common bounty. Or that helping others is of greater value than helping ourselves.

These more socially oriented intuitions about the distribution of income are no less valid than the individually oriented intuitions that underlie Nozick's claims for free exchange and just deserts. A modern economy often requires us to sacrifice individual rights and liberties in order to achieve cooperative arrangements that make us all better off—paying taxes to pay for common defense, for example, or submitting to the rule of law. Our moral instincts evolved to encourage and enforce such mutually beneficial cooperation and ensure that such sacrifices are fairly apportioned.

Of course, even if we could agree that a particular distribution of income is unjust, we would be hard-pressed to declare what the right distribution would be.

Which commissars would we choose to set the morally correct levels of income and what moral algorithm would we instruct them to use to determine the distribution?

Would an alternative distribution provide sufficient incentives for individuals to work hard, take risks and develop their talents so that the economic pie becomes as large as possible before it is divided?

Must any distribution guarantee that even the least advantaged among us is made better off—the standard proposed by John Rawls, Nozick's greatest rival?[3]

Such questions complicate our consideration of distributional justice.

For the most part, even those of us who are uncomfortable with the current income distribution do not begrudge Bill Gates or Oprah Winfrey or LeBron James their fortunes. We believe ourselves to be better off as a result of the software, entertainment and thrilling performances they produce and that we are willing to pay for—that was Nozick's point. We believe they earned their fortunes fair and square, through hard work, risk-taking, talent and ingenuity, while following the same rules that are meant to provide all of us with the same opportunity to succeed. And we don't begrudge them their fortunes because the market system that produced them also provides the great majority of us with a higher standard of living than any other system.

But what if those things are not true? What if the incomes earned in market exchange are not just an objective measure of individual contribution? What if we were to discover that markets do not provide everyone with anything close to an equal shot at success? What if the market system no longer offers high and rising living standards for most people or leaves some trapped in abject poverty?

If those presumptions are not true, then our moral intuitions might tell us that the distribution of income may not be fair and just. And it is to those fundamental challenges to the concept of market justice that we now turn.

How Unequal Have Incomes Become?

Over the past 35 years, incomes have become more unequal in all advanced countries, but that has been truer in the United States than any other country. The most compelling calculation I've found was offered by former Treasury secretary Lawrence Summers, who estimated that if income distribution in the United States had remained the same as it was in 1979, about *$1 trillion* more would be going each year to the bottom 80 percent of households, increasing their current incomes by almost 25 percent.[4]

One problem in talking about inequality is that there are lots of different data sets to choose from, each imperfect in its own way.

Start with the most basic question: What is income? There are data sets that measure wages and salaries, but ignore things like bonuses, pensions, profits from the sale of stocks or real estate or the value of employer-paid health insurance. Some income data include the value of government payments like food stamps, housing vouchers or government-provided health care; others do not. Some data sets focus on market income, others after-tax income and still others on income after taxes and government transfers— what is often referred to as disposable income.

Then there's also the question of whose income you want to measure—should it be individual or household income? In thinking about what matters for standard of living, household income is clearly superior, but that can be tricky because the size of the average household has been shrinking as more people have divorced or never married. That complicates making comparisons over time.

Measuring income is one thing, measuring income inequality quite another. The most popular measure of income inequality is what scholars call the "Gini coefficient," named after the Italian sociologist Corrado Gini, which calculates the deviation from perfect equality. Sometimes, however, it is more useful to look at the ratio of incomes between those at different rungs of the income ladder—the 90–10 ratio is a common one, looking at the gap between the very rich and very poor, or the 90–50, which focuses on the gap between the very rich and the middle class.

The choice of data set, it turns out, can have a significant impact on calculations of how unequal incomes have become. So it is not surprising to find some analysts who use the set that best conforms to their ideological inclinations.

For my money, the most reliable, comprehensive and ideologically neutral information on American incomes comes from the nonpartisan Congressional Budget Office (CBO), which uses both tax and census data to come up with a broad measure of market income of households that includes employer-paid fringe benefits and realized capital gains. In calculating disposable income, the CBO accounts for all federal taxes paid and government benefits received, using the most comprehensive inflation gauge and adjusting its results to reflect the decline in household size.[5]

The CBO divides the country into five groups, or quintiles, with the bottom quintile consisting of the poorest 20 percent of households and the top those households with the highest income. In a perfectly egalitarian world, each quintile would have 20 percent of the nation's income. In the real world, however, those income shares in 2013 ranged from less than 2 percent for the bottom quintile to 57 percent for the top, as shown in the first figure. After taxes and government benefits are factored in, the distribution of income becomes slightly more equal, with the bottom quintile receiving 7 percent and the top quintile receiving 49 percent. The CBO also breaks out the income shares for the top 1 percent: roughly 17 percent of market income, 13 percent after taxes and transfers.

The second figure shows growth in average market incomes in each quintile between 1979 and 2014, adjusted for inflation. You'll see that there has been very modest growth in market income for the bottom quintiles—less than half a percent a year—while the average income in the top quintile

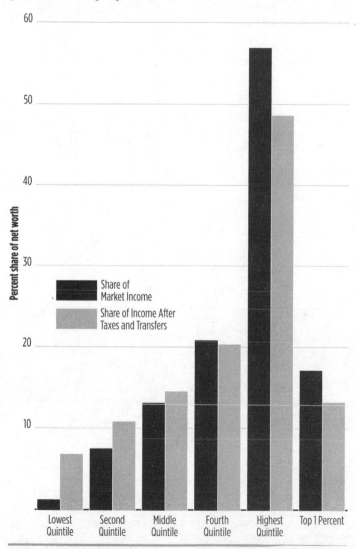

Figure 2.1 **Unequal Shares**

Share of national income that went to each income class in 2014

Income in the United States is heavily skewed toward the top—in particular, the top 1 percent.

Percent share of net worth

- Share of Market Income
- Share of Income After Taxes and Transfers

Lowest Quintile · Second Quintile · Middle Quintile · Fourth Quintile · Highest Quintile · Top 1 Percent

Source: Congressional Budget Office, "The Distribution of Household Income, 2014," March 19, 2018, https://www.cbo.gov/publication/53597.

Figure 2.2 **The Rich Get Richer**

Cumulative percent change in average market income

Since 1979, most of the benefits of economic growth have gone to those at the top, with very little growth for the poor and working-class households.

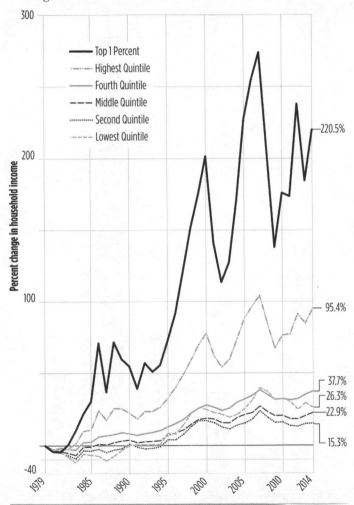

Percent change in household income, by class, 1979–2014, taxes and government transfers, adjusted for inflation.

Source: Congressional Budget Office, "The Distribution of Household Income, 2014," March 19, 2018, https://www.cbo.gov/publication/53597.

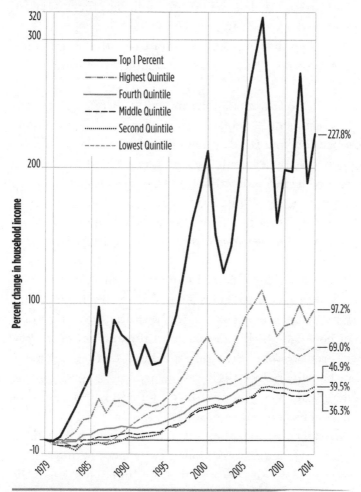

Figure 2.3 **Redistribution Is Modest**

Cumulative percent change in average after-tax income

For households at the bottom, increases in income have come largely as a result of the government's progressive system of taxes and transfers.

Percent change in household income

- Top 1 Percent
- Highest Quintile
- Fourth Quintile
- Middle Quintile
- Second Quintile
- Lowest Quintile

320
300

200

100

-10

1979 1985 1990 1995 2000 2005 2010 2014

227.8%
97.2%
69.0%
46.9%
39.5%
36.3%

Percent change in household income, by class, 1979–2014, after taxes and government transfers, adjusted for inflation.

Source: Congressional Budget Office, "The Distribution of Household Income, 2014," March 19, 2018, https://www.cbo.gov/publication/53597; National Bureau of Economic Research Working Paper 24085, 2016, http://www.nber.org/papers/w24085.

has risen steadily. For the top 1 percent, however—those with incomes above $450,000—the increase has been nothing short of spectacular.

The story is somewhat less bleak when you look at cumulative growth in income after taxes and transfers, as shown in the third figure. For the bottom quintiles, the annual income growth exceeds 40 percent for the 35-year period.

How does the United States compare with the rest of the world? In terms of inequality, we're pretty much the world champs.

Using the Gini inequality index for income after taxes and government benefits, the Organisation for Economic Co-operation and Development finds that, among more developed economies, only Brazil, Mexico and Chile have more income inequality than the United States, as shown in the fourth figure. While other countries' Gini ratios have also increased over time, ours has increased more.[6] That inequality will be even more pronounced once the new tax law takes effect.

One reason for greater inequality in the United States is the wide gaps in market incomes. But an even bigger factor is that our taxes are lower, along with the level of government benefits, which together limit the amount of income that is redistributed. Roughly speaking, taxes and government benefits reduce the level of income inequality in the United States by about one third, noticeably less than they do in other advanced economies.

What is clear from all this is that inequality in the United States is not being driven so much by the poor falling behind the middle class—it's because the rich, and in particular the super rich, are pulling away from everyone else.

A word of caution, however. When thinking about all this data, it is important not to confuse quintiles with actual people. When someone says that income has stagnated in

Figure 2.4 American Exceptionalism

Income inequality by country

While the United States is one of the most unequal in terms of how market national income is distributed, it does less than other countries in equalizing those incomes through taxes and government transfers.

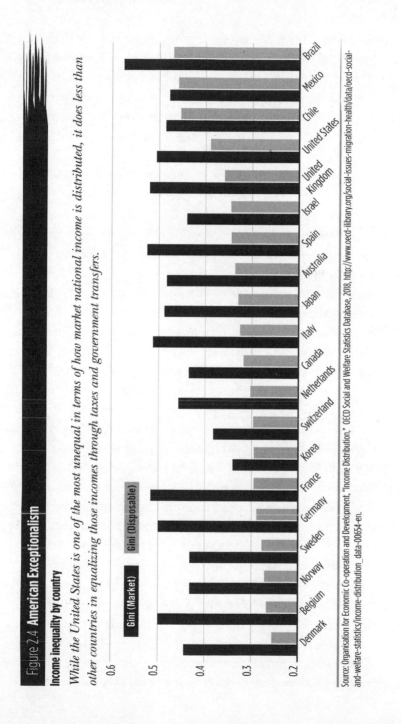

■ Gini (Market) ▨ Gini (Disposable)

Source: Organisation for Economic Co-operation and Development, "Income Distribution," OECD Social and Welfare Statistics Database, 2018, http://www.oecd-library.org/social-issues-migration-health/data/oecd-social-and-welfare-statistics/income-distribution_data-00654-en.

the bottom quintile over 30 years, or soared for the top 1 percent, it doesn't refer to an identifiable, consistent set of households. In fact, the households represented in each quintile change quite a bit over time as people move from one to another in response to immigration, changes in economic conditions or the normal progression of lives and careers. The data is merely a snapshot of incomes at different moments in time. A Treasury study, for example, found that of taxpayers in the top 1 percent in 1987, more than half were not there a decade later.[7]

There are other data sets that do track the income of the same households over time. Using this so-called panel data, Stephen Rose of the Urban Institute compared the incomes of married couples who were in their 20s in 1979 with their incomes in 2007, when they were in their 50s. Slightly more than a quarter experienced an income decline over the period, while a third had at least doubled their incomes. The typical couple saw its income grow by 56 percent.[8]

All the income measures mentioned so far are adjusted for inflation. The indexes on which these adjustments are based are quite good at tracking the changes in prices of the same basket of goods, but not as good at adjusting those prices in a way that captures improvements in quality that allow us to get more value for the same or less money. Yesterday's cell phones allowed us to make phone calls, while today's allow us to call and text anyone almost anywhere at any time while accessing anything on the Internet. We also know that what we buy—the basket of goods—is changing, and that the average household has more cars, takes more trips, eats out more often and is able to buy more fruits and vegetables out of season. In terms of material possessions and comfort, it is hard to argue that we are worse off than we were 30 years ago, which is why a number of conservative analysts have argued that what really matters isn't income, but consumption. The most thorough of recent studies finds that inequality of consumption is a third less than inequality of income.[9]

Moreover, to the degree that households in the top quintile are spending more, much of it is on "status goods"— fancy clothes and accessories, houses in the most desirable neighborhoods and vacation spots, luxury cars, visits to first-class hotels and restaurants and tuitions at top private schools and colleges. Prices for status goods have risen faster than prices of other goods, which means that, in terms of their consumption, the super rich have been getting less bang for all those extra bucks they've been earning. The hedge fund manager might get more pleasure from his $7,000 Rolex than you get from your $52.99 Timex, but we also know that both watches are equally good at keeping time. It's hard to argue that this is the kind of inequality we ought to care about.[10]

Finally, what are we to make of the commonly voiced concern that rising income inequality is eroding the American middle class?

There is, in fact, no official definition of the middle class, but one common way to describe it is as those households clustered around the median income, the 50th percentile or the precise middle rung of the income ladder. Whatever range around the median you want to use, the middle-class share of the population has shrunk by about 15 percent since 1979, with a bit over half of the decline caused by people falling down into the working class. The rest is the result of people climbing to the upper middle class.[11] The "decline" of the middle class, in other words, turns out to be a decidedly mixed blessing.

All of the data so far concerns annual income—the money flowing into households during a year. Wealth, on the other hand, is the money that households save and invest

Figure 2.5 **American Plutocracy**

Share of net worth—assets minus debt—held by each class in 2016

Wealth in the United States is skewed more than income, with the top 1 percent of households holding more wealth than the bottom 95 percent.

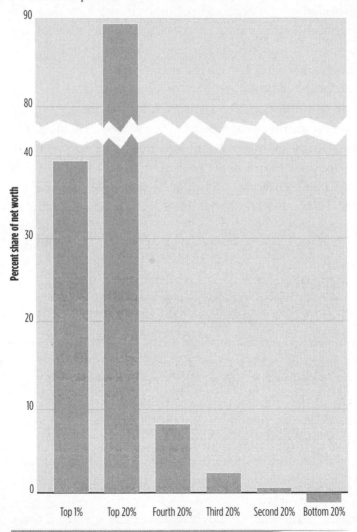

Source: Edward N. Wolff, "Household Wealth Trends in the United States, 1962 to 2016: Has Middle Class Wealth Recovered?" National Bureau of Economic Research Working Paper 24085, 2016, http://www.nber.org/papers/w24085.

after earning it or inheriting it. Since lower-income households save or inherit very little, inequality of wealth has always been significantly greater than that of income. In the United States, the richest 1 percent of households holds more wealth than the bottom 95 percent.[12] And because wealth that is invested generates income each year, over time high levels of wealth inequality have the effect of turbocharging inequality of income, particularly between households at the top and everyone else. Thomas Piketty, the French economist who most recently called attention to this dynamic, estimates wealth inequality is already responsible for 30 percent of the recent increase in income inequality. With the elimination of the inheritance tax by the Republican Congress, that impact is almost certain to grow.[13]

No matter what measure you want to use, however, it should be clear that the United States is now in the middle of a new Gilded Age in which the benefits of economic growth are being distributed more unequally than they have been at any time since before the economic reforms of the Progressive Era and the New Deal.

Why Have Wealth and Incomes Become More Unequal?

Although incomes in the United States have been becoming more unequal for almost four decades, the reasons have changed over time.

In the early 1990s, the consensus among economists was that rising inequality was driven by a decline in demand for lower-skilled workers. Most put the blame on advanced technology that made it possible for machines to more efficiently do the work that had previously been done by workers. That was particularly true for workers with only a high school education.

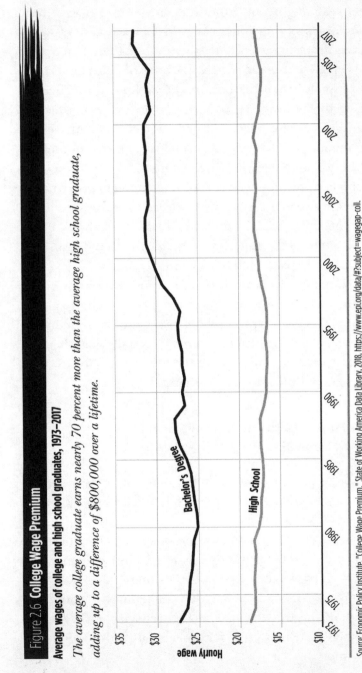

Figure 2.6 College Wage Premium

Average wages of college and high school graduates, 1973–2017

The average college graduate earns nearly 70 percent more than the average high school graduate, adding up to a difference of $800,000 over a lifetime.

Bachelor's Degree

High School

Hourly wage

$35

$30

$25

$20

$15

$10

1973 1975 1980 1985 1990 1995 2000 2005 2010 2015 2017

Source: Economic Policy Institute, "College Wage Premium," State of Working America Data Library, 2018, https://www.epi.org/data/#?subject=wagegap-coll.

Even as technological change was lowering demand for unskilled workers, it created additional demand for skilled workers who could create, maintain and operate all that new technology. That increase in demand, moreover, came at precisely the moment when the supply of workers with college degrees was beginning to level off after years of steady growth.

These simultaneous shifts in supply and demand both for workers with and without college degrees came to be reflected in the so-called college wage premium—the gap between the incomes of the average high school and college graduate. That gap has been steadily increasing since the 1970s, and now amounts to a difference of around 70 percent. Over a lifetime, that means a college degree, on average, is worth an extra $800,000 in income.[14]

By the mid-1990s, globalization was also beginning to be recognized as a culprit in the inequality story. The spur of competition from imports that initially prompted American manufacturers to invest heavily in computers, robots and other high-tech equipment led some to outsource more and more of their production overseas, further decreasing demand for blue-collar workers.

Globalization doesn't just involve the flow of goods across borders. It also involves the flow of people, some legal, but during the 1980s and '90s, much of it illegal, bringing waves of low-skilled workers. The negative effect on the wages of low-skilled workers who were already here is still hotly debated, but if there has been any effect, it is likely to have been modest, with the greatest impact on other recent immigrants. There is general agreement, however, that by reducing the cost of personal services and increasing overall economic output, immigration has generated higher living standards for other Americans.[15]

Today, however, the dramatic rise in inequality in the

United States cannot be adequately explained by simple supply-and-demand stories related to technology and globalization.[16] These factors cannot account for the widening gap in household incomes among those with the same education, skills and experience. Nor can they fully account for the stagnation in market wages in industries not subject to global competition or rapid technological change.

Demographics offer some of the answer. Consider four developments since 1960:

(1) *Fewer people are getting and staying married, particularly among the poor and working class.* Marriage rates for men have fallen by about 30 percent for those on the bottom half of the income scale, while only half that much for those in the top half.[17]

(2) *More people are marrying within class.* Executives marrying their secretaries? Not so much anymore. People are now more likely to marry spouses with similar levels of education and similar earning power.[18]

(3) *More married women are working, particularly those who are college educated.* The probability that that college-educated wife will be employed rather than stay at home has doubled.[19]

(4) *The college wage premium has increased.* The economic value of both of those college degrees has doubled.[20]

The combined effect of these trends has turbocharged the widening of the gap in household incomes. Incomes of families headed by single parents, or married households where the wife remains at home, have been relatively stagnant since the 1970s, while those of families with married working couples have more than doubled—even more than that for couples with college degrees.[21] Indeed, some analysts estimate that changes in workforce participation and family structure account for as much as a third of the increase in measured inequality.[22]

In addition to demographics, changes in government policies have dramatically altered the balance of power in labor markets. These include deregulation, a decline in the value of the minimum wage, the shrinking of private-sector labor unions and unchecked mergers and acquisitions that have allowed a handful of companies to dominate many industries.

Beginning in the late 1970s, Congress set out to deregulate much of the communication, transportation and energy sectors, where for decades government agencies had determined which companies could participate, which markets they could serve, what they could charge and how much profit they could earn. For generations of Americans, getting a job as a lineman with the phone company or a conductor on the railroad was a ticket into the middle class. Because their prices were regulated and their profits guaranteed, regulated companies could offer generous wages and benefits and job security and be certain they could pass on the higher costs to their customers.

By the late 1970s, however, those customers began pressing for more competition and the lower prices and wider choices that it would bring. One by one the industries were deregulated. And as lower-cost, non-unionized companies entered the market, the old regulated companies were forced to bring wages and benefits in line with the rest of the labor market.[23]

A similar dynamic took hold in the public sector, where a tax revolt that began in the 1980s strained government budgets and put downward pressure on the wages and benefits of government workers.[24] For decades, unions had tremendous success in organizing government workers and protecting the compensation packages of their

largely middle-class members. But with government budgets strained and Republicans hell-bent on crushing the
union movement, public-sector unions have begun to face
serious challenges to their bargaining power and wage and
benefit levels. Both Wisconsin and Michigan, once cradles
of the union movement, recently restricted the collective
bargaining rights of government workers.

In the private sector, meanwhile, it's pretty much game
over for union organizing. Today, less than 7 percent of
private-sector workers are union members, down from
22 percent in 1979 and 35 percent at the end of World War
II. Some decline in union density was almost inevitable given
the secular shift in the labor force from the heavily unionized
manufacturing sector to the less easily unionized service sector. But just as important has been the relentless and largely
successful campaign by the business community to weaken
unions by moving operations to states with anti-union, right-
to-work laws. Businesses have also used the courts and the
regulatory process to erode the legal rights of workers and
unions. The reality today is that non-union companies face
little threat that their workers will vote in a union, while
those with unions face little threat from strikes. The result
has been a noticeable shift in bargaining clout from workers to employers.

The erosion in the value of the federal minimum wage
is another part of the inequality story, albeit a smaller one.
In today's dollars, the federal minimum wage was about
$9.70 back in 1979. Today, it is $7.25, although higher in a
number of states and cities. Back then the minimum wage
was nearly half the median hourly wage of all workers; today
it is a third.[25]

While weaker unions and a lower minimum wage may
help explain the slow growth in wages for lower-skilled workers, they cannot explain the runaway incomes of those at

the top of the income scale. Something else is going on there.

The most benign explanation is the so-called superstar effect, in which technology and globalization have together conspired to raise incomes of the top performers in areas ranging from sports and entertainment to the law, medicine and even academics.[26]

As the economist Robert Frank explains it, a century ago, the income of opera tenors, for example, was determined by how many opera fans bought tickets to hear them sing. The better tenors might charge more than the average ones, and get booked for bigger halls, but even so, the best tenor could earn only four or five times what a mediocre tenor could.

With the advent of records, however, all that changed. The pool of paying customers was no longer limited by the number who could hear the singer in person. But these new customers, who could be anywhere in the world, weren't so interested in listening to just any tenor—the new technology made it possible for anyone to hear the best. As a result, the pay gap between the best and everyone else turned into a chasm. With the advent of radio, movies, TV and the Internet, all manner of entertainers and sports figures have felt the impact of this superstar effect.

This superstar effect, however, now extends well beyond sports and entertainment. These days, the very best lawyers, doctors and management consultants are also pulling away from the pack as they find new ways to leverage their global reputations for being the very best. If you are planning a $5 billion stock offering for your social media company, you're probably going to spend the extra $10 million to hire the very best investment banker rather than save money by hiring one who is merely competent. People from all over the world travel to the Mayo Clinic or major teaching hospitals in Boston, Baltimore and San Francisco to get what they believe to be the best and most cutting-edge treatments. And in a world in which millions can take the same course online, or anyone in the world can read the same blog post, even college professors and journalists can become superstars. This winner-take-all dynamic can be found in almost any market in which reputation plays an outsized role.

When researchers looked at the tax returns, however, they found that these "rock stars" account for a minority of those in the top 1 percent. About half of the members of the top 1 percent were corporate executives and Wall Street financiers.[27]

As a rough rule of thumb, the pay of the top five executives at large corporations since 1980 has grown twice as fast as their firms' sales, profits and overall share prices. One study found that in the largest corporations those five officers now typically capture 12 percent of annual profits.[28] Even after adjusting for firm size and stock returns, chief executives of U.S. corporations are paid 88 percent more than those in Europe and Asia.[29]

The initial impetus for the dramatic escalation in executive pay, as discussed in the last chapter, came not from the executives but from Wall Street, which relied on bonuses and stock options to focus corporate managers on the single-minded goal of maximizing shareholder value. But it wasn't long before a generation of corporate executives learned how to manipulate the system to their benefit, convincing compliant directors—many of them chief executives of other companies—that their pay had to be above the average of that in a "peer group" of companies cherry-picked by cooperative compensation consultants. The result has been a perverse arms race in which no company wants to think of itself or its chief executive as below average and companies compete to see who can pay their executives the most. Even

Figure 2.7 **Why They Call It Capitalism**

Share of national income earned by workers and holders of capital, 1979–2015

The increased share of national income going to capital—owners of businesses, property and other financial assets—has reduced workers' wages and salaries by shifting half a trillion dollars annually.

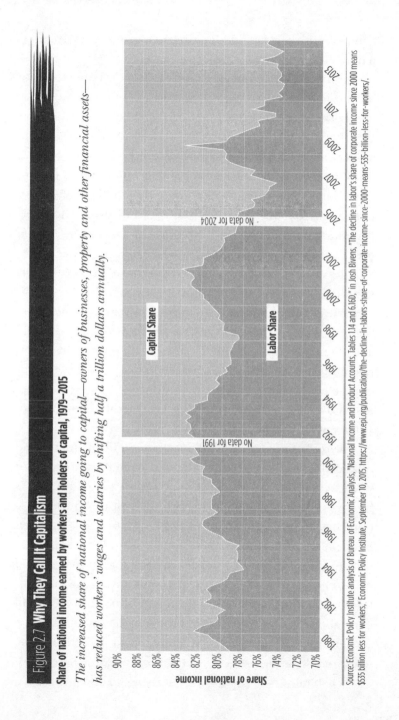

Share of national income

90%
88%
86%
84%
82%
80%
78%
76%
74%
72%
70%

Capital Share

Labor Share

No data for 1991

No data for 2004

1980 1982 1984 1986 1988 1990 1992 1994 1996 1998 2000 2002 2005 2007 2009 2011 2013

Source: Economic Policy Institute analysis of Bureau of Economic Analysis, "National Income and Product Accounts, Tables 1.14 and 6.16D," in Josh Bivens, "The decline in labor's share of corporate income since 2000 means $535 billion less for workers," Economic Policy Institute, September 10, 2015, https://www.epi.org/publication/the-decline-in-labors-share-of-corporate-income-since-2000-means-535-billion-less-for-workers/.

chief executives acknowledge that, as a group, they are over-paid.[30]

If the aim of paying executives more was to get them to increase profits by paying workers less, then the strategy has been a smashing success. The Economic Policy Institute has calculated that the share of corporate gross income going to compensation for labor had fluctuated around 80 percent until the early 1990s. Since then, it has fallen to 75 percent. That alone represents a shift of more than half a trillion dollars a year from workers to shareholders, disproportionately benefiting those at the top.[31] Nothing that liberals have done over the years to redistribute income from the haves to the have-less comes anywhere near this tectonic shift of the distribution of income from "labor" to "capital."[32]

Shareholders and top executives, however, have not been the only winners from the shift from labor to capital. A sizable chunk of capital's share of economic output has been raked off the top by the financial services industry, including the top Wall Street bankers, traders and money managers who now constitute one in seven members of the top 1 percent.[33]

Skyrocketing pay on Wall Street might be justified if the financial sector had become more efficient in transforming savings into productive investment, which is what finance is supposed to be about. But, in fact, the cost of "intermediation" has increased from about 1.5 cents for every dollar of financial sector assets in 1980 to 2.3 cents today—and that despite dramatic improvements in technology that should have lowered costs. The reason: a dramatic increase in industry profits and compensation. By one recent estimate, the financial sector now extracts $280 billion each year in excess surplus from the U.S. economy, more than 1 percent of GDP, much of it winding up in households of the top 1 percent.[34]

When most people think about rising income inequality,

what generally comes to mind is the income gap between the chief executives and the marketing manager and between the marketing manager and the janitor—widening gaps, in other words, between employees with different skills and education within the same firm. And, indeed, this was the inequality story during much of the 1980s and '90s as markets became more competitive and efficient.

But more recently, the increase in inequality has taken on a different character. Rather than greater wage dispersion *within* firms, there has been a noticeable increase in the wage gap between the chief executives, marketers and janitors in one firm and those in another. What you make, in other words, is determined not simply by the skills you bring to a job, but increasingly by which industry—and which company within that industry—you work for.

What these variations suggest is that competition in some industries is less robust than economic theory imagines. Such markets are dominated by a handful of large players who are able to charge higher prices and earn outsized profits—what economists call "rents." Often, a portion of those rents is shared with employees in the form of wages and salaries that are higher than paid to workers with similar talent and experience in other companies and other industries.

There are lots of reasons why firms earn rents. In the technology, telecom and transportation sectors, the natural desire for consumers and businesses to have compatible equipment or be on the same network creates a winner-take-all competition. Think Facebook and Craigslist. In other industries—automobile and airplane assembly are examples—economies of scale are so powerful that the market can only support a handful of firms that can tacitly agree not to compete too fiercely on the basis of price. In industries such as pharmaceuticals and software, patents designed to spur innovation intentionally limit competition, while in others, such as power generation and cable television, politically connected firms have used regulation to make it hard for new firms to enter the market. And, of course, without vigorous antitrust enforcement, mergers and acquisitions can lead to excessive consolidation in any industry.

We also see that excessive consolidation in one industry leads to excessive consolidation in others. The big banks that now dominate finance prefer to make loans to big firms, not small ones. And as big real estate firms have come to control most of the desirable locations in metropolitan areas, large national tenants are favored over small local ones. Consolidation of the hospital and drug industries has forced consolidation among health insurers who bargain with them, just as consolidation among retailers has led to consolidation among their suppliers.

A study by the White House Council of Economic Advisers during the Obama administration showed that more industries today are more highly concentrated than ever before, allowing dominant firms in those industries to earn rents.[35] One recent paper suggests that these rents explain much of the shift of national income from labor to capital, while another argues that they now explain 80 percent of the recent increase in income inequality.[36]

The search for explanations for rising income inequality would be incomplete without considering one final and often overlooked culprit: changes in social norms, or what people consider to be socially acceptable business behavior. In the period after World War II, it would have been considered inappropriate for chief executives to pay themselves 270 times what their frontline workers made, or for one full professor in a department to earn twice what another was paid, or for one partner in a law firm to demand three times what a "less productive" partner was making. It would have been equally unthinkable for a highly profitable company to pay its top executives and engineers above the market rate without also paying secretaries and janitors a similar premium.

The 1950s and '60s were, in that respect, a golden era of income equality. The U.S. economy was growing like gangbusters as firms expanded to meet the pent-up demand of American consumers and the massive rebuilding efforts overseas. In such a booming economy, there was plenty to go around for everyone.

The country was also emerging from a prolonged period of shared sacrifice during World War II, and it would have been unseemly for men who had served together on the front lines, or women who had worked side by side on assembly lines, to suddenly be paid significantly more than their colleagues. With communism a growing threat, the business community was also eager to demonstrate that the benefits of a market economy were widely shared.

It was only once memories of the wartime period had faded, and American firms began to feel pressure from foreign competition, that the communal and egalitarian instincts of the postwar era gave way to a more individualistic, get-all-you-can ethic reminiscent of the Gilded Age or the Roaring Twenties.[37] That some people were beginning to earn vast sums suddenly came to be thought of as not just economically necessary, but socially and morally acceptable.

The Myth of Marginal Productivity

What should be apparent from this brief review is that incomes in the United States over the last 40 years didn't just become more unequal because the market, for its own reasons, suddenly started valuing work and workers differently. Rather, in response to changes in technology and the economic challenge from Europe and Asia, Americans chose to alter the rules and norms that govern the marketplace—or allowed them to be altered—in ways that either were designed to make incomes less equal, or could have been predicted to have that effect.

In the theoretical models favored by economic textbooks, pay is assumed to be set in perfectly competitive labor markets that precisely calculate how much each employee adds to the output of the company—what economists call the worker's "marginal productivity." And if we still had an economy of independent, self-sufficient farmers and hunters that might be true. Someone could rightfully point to a bushel of tomatoes or a butchered deer or a hand-knit sweater and credibly make the claim, "I produced that. That's the fruit of my labor. My income is just desert." That is essentially the simple model used by Robert Nozick in his example of the basketball star offering his services directly to his appreciative fans.

But in a modern economy, creating products and services is a team sport, with individuals working and interacting with other individuals and firms. Such complex arrangements make it much more difficult to pinpoint with any certainty the economic contribution of each person along the value chain. In the real world outside of economic theory, those markets are characterized by significant differences in bargaining power between firms, and differences in bargaining power within firms between employers and employees, all having an impact on what people are paid. In the real world, wages also reflect employers' subjective judgment about the performance of individual employees, just as they reflect the different motivations and demands of individual employees. And, as we've just seen, what anyone earns reflects rules and norms that are constantly changing. Given all that complexity, variation and contingency, the idea that market income is a precise and objective measure of individual contribution to economic output is absurd. Or as the Nobel Prize–winning economist Amartya Sen once put it, the whole concept of "marginal product" is nothing more than a "convenient fiction."[38]

As a thought experiment, imagine we are in Virginia back in the eighteenth century, where tobacco was grown on great plantations on the fertile banks of the James River. In those days, there were laws and customs that helped to determine how the proceeds from the sale of each barrel of tobacco should be split between the plantation owner and those who had participated in producing it. And because those laws and customs permitted slavery, the market determined that the wages of those who actually planted and harvested the crop were something close to zero.

Today, Virginians still grow tobacco along parts of the James River, but over the years the distribution of proceeds from each barrel has changed. It changed quite dramatically when slavery was abolished. It changed again when laws were enacted protecting sharecroppers from the exploitive practices of landowners. It changed again when farmhands were given the right to form a union and bargain collectively. And it changed when farmers were required to pay a minimum wage and an overtime premium. With each change in public policy, the distribution of income became more equal.

Consider the implications of this for the traditional defense of market justice. At every stage of history, the owner of that tobacco farm would have surely argued that the profit he earned in the marketplace was his just desert. Yet, as this little example makes clear, the amount of money he earns, and the amounts those who work with him earn, are determined in no small part by laws, regulations and customs that were not

conjured up by some magical "invisible hand," but were
politically and socially determined. Wars have been waged
over such questions, election campaigns have been won and
lost because of them and legislative battles have been fought
over them.

Recall the factors that are behind the recent increase in
inequality.

The decisions to allow open and free trade with low-
wage countries, to deregulate the transportation and communications sectors, to allow the erosion of the minimum
wage, to use a light touch in regulating the financial sector,
to make it easier for businesses to fire union organizers and
sympathizers—all of these were deliberate policy choices.
So, too, is the embrace by business executives and directors
of the notion that the only purpose of a corporation is to
maximize shareholder value, which provided the rational-
ization and impetus for hostile takeovers, outsourcing of
jobs, widespread layoffs, cuts in wages and benefits for workers and the explosion of compensation for executives. I will
be the first to acknowledge that many of these choices have
made the economy more efficient and innovative, and increased the size of the economic pie. But there can be little
doubt that they have also had the effect of changing the
formula by which the pie is divided, increasing the incomes
of some at the expense of others in ways that are unrelated
to any differences in individual performance or attribution.

"To even a greater extent than other markets, the labor
market is not a mathematical abstraction whose workings
are entirely determined by natural and immutable mechanisms and implacable technological forces," writes Thomas
Piketty in his surprise and weighty bestseller, *Capital in the
Twenty-First Century*. "It is a social construct based on specific
rules and compromises."[39] The idea that there is a neutral,
objective labor market that generates a perfectly fair and ob-

jective distribution of market income based on the relative economic contribution of each worker, he writes, is nothing more than a "pure ideological construct."[40]

The subjective and contingent nature of market incomes undermines the simplistic case for just desert offered by Nozick and his story of the superstar basketball player. To use his example, there are issues relating to the monopoly that the National Basketball Association enjoys in the market for professional basketball, and the public subsidies for stadium deals that the league is able to extract from municipalities, and the monopoly power of the networks that broadcast NBA games to the public. And there are the various rules the NBA imposes on teams and owners regarding salaries and salary caps, and the contract that the league has negotiated with the players' union. All of these arrangements have a direct impact on the amount of revenue flowing to the league, how the league distributes that revenue among its teams and how each team distributes the revenue among its players and owners. To a significant degree, they explain why LeBron James earns $30 million a year rather than $20 million, and why, even after adjusting for inflation, James earns 15 times what Wilt Chamberlain ever did.[41]

The same logic applies in other industries. Does anyone really think that the $1 billion a year earned by top hedge fund managers actually reflects their economic contribution? Are financial and labor markets so perfectly rational and competitive that we know there isn't someone every bit as brilliant, cunning and hardworking who would be willing to do it for $750 million? If they were paid a mere $500 million, would these masters of the universe decide to withhold their excellence and head for the beach? Somehow I doubt it.

To point out the subjective and contingent manner in which pay is set and income is distributed by the market is not to suggest that I know of a more objective system. Rather, it is to suggest that if we, as a society, don't feel right about the distribution of income generated by the market—if that distribution offends our moral intuitions—then it violates no economic law or moral imperative if we decide to alter that distribution. When it comes to the distribution of income, there is no pure market and any distribution is, by its nature, subjective and political.

If we decide to change the current distribution of income, there are basically two ways to go about it. We could alter the rules and norms that govern those markets—change the minimum wage, for example, or encourage unions or restrict trade with China—so that markets generated different outcomes. Or we could leave the rules and norms as they are and alter the distribution after the market has delivered its judgment, through more progressive taxation and government spending. The first has been called "predistribution," the second "redistribution."

In the United States, our preference has been to alter the distribution of rewards primarily through predistribution because the effects are more hidden and indirect and more consistent with our political inclination toward limited government. Other successful countries prefer to rely more on government redistribution. From a moral viewpoint, however, there is no meaningful distinction between the two approaches. They both are a form of collective action to "tamper" with market outcomes to make them better conform to our collective intuitions about what is fair and just.

As a moral concept, just desert is inadequate and incomplete. In determining whether any distribution of income is just, it is not enough to simply inquire whether someone has earned his income through voluntary market exchange, playing by the rules. We must also look at the distribution of income and ask whether the rules themselves are just.

3

Is Equality of Opportunity Possible or Even Desirable?

No moral intuition is more hardwired into Americans' conception of economic justice than equality of opportunity. While some of us may be rich and others poor, we are willing to accept such outcomes as long as everyone has an equal shot at success. The moral legitimacy of the market's distribution of income rests on a presumption that our system rewards ingenuity, hard work, talent and risk-taking, rather than race, class, family connections or some other advantage we consider unearned, illegitimate or unfair.

"In every wise struggle for human betterment one of the main objects, and often the only object, has been to achieve in large measure equality of opportunity," declared President Theodore Roosevelt in a speech in Osawatomie, Kansas, in 1910, laying out the "square deal" he believed was due to all Americans.

In a speech later that year, Roosevelt took pains to reassure members of the New Haven Chamber of Commerce that his notion of equal opportunity fit squarely within the context of a market economy. "I know perfectly well that men in a race run at unequal rates of speed. I don't want the prize to go to the man who is not fast enough to win it on his merits, but I want them to start fair."[1]

A century later, another president would pick up on Roosevelt's meritocratic theme in his second inaugural address: "We are true to our creed," declared Barack Obama, "when a little girl born into the bleakest poverty knows that she has the same chance to succeed as anyone else, because she is an American, she is free, and she is equal, not just in the eyes of God but in our own."

These days, however, it is not just progressives who champion the ideal of equal opportunity. When confronted with evidence of the widening gap between the rich and everyone else, defenders of market justice invariably invoke the metaphor of the race fairly won. We need not concern ourselves with the level of equality of wealth and income, they argue, because all that really matters is equality of opportunity. To complain about how things turn out after the race is over, in their view, is merely class envy or sour grapes.

Equality of opportunity, of course, taps into the conception Americans have of themselves as a people who fought one war to shake off the tyranny of a British monarchy and aristocracy and another to shake off the chains of slavery, a people who welcomed wave after wave of ambitious immigrants yearning for a better life. Yet there is now a sizable and growing body of evidence that, despite elimination of most legal barriers to equality of opportunity, the luck of which parents you were born to continues to play an outsized role in determining economic success. Whether it's by way of the genes we inherit (nature) or the circumstances in which we are raised (nurture), the results of this parental lottery are more important than ever in determining our natural capabilities and the degree to which we are able to develop those capabilities and bring them to an increasingly competitive marketplace. Indeed, for the first time in American history, the steady march toward greater equality of opportunity seems to be headed in the opposite direction.

Accidents of Birth

Let us begin with nature, and the question of inherited intelligence. This remains a highly controversial topic, but one that cannot be ignored in any discussion about economic outcomes. As a broad generalization, the evidence suggests that somewhere between 35 and 75 percent of our intelligence comes genetically from our parents, with the lower end of the estimates applicable to children and the higher end to adults.[2]

And how much does intelligence affect adult income? A recent review of the literature found that about a quarter of the variation in people's incomes could be accounted for directly by natural intelligence, a slightly better predictor than parents' income or education.[3] Holding a range of other factors constant, one study found that the difference between having an average IQ score and one at the 98th percentile translates into an income difference of anywhere between $6,500 and $20,000 per year.[4] Why such a large range? Because the economic value of intelligence rises as you move up the income ladder. Intelligence turns out to be a bigger factor in determining the incomes of a smart and less-smart lawyer or engineer than it does in determining the incomes of a smart and less-smart auto mechanic or insurance agent.[5]

Other highly heritable traits also have economic consequences.

Based on studies of identical and fraternal twins, researchers have concluded that between 60 and 80 percent of differences in height can be explained by heredity, with each inch of height worth as much as $1,000 a year in added income.[6]

Equally heritable are good looks, which also lead to income differences, particularly among men.[7] Attractive people have wider social networks, are more likely to attend and graduate from college, have greater self-confidence and are thought, without reason, to be smarter, more competent and have more leadership potential.[8] One study of Canadians found that, on a five-point attractiveness scale, each point translates into more than $2,500 in annual income.[9]

As any parent will attest, personality also turns out to be inheritable, including traits that have a significant impact on economic outcomes: empathy, reliability, ambition, impulsiveness, orientation toward the future, an appetite for risk and an aptitude for leadership. One recent study found that inherited personality traits explain a quarter of earnings differences, an effect comparable to that of inherited intelligence.[10]

My purpose in citing these studies is to emphasize that it's not just brainy mathematicians, beautiful supermodels and elongated basketball stars who benefit economically from inherited traits and capabilities. To varying degrees, genes play a significant role in determining everyone's relative economic success. Those who succeed may argue that there are many others who inherited the same traits and capabilities as they, but didn't put in the time or effort to leverage their endowments to maximum advantage—and it is that difference which justifies their higher earnings. But that is a straw man argument. Nobody denies that how you play your cards is important—and should be important—to the outcome of the game. That doesn't mean, however, that the cards you are dealt aren't important as well.

The issues raised by the parental lottery do not stop with genetic inheritance. No less important in shaping opportunity and outcomes are the things parents do to nurture their children's innate capabilities.

In considering such environmental factors, conservatives tend to focus on the importance of family structure, character development and community values, while liberals focus on nutrition, psychological stress, crime, role models and social connections—"red truths" and "blue truths," as Harvard's Robert Putnam has called them. Both sets of truths, however, acknowledge the vital role of upbringing in determining a person's future.

The latest research confirms that it is the earliest environmental influences that matter most. "Virtually every aspect of early human development, from the brain's evolving circuitry to the child's capacity for empathy, is affected by the environments and experiences that are encountered in a cumulative fashion, beginning in the prenatal period and extending through the early childhood years," a panel of the National Academy of Sciences concluded in a landmark study published in 2000.[11]

For infants, the type of food they eat and the toxins they are exposed to, the amount of touching and cuddling they receive, the quality and quantity of interactions with adults— all of these have a significant effect on how a child's brain evolves and develops the capacity to learn.

Between the ages of one and four, physical, intellectual and psychological development can be significantly affected by the amount of time children have with parents and the degree of exposure to stimulating environments outside the home. The level of stress in the household, the mental health of parents and the exposure to violence and chaotic surroundings can have significant negative effects. It is also in these early years that the emotional and biological foundations are laid for traits such as self-esteem, confidence, emotional stability, curiosity, optimism and grit, in addition to verbal and mathematical skills.[12]

There is a now-famous study of Kansas families that showed that three-year-olds with upper-income, college-educated parents had heard 19 million more words than the children of working-class parents, and 32 million more words than the children of parents on welfare.[13]

Other researchers have found that 72 percent of middle-class children show up in kindergarten already knowing the alphabet, compared to only 19 percent of poor children.[14]

Chaos and stress are more prevalent in poor households than rich. Children living in poor households were found to have elevated levels of cortisone in their brain, a hormone that inhibits development of memory and logical thinking. Studying brain waves, Canadian researchers found that lower-class kids had more difficulty concentrating on a simple task because their brains were conditioned to be constantly on the lookout for new threats.[15] Other brain researchers have found a significant correlation between parental income and the size of the surface area of their children's cerebral cortices, the outer layer of the brain that controls language and executive functions. The study was based on scans of more than a thousand subjects after controlling for race and genetic ancestry.[16]

In his book *Our Kids*, Robert Putnam cites numerous studies to demonstrate that richer and better-educated parents aim to raise "autonomous, independent, self-directed children with high self-esteem and the ability to make good choices, whereas less educated parents focus on discipline and obedience and conformity to pre-established rules"— good traits for an industrial economy, but less so for one that pays a premium for innovation and problem solving. Upper-class parents are more likely to use reasoning and guilt to discipline their children, while lower-class parents incline toward physical punishment.[17]

In a paper for the Brookings Institution, Richard Reeves and Kimberly Howard found strong correlations between the quality of parenting and the income, education, age and marital status of those parents.[18] One factor that may explain such a link is the greater time pressures facing low-income households. In *Scarcity*, poverty researchers Sendhil Mullainathan and Eldar Shafir argue that what may look like a parent's lack of attention, patience and care might be explained by simply having an ordinary mental bandwidth and an extraordinary number of things to worry about—problems that would disappear or be dealt with more easily if only there were more financial capacity.[19]

One of the first researchers to call attention to the importance of family and environmental factors on educational and social outcomes was James Heckman, a Nobel laureate in economics. Heckman and colleagues have conducted a 35-year study of what happened to three- and four-year-old black children from low-income families randomly chosen to attend the high-quality Perry preschool in Ypsilanti, Michigan, in the 1960s. Like similar studies of Head Start programs, Heckman found that those attending the school experienced an increase in cognitive abilities (IQ scores) that faded over time. What endured, however, was a positive impact on character traits that increased motivation to learn and succeed while reducing lying, cheating, aggression and disruptive behavior. These non-cognitive skills not only improved educational achievement during childhood, but also led to higher incomes, better health and less criminal behavior later in life.[20]

The link between family income and educational

achievement, of course, has been known for a long time. What is new and disturbing is that, after a period of stability from the 1950s to the mid-70s, the educational achievement gap between high- and low-income students has grown wider—not, as you might have thought, because the income gaps between parents have gotten wider, but because family income has become even more important in determining academic success.

Sean Reardon, a leading researcher at Stanford University, calculated that in 1978 the difference in scores between eighth graders of rich and poor families was 96 points on an SAT-type scale, which roughly translates into three or four years of schooling. By 2008, the gap had grown to 131 points, with the poor kids falling another year behind.[21] While Reardon found that the scores of poor kids had improved slightly over the 30 years, the scores of rich kids had improved a lot more.

The liberal instinct is to assume that what accounts for this widening achievement gap is the unevenness of funding between higher-income school districts and poorer ones. Given the difference in cognitive and non-cognitive skills with which children enter the school system, poorer students should, if anything, require higher levels of spending if equality of opportunity is to be achieved. In fact, the spending is often less.

According to the Education Law Center's 2014 annual report, in only 14 states do schools with high concentrations of poverty households get more in per pupil funding than districts with no students in poverty. The rest either have regressive state and local funding structures, with high-poverty schools receiving less per pupil than no-poverty schools (19 states), or are neither regressive nor progressive (15 states).[22] Analysis from the Organisation for Economic Co-operation and Development indicates that, among advanced economies, only the United States, Turkey and Israel have school funding structures that are this regressive.[23]

That said, there remains considerable debate about the link between per pupil spending and educational outcomes.[24] For starters, it is fairly well established that the gap in test scores between rich and poor grows only modestly during the K–12 school years.[25] Differences in educational achievement based on socioeconomic factors are pretty much baked into the cake by the time kids enter kindergarten.

Moreover, to the degree schooling does widen the gap, the evidence suggests that it has less to do with how much is spent than with how much students are segregated by class. Students from all socioeconomic backgrounds do better in schools where there are lots of middle- and upper-class students, and do worse in schools where poor students dominate, even after controlling for per pupil spending.[26] There are a number of possible explanations for this: more successful peer and parental role models, more involved and demanding parents, the ability to attract and retain better teachers, less disruption from students with behavioral problems, less turnover among students. In fact, the socioeconomic background of a student's classmates is actually a better predictor of academic success than his or her own socioeconomic background.[27]

The role of classmates takes on increasing importance now that Americans are increasingly sorting themselves into economically homogenous neighborhoods.[28] Schools with high concentrations of low-income students are becoming more prevalent. A recent survey by the U.S. Department of Education found that 20 percent of public schools— 40 percent in urban areas—have at least 75 percent of their students coming from households with incomes low enough to be eligible for free or reduced-price meals.[29]

The widening income–educational achievement gap is

also being reinforced by what's going on at home. Anyone who has watched the spread of helicopter parenting among the urban professional class knows, as Edward Kleinbard recently put it, how much can be accomplished on behalf of a moderately able child who is "coached, prodded, cajoled and bribed all the way into a top tier university."[30] Greg Duncan and Richard Murnane, two leading researchers on inequality and education, used consumer expenditure surveys to estimate that lower-income families, on average, now spend about $1,400 a year on things like music lessons, summer camp, travel, books, and sports teams for their kids, while the richest families spend $9,600.[31]

This arms race in enrichment spending probably has less impact on the prospects of their coddled children, in school or in life, than many parents believe. At the same time, given the sums involved, the sophistication of the parents and the degree to which the parents themselves were the beneficiaries of such enrichment, it's hard to imagine that such spending confers no advantage. These overeager parents may be crazed, but they're not stupid.

Nowhere is the connection between family income and educational opportunity more visible than within the gates of America's universities.

Much has been written about how the rapid rise in tuitions has put a college education out of reach of the poor and working class. Reduction of state support per student has more than doubled the posted tuitions and fees at four-year state colleges and universities, putting them beyond the financial means of some students. The effect of those increases, however, has been somewhat dampened by an increase in student aid. The average tuition and fees actually paid by full-time students at four-year public universities— net tuition, as it is called—has increased about 90 percent over the last 20 years after accounting for inflation, from

$2,180 to $4,140 a year. (With room and board, that rises to nearly $15,000.) For private nonprofit colleges and universities, the increase in net tuition has been about the same in dollar terms, but much less in percentage terms—19 percent—and now stands at $14,530 per year ($26,740 with room and board).[32]

Lack of affordability, however, may not be the main reason why so many low-income kids never make it to, and through, college. Some who are qualified simply assume that they are unable to afford the testing and admission fees, unaware of the financial aid that would be available to them, and never apply. One study found that among low-income students who had a decent shot at being accepted to top-ranked universities because of strong SAT scores, the vast majority applied only to second- and third-ranked colleges, or none at all.[33]

But surely the biggest reason kids from low-income households don't attend and complete college is that their public schools have failed to adequately prepare them. Fewer low-income students graduate from high school, even fewer apply to college and are accepted, and fewer still go on to graduate.[34] One study found that, among students graduating from high school, only 21 percent from the lowest-income households were prepared to do college-level work, compared to 54 percent from middle- and upper-class households.[35]

Whatever the reasons, while more kids than ever are graduating from college, that increase has disproportionately come from those born into households at or above the median income. In the United States today, the probability of someone born into the top income quartile earning a bachelor's degree is now eight times that of someone born into the bottom quartile.[36]

The undergraduate roster at Harvard University provides

a good window through which to see how the dynamics of unequal wealth and education are playing out. Several years ago, Harvard announced that, because of the growth in its endowment, its undergraduate admissions decisions would be made on a needs-blind basis, without regard to how much financial aid a student would need. It also announced a new tuition structure that ensured no family would pay more than 10 percent of its income in tuition and fees, with families with incomes under $65,000—roughly, the national median—paying nothing.

Harvard's admirable intention was to ensure that any qualified student from any economic background could afford to attend what some believe to be the country's best university. But despite a concerted push by the admissions office to recruit qualified lower-income applicants, the undergraduates at Harvard could hardly be said to look like America. A recent analysis by Raj Chetty and colleagues at the Equality of Opportunity Project found that just 21 percent of Harvard students came from households in the bottom 60 percent of households by income, with less than 5 percent coming from the bottom quintile.

As it turns out, Harvard has done a modestly better job at attracting low- and middle-income students than other elite private universities—the Ivy League plus MIT, Duke, Stanford and the University of Chicago. But it is hard to say that any of these institutions has been able to make much headway in giving every American an equal shot at higher education, regardless of income. At all of these elite schools, there are still as many students from households in the top 1 percent—incomes above $450,000—as there are from students in the bottom 50 percent.[37]

Since the days when Horace Mann advocated for free and compulsory public schools, Americans have looked to education to be, in his words, "the great equalizer," the primary mechanism for breaking down class barriers and equalizing economic opportunity. But the harsh reality is that the education system today is having the unintended effect of reinforcing class lines rather than blurring them, helping to further widen the lead enjoyed by those already advantaged by natural talents and family income. As the *Chronicle of Higher Education* recently put it, the American education system has become "an inequality machine."[38]

Moreover, even as the link between a child's family income and educational achievement has become stronger, so too has the link between educational achievement and adult income. We need to recognize this for what it is: a vicious cycle in which wealth and educational achievement, just like poverty and educational failure, reinforce each other from one generation to the next. We have created a new aristocracy—a "meritocratic" aristocracy—that is no less persistent, and only slightly less unjust, than earlier aristocracies based on inherited land and title.

Back in 1958, British sociologist Michael Young foresaw all this with uncanny accuracy in a now largely forgotten satire, *The Rise of the Meritocracy* (the word "meritocracy," in fact, was Young's invention). His fable describes a Britain in the year 2033 that has come to be dominated by an elite upper class, selected for its intelligence and skill, that comes to wield all political power and captures for itself all the benefits of economic growth. Because members of the elite marry each other and live apart from the hoi polloi, social scientists determine that only a few random children from the lower classes have the potential to succeed. For that reason, common schools are abolished and only the children of the elite are eligible for universities and top jobs. And while equality of opportunity remains official government policy, that is merely propaganda used to placate the increasingly restless lower classes. Within the elite, genuine equality of opportunity is considered an outmoded idea.

Suffice it to say that we may have not yet achieved Michael Young's dystopia, but we are well on our way.

Opportunity and Mobility

The fact that some people born at the bottom can and do rise to the top—or that those born at the top sometimes wind up nearer to the bottom—does not, by itself, demonstrate equality of opportunity. What matters is the overall likelihood of such outcomes. And the best yardstick for assessing that likelihood is to look at the data on where people start and where they end up—intergenerational mobility, in the argot of social science. In a rigid class society, there is very little mobility and very unequal opportunity, while in a society with perfectly equal opportunity, economic outcomes would be random: there would be so much mobility that where you start out would have no bearing on where you end up.

There are, however, different conceptions of mobility and different ways to measure it.

When Americans think of the American Dream, they often think in terms of people having higher incomes or living standards than their parents. Economists refer to that as *absolute* intergenerational mobility, and by that measure, America has traditionally been a land of opportunity, with four in five Americans achieving incomes higher than their parents.[39]

Last year, however, our belief in this dream was called into question. Another team of researchers led by the prolific Raj Chetty, using information from tax records, found that absolute intergenerational mobility has been steadily *declining* since the 1960s, to the point that among those born in the 1980s, only half are doing better than their parents at this point in their lives.[40] While this is a preliminary finding—those born in the 1980s are still in their 30s—it suggests a sea change in the American experience.

Absolute mobility may be what most of us care about as individuals or even as a society. After all, why should it matter if hedge fund managers or tech execs are becoming fabulously rich if I am the first in my family who is able to own my own home, drive a late-model car, take three weeks at the lake and put two kids through college? No matter that some may be doing even better, my standard of living is still much higher than my parents'.

That kind of mobility, however, is not particularly useful in measuring equality of opportunity. That's because what absolute mobility often reflects is simply growth in the overall economy—a rising tide that has lifted all boats. To measure opportunity, we need to filter out the effect of the rising tide in order to focus on changes to people's *relative* position on the economic ladder, their income relative to everyone else's.

For years, the most common way to measure relative mobility has been to capture, in a single number known as "income elasticity," the degree to which fathers' earnings accurately predict those of their sons, even if almost all sons earn more than their fathers. (Data on mothers and daughters is not used because of changes in how many women work outside the home and levels of female pay.) An elasticity of 0.0 means that parental income has no statistical correlation with the economic success of their children—in other words, perfect mobility and perfectly equal opportunity. An elasticity of 1.0 means that you can perfectly

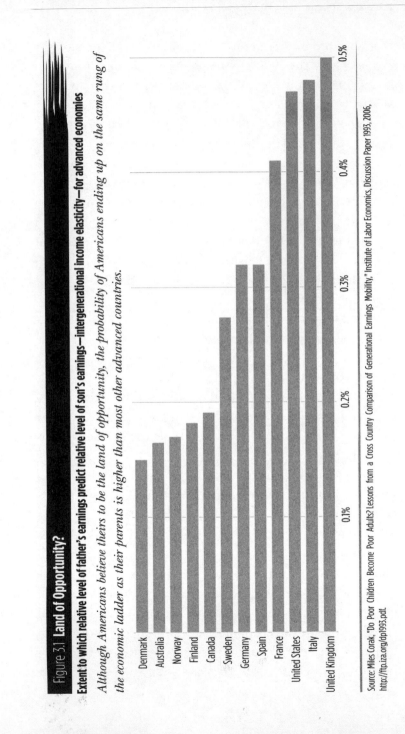

Figure 3.1 Land of Opportunity?

Extent to which relative level of father's earnings predict relative level of son's earnings—intergenerational income elasticity—for advanced economies

Although Americans believe theirs to be the land of opportunity, the probability of Americans ending up on the same rung of the economic ladder as their parents is higher than most other advanced countries.

Denmark
Australia
Norway
Finland
Canada
Sweden
Germany
Spain
France
United States
Italy
United Kingdom

0.1%   0.2%   0.3%   0.4%   0.5%

Source: Miles Corak, "Do Poor Children Become Poor Adults? Lessons from a Cross Country Comparison of Generational Earnings Mobility," Institute of Labor Economics, Discussion Paper 1993, 2006, http://ftp.iza.org/dp1993.pdf.

predict a son's income from that of his father—in other words, no mobility and perfectly unequal opportunity.

The accompanying chart shows the intergenerational income elasticity for the richest advanced countries. The United States has an elasticity of somewhere between 0.4 and 0.5, which hardly squares with the notion that ours is the land of opportunity. With the exception of Britain and Italy, other advanced countries have more relative mobility.[41] The only thing exceptional about America is that it is now less mobile than many other societies with long histories of rigid social and class structures.

Moreover, this measure of equality of opportunity appears to be getting worse. Researchers at the Federal Reserve Bank of Chicago, looking at intergenerational elasticity from 1940 through 2000, calculated that the influence of parental income, which had remained steady for many decades, rose sharply after 1979 as economic growth began to slow and inequality began to rise.[42]

From a statistical standpoint, there are some shortcomings to using wage elasticity as a measure of intergenerational mobility. The most serious is that, as an average number for all fathers and sons, we can't tell whether mobility is uniform at all points on the income ladder. So other researchers have come up with different methods for analyzing the data that provide a more granular look at where mobility occurs.

Richard Reeves and Isabel Sawhill of the Brookings Institution recently updated their "social mobility matrix," which shows the odds that an American born into one income quintile would end up in any of the other quintiles. In this graphic, each of the vertical bars tells the story of the sons born into that quintile. The squares that make up the bars tell where those sons ended up as adults.

In a world of perfect mobility, where you end up would

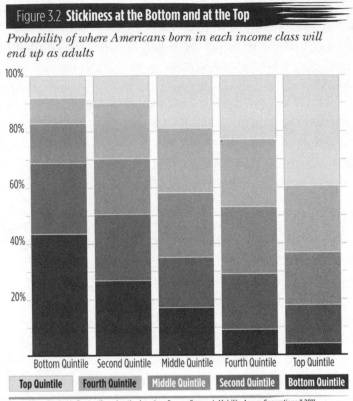

Figure 3.2 **Stickiness at the Bottom and at the Top**

Probability of where Americans born in each income class will end up as adults

Source: Pew Charitable Trusts, "Pursuing the American Dream: Economic Mobility Across Generations," 2011, http://www.pewtrusts.org/-/media/legacy/uploadedfiles/wwwpewtrustsorg/reports/economic_mobility/pursuingamericandreampdf.pdf.

be totally unaffected by where you start, the results would be random, and all the squares would be the same 20 percent. And, indeed, in the middle squares of the middle bars—in other words, in the broad middle class—that's pretty much how things turn out. The big exceptions are found among those born at the top and the bottom of the income ladder, where relative position tends to be rather more persistent, or sticky, from one generation to the next. Forty-three percent of those born in the bottom quintile wind up there, while 40 percent of those born in the top quintile remain there.[43] This stickiness at the top and bottom is less pronounced in Britain, Canada and the Nordic countries, and goes a long way toward explaining the lower mobility now found in the United States.[44]

Why is American mobility so low? One hypothesis is that higher income inequality leads to lower mobility; that the bigger space between the rungs in the ladder makes it harder to move up or down. It was Canadian economist Miles Corak who first plotted the correlation between income inequality and intergenerational mobility, based on data from numerous countries, but it was Alan Krueger, then serving as top economic adviser to President Obama, who cleverly dubbed it the "Great Gatsby Curve."[45] Based on that significant correlation, Krueger predicted that the surge in inequality in the United States during the last 40 years will wind up reducing mobility in the next generation—those born after 1980—by 20 percent. Krueger's curve created an immediate controversy because it seemed to undermine the standard conservative argument that the only thing that matters is equality of opportunity. Here was evidence that inequality of income was indeed important, precisely because of its negative impact on equality of opportunity.

Krueger's curve, however, is hardly the definitive word on that question. While the data used by Corak and Krueger demonstrated a statistical link between income inequality and mobility, like all correlations it does not answer the question of which way the causality runs. Is it that less income equality leads to less mobility, or does less mobility lead to more inequality? Or is there some third factor, such as the pace of economic growth, that drives both inequality and mobility? If your head is spinning right now, it's because like many important and interesting questions in economics, the answers are never simple. But it's a good guess that, on this one, the right answer is all of the above.

Figure 3.3 **The Great Gatsby Curve**

Less equality, less mobility

A country's inequality, as measured by the Gini coefficient, is plotted against its intergenerational mobility, as measured by intergenerational earnings elasticity. Perfect correlation would show dots arrayed along a line at 45 degrees. The data shows a significant correlation between the level of a country's income inequality and the amount of class mobility from one generation to the next.

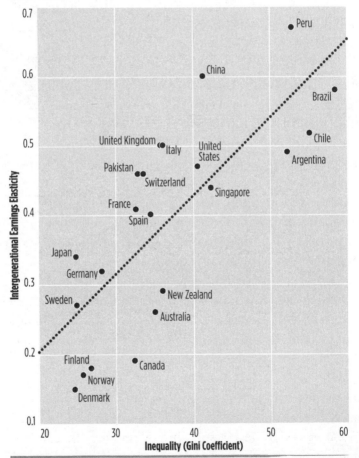

Source: Miles Corak, "Here Is the Source for the 'Great Gatsby Curve,'" in the Alan Krueger Speech, Center for American Progress, Economics for Public Policy (blog), January 12, 2012, https://milescorak.com/2012/01/12/here-is-the-source -for-the-great-gatsby-curve-in-the-alan-krueger-speech-at-the-center-for-american-progress/.

One thing we do know is that, despite the recent rise in income inequality in the United States and elsewhere, most measures of relative intergenerational mobility have continued to remain remarkably stable.[46] That is hardly surprising. The surge in inequality didn't really gain traction until the early 1990s, and the children born in the early '90s won't reach their prime earning age until at least 2030. It is only then that it will be possible to measure the impact of inequality in one generation of Americans on incomes and mobility in the next.

There are, however, good reasons to worry. We can already see that rising inequality of income is leading to widening inequality in such things as physical and mental health, educational achievement and marriage rates, all of which have a well-documented effect on economic success later in life.[47] So it would be surprising if the recent widening of the income gap does not reduce mobility and erode overall equality of opportunity.

At the same time, we should also be mindful that mobility and opportunity in any society is determined by factors other than parental income. Gregory Clark, an economist at the University of California, Davis, makes this point in his cleverly titled book *The Son Also Rises*, which takes a more sociological approach to thinking about class. Digging deep into institutional archives in various countries, Clark searched for lists of people who, by virtue of simply being on the lists, could be said to have high or low social status. He then reviewed those lists looking for distinctive surnames that were over-represented, and calculated how long those surnames continued to be over-represented on those same lists in subsequent generations. The longer those family names continued to be over-represented, he reasoned, the less social mobility.

In Sweden, for example, Clark combed through lists of

physicians, university students and members of the Royal
Academy, focusing on names associated with Sweden's an-
cient noble families. In the United States, he scoured professional and club membership lists looking for names of
Ashkenazi and Sephardic Jews, French Canadians, early
black slaves and Native Americans. In England, he looked
for names dating back to the Norman conquerors; in India,
it was names associated with high and low castes.

But no matter what the country, which lists or what time
period he looked at, Clark found a surprisingly universal
pattern: that it took from eight to ten generations for the
over-representation of those names on high- or low-status
lists to disappear. Based on this data, Clark concluded that
social status is significantly more heritable—and social mobility significantly lower—than suggested by one-generation
studies that focus only on income. Indeed, according to
Clark's calculation, social status is no less heritable than
height.

Clark undoubtedly overstates his case. As he himself has
acknowledged, in order for his iron law to be true, you'd
have to believe that the end of primogeniture, the introduction of free universal public education, the outlawing
of race and religious discrimination, the decline in occupational nepotism and the rise of government welfare
programs had no appreciable effect on class mobility or
equality of opportunity. Logic and experience suggest
otherwise.

But Clark's finding also offers some useful reminders as
we think about mobility and opportunity.

The first is that most of the mobility that people have
experienced over generations turns out to have been absolute mobility, not relative. Clark's point about all those progressive reforms is not that they haven't improved people's
lives. Rather, it is that their greatest impact has been to raise

the living standards for everyone in the society—the rich, the poor and everyone in between.

The work of Clark and others also points to the importance of culture on mobility.[48] Parents from different cultures often pass on to their children distinctive values, attitudes and norms about work, savings, ambition, education and family that are important in shaping character and behavior. In subsequent generations, these cultural differences may manifest themselves statistically as differences in educational achievement or household income, about which data is readily available. But it is a mistake to conclude that a child's prospects are exclusively determined by such easily measurable variables while ignoring the persistent influence that culture might have on them.

Most significantly, Clark's research also offers a reminder about the importance of talents, character traits and social connections that are passed on genetically and through upbringing.[49] One son in a rich and prominent family might follow in his father's footsteps and become a successful financier, while another might choose the impecunious life of a preacher. Both sons, however, inherit the same genes, the same upbringing and the same social connections and, notwithstanding their eventual differences in occupation and income, pass these advantages on to subsequent generations. That is the simplest explanation for why social and economic advantage is so persistent over the generations, why mobility hasn't changed much over time and why rates of mobility are so similar across countries.

The Chimera of Equal Opportunity

The scientific literature is unambiguous: because of heritability and culture and the effects of parenting and home environment, there can never be genuine equality of opportunity, as much as we might wish it otherwise. As a matter of rough approximation, about half of the difference in income between one person and the next is due to the persistence of advantages relating to genes and family—in other words, of luck rather than just deserts. Some advanced countries have gone a long way toward equalizing access to health care, education, nutrition, childcare and even disposable income, and yet, for all their success, they have not come close to eliminating the transmission of family advantage or disadvantage. We might agree that, for both moral and economic reasons, still more should to be done to equalize opportunity even further, particularly in the United States, Britain and other countries where mobility is lower. But we should do so realizing that there is a point beyond which the consequences of the parental lottery can never be overcome.

"Hardly anyone who has raised children believes that equalizing parents' income or providing more social services would fully equalize children's development opportunities," write Harvard sociologist Christopher Jencks and three coauthors in a recent essay about family background and economic success, a topic Jencks has been studying for decades. "Nor do many people think that schools can fully compensate children for being shortchanged at home."[50]

Indeed, the irony is that to the degree we are successful in making family income and home environment less important in shaping economic outcomes, the effect is to make more important those *genetically* inherited skills and traits that no amount of social engineering can alter. A meritocratic society that reduces the role of "nurture" only winds up increasing the role of "nature," reducing one form of injustice only to increase another.[51]

We might agree, for example, that conventional equal opportunity requires that poor and rich children with high intelligence have an equal chance to succeed, but that begs the question of why the naturally intelligent child should have far more success than the naturally doltish one. If it is important from a moral standpoint to correct for success based on the luck of having grown up in the home of wealthy parents, why isn't it just as important to correct for success based on the luck of having been born with a photographic memory, or the good looks of a matinee idol or the height to dunk a basketball?

Luck or other arbitrary factors, in other words, will inevitably play a role in shaping individual opportunity, and any systematic effort to eliminate it will put us into tricky territory—what's been called "luck egalitarianism."[52] It becomes apparent very quickly that trying to achieve this kind of deep equality of opportunity presents a series of practical and moral conundrums that are not easily resolved.

For starters, there's room for disagreement over what qualities people can or can't change. We're pretty sure height and intelligence are significantly heritable, but what about ambition, self-discipline, grit or an appetite for risk-taking? Clearly these character traits affect how productively we make use of the intellectual or physical talents we have inherited, but what if these character traits are themselves largely inherited? Wouldn't that transform a lot of what looks like just deserts into something that looks a lot more like dumb luck?

Moreover, even if we could decide which skills and traits are heritable and require some evening up, there would still be the question of how the evening up should be accomplished. In his dystopic satire "Harrison Bergeron," Kurt Vonnegut conjures up a society in which an egalitarian-obsessed

government hangs bags of lead birdshot around the necks
of the physically strong and athletically gifted to slow their
movements, while the highly intelligent are forced to wear
earphones that play distracting noises to prevent them from
thinking clearly. A Handicapper General requires that only
people with speech impediments be hired as newscasters,
and people with two left feet as ballerinas, so that nobody
rises above average. Vonnegut means us to see that this kind
of deep equality of opportunity isn't in the least bit tempt-
ing since the extraordinary contributions of the talented
would be lost while the happiness of everyone would be
reduced.

Perhaps the biggest barrier to achieving deep equality
of opportunity is that it would require undermining the role
of families in providing the basic social structure of society.
The instinct to protect and nurture one's own offspring has
been naturally selected through the evolutionary process,
and from that flows the importance we assign the family in
rearing children and shaping their values, characters and
personalities. Would deep equality of opportunity require
us to restrict the freedom of some parents to read to children
before bedtime, to cheer for them at soccer games or teach
them to be hardworking and frugal, simply because other
parents will not?

And there's the conundrum. We know that differences
in parental income, education and parenting skill are significant factors in determining the success of children. We
also know that the assignment of parents is a matter of luck.
What that means is that, short of taking children away from
their families and rearing them in government-run residential schools, public policy can't eliminate the differences in
nurture any more than it can eliminate all differences in
nature.

The implications of these insights for economic justice

are profound. If genuine equality of opportunity is neither possible nor even desirable, then we must acknowledge that luck must always play a significant role not only in who achieves economic success, but who has the opportunity to succeed. No matter how hard we might try to make it otherwise, we cannot all start on the same starting line. We are not endowed by our Creator with equal talents and capabilities and, just as significantly, we do not have an equal opportunity to develop those talents and capabilities. And because of that, there is a fundamental and irreducible level of unfairness to market competition, one that undermines the moral legitimacy of market outcomes.

Jencks, along with fellow sociologists James Coleman and Daniel Bell, warned about the false promises of meritocracy back in the late 1960s and early '70s, before it became the received wisdom that equalizing opportunity was the only legitimate aim of social policy and redistribution must be rejected as socialist rubbish.[53] The meritocratic dynamic has played out pretty much as they warned it would, with the rise of a new aristocracy based on talent that is no less arbitrary than those based on race and class. And, as they did, we must conclude that if we want an economic system that is fair and just, we have to go beyond equalizing opportunity to acknowledge the moral necessity of equalizing incomes in ways that make economic and moral sense.

* * *

So where does this leave us?

Recall that the moral argument for accepting the market's determination of the distribution of income is that (1) it reflects our individual contribution to an economic system that (2) gives everyone an equal chance to succeed and (3) makes all of us better off. Cheerleaders for American capitalism have relied on that argument to justify the widening gap between the rich and everyone else and to condemn government efforts to correct it.

We learned in the last chapter that the way the market divides the pie does not, in fact, reflect a purely objective measure of economic contribution but is, and always will be, influenced by political decisions and prevailing social norms. Or to use the sporting metaphor, no matter what rules are chosen for how the race is run, the choice of rules inevitably skews the results.

In this chapter, we are reminded that the outcome of the race is, to a substantial and unacceptable degree, determined even before the race begins, based on a parental lottery that gives some competitors a head start over the others. Despite our best efforts to even the odds, the results can never be purely a reflection of individual merit. Our moral instinct is to try to compensate for that reality by redistributing the prize money in a more equitable way.

But that still leaves us with a third and final rationale for market justice, the one that holds that inequality of income and opportunity, though unfortunate, are necessary features of a system that has proven itself the best at growing the economic pie and making everyone better off. As we will soon discover, however, that is only true until it isn't.

4

Fairness and Growth—A False Choice

Before and after the state of Israel was founded in 1948, a small but important segment of its economy was organized around kibbutzim, socialist collectives in which the land, housing, buildings and equipment were owned by all residents, who shared equally in what was produced and how the commune was governed.

Initially, the kibbutzim were successful in helping to make the desert bloom and lay the foundation for a successful society and a successful economy. But in time—or so the standard story goes—their egalitarian solidarity began to erode. The most productive workers came to resent carrying those who were less talented or hardworking, so they moved to the cities where they would get a better reward. As they did, the average productivity and standard of living back on the kibbutzim began to decline, prompting the next-most-productive workers to defect. Eventually, this vicious cycle led many kibbutzim to close as all but the most ideologically committed members concluded they could do better in the more market-like economy.[1]

Among defenders of free markets, the story of the kib-butzim is a parable of the failure of egalitarian income distribution. The lesson they draw from it—and more broadly from the failure of communist and socialist economies during the twentieth century—is that without significant differences in income, the productive will expect no extra reward for their dedication and creativity and the unproductive no punishment for their sloth and lack of ambition. Inequality, they believe, and a good amount of it, is the inevitable consequence of an incentive structure that rewards the hard work, innovation, risk-taking, skills development, savings and investment that raise everyone's standard of living. By that standard, the distribution of income in a market economy must be judged to be fair and just.

As students of philosophy have long recognized, however, the utilitarian criterion of creating the greatest good for the greatest number demands more than just producing the largest economy. Overall well-being would also be increased if money were redistributed from those who had more than enough to satisfy their worldly needs and desires to those whose needs were still unmet. After all, the last dollar of income earned by Bill Gates will do much less to improve his happiness than it would for a working single mom struggling to feed her children. And, if that is the case, providing the greatest good for the greatest number also must involve redistributing at least some income from those who have so much to those who have so little.

This tension between wanting to generate a bigger pie and wanting to cut the slices more equally has long bedeviled both moralists and economists—"the big tradeoff," as economist Arthur Okun famously called it.[2] We can either have faster growth and higher incomes by allowing the market to reward individual effort, however unequal the distribution, or we can have a more equal distribution of income that better comports with our other moral intuitions about fairness and need. Our dilemma, identified long ago by Bernard Mandeville and his fable of the bees, arises from the fact that having more of one seems to lead inevitably to having less of another.

There is reason to believe, however, that this choice between growth and equality can be a false one—that at some point, more inequality stops producing a bigger pie and begins to *slow* economic growth, and that, under such circumstances, redistribution might actually *enhance* growth rather than diminish it.

Inequality and Work Incentives

The economist Arthur Laffer is famous for having drawn a graph on a cocktail napkin that illustrated what has since become a cherished conservative nostrum: that raising income tax rates doesn't necessarily generate more revenue for the government. Laffer's insight was that a tax rate of 100 percent, just like a tax rate of zero, would raise no money—at one extreme because the rate was so low, at the other because it was so high that nobody would work and produce any income to tax.[3] Laffer's famous curve, in this rendition with tax rates set out on the horizontal x-axis and revenue raised on the vertical y-axis, is in the shape of an upside-down "U." It is meant to demonstrate that high tax rates are both economically inefficient and fiscally self-defeating.

Using a similar logic, imagine a curve that plots two other variables, income inequality and economic growth. In this thought experiment, let the level of income inequality be represented on the horizontal x-axis and economic growth

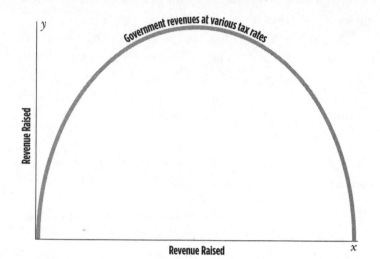

Figure 4.1 **The Laffer Curve**

Economist Arthur Laffer's insight was that a 0 percent tax and a 100 percent tax brought in the exact same revenue—zero—from which he inferred that high levels of taxation were self-defeating.

Government revenues at various tax rates

y

Revenue Raised

Revenue Raised   x

rates on the vertical y-axis. Experience and logic tell us that in a world in which incomes are guaranteed to be perfectly equal, at the far left of the x-axis, there would be little incentive for anyone to produce any more than the bare minimum, since workers are guaranteed an equal income no matter how they perform—a recipe for Soviet-like economic stagnation. At the opposite end, at the far right, where inequality is extreme, a handful of oligarchs capture all the income, leaving everyone else with little incentive to work hard or smart. The curve provides a graphic illustration of our intuition that too much inequality, no less than too much equality, can be economically self-defeating.

Richard B. Freeman, a labor economist at Harvard University, conducted an experiment with a group of students to test the validity of this intuition. He and a colleague ran-

Figure 4.2 **The Pearlstein Curve**

An economic system that guarantees everyone an equal income would generate roughly the same economic output as one in which a handful of people earned virtually all the income.

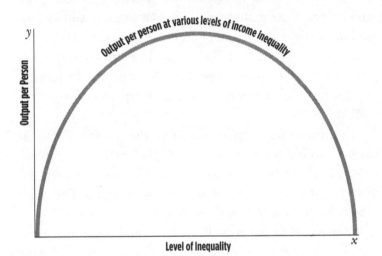

domly divided the students into three groups and tasked each group with solving a set of puzzles. The group that solved the most puzzles would win a prize, but the way the prize would be distributed was different in each group. In the first, the students were told they would all receive equal shares of the prize. The second group was told that the person in the group who solved the most puzzles would get the entire prize. And those in the third group were told that everyone would receive some portion of the prize, but the amounts would be incrementally higher for those solving more puzzles.

When the experiment was completed, the results roughly confirmed the upside-down "U" configuration. The equal-pay group had the lowest "output," solving the least number of puzzles. The winner-take-all group was only slightly better.

But far and away the most productive group was the one in which an egalitarian reward structure was blended with a meritocratic one.[4]

As with Laffer and his curve, we are probably pretty safe in intuiting where the extreme and unlikely endpoints of the growth-versus-inequality curve are likely to be. And as with the Laffer curve, the trickier and more significant task is figuring out the shape of the curve in-between—where it peaks and how steep the slopes are on either side. Determining that shape is what the debate about equality and growth is all about.

Central to that debate has been the question of what happens to economic growth if the incomes at the top are reduced in some way because of society's desire to alleviate poverty or make economic outcomes more equal. There are two ways to go about doing that.

One way is to tinker with the rules and institutional arrangements that govern the way markets operate and have an impact on how the pie is divided—things like raising the minimum wage, making it easier to form labor unions, limiting trade with low-wage companies or requiring all employers to provide pensions and health insurance. This is what was referred to earlier as predistribution, a term originally coined by Jacob Hacker of Yale University.[5]

The other strategy is to wait until after the market has made its distribution and do the evening up later, by taxing those with higher incomes and redistributing the proceeds to those whom the market has judged to be less productive, either in cash or in the form of basic services such as health care.

The standard free market argument against both forms of redistribution is that the more you do of either, the more likely it is that you cause the economy's most productive workers to decide to curb their ambition, withhold their excellence and head for the beach.

As it turns out, both economic theory and experience are ambiguous on this point.

If my compensation is reduced or taxed away so that working is no longer worth as much, I might decide to work less hard—to substitute leisure for work—and thereby reduce my output. Or I might respond in just the opposite way, by working longer and harder to make up for the income that I've lost and thus maintain my previous lifestyle. One is called the "substitution effect," the other the "income effect," and among economists there is general agreement that both come into play. The answer to the question of which is more powerful depends on various factors, but the evidence is that the net effect is fairly modest.[6]

Those who want to rely on markets and oppose redistribution tend to assume that, for very-high-income people, the substitution effect—the instinct to head to the beach—would be the stronger one. After all, they will ask, does Bill Gates really need to replace the last $50,000 of income if it were taxed away?

But then ask yourself: Why, even in high-tax places like New York and California, do we see billionaire hedge fund managers and movie moguls driving their Range Rovers to work each weekday, or working the phones on the weekend from beach houses in Malibu or the Hamptons? If you ask them why—and I have—many will acknowledge that they are motivated by non-monetary considerations such as power and fame, or the intellectual and competitive challenge of playing the game, or merely the satisfaction of doing a job well. The additional income is important to these hypercompetitive people not so much because they want to buy things with it, but because it is how they keep score. As Adam Smith put it in *The Theory of Moral Sentiments*, "It is the vanity, not the ease of the pleasure, which interests us."[7]

But in thinking about the effect of equalizing incomes on work effort and output, we cannot focus solely on the impact on the behavior of entrepreneurs, executives and other so-called job creators. To do a truly thorough analysis, we also have to consider the impact on the behavior of the much larger number of people who would be at the receiving end of the income adjustment.

Let's start with predistribution—that is, raising the pay of frontline employees. Once again, the income and substitution effects both come into play. Higher pay might encourage middle-class and lower-wage workers to put in more hours, substituting work for leisure—think of the incentive effect of time-and-a-half overtime pay. Or higher wages could give some workers enough extra money that they feel financially secure enough to work less and spend more time on their hobbies or with their grandchildren—that's the income effect. Given how much more an extra dollar means to those near the bottom of the income scale, it's a good guess that the instinct to work longer and harder would be the more dominant response.

"The liberal reward of labor . . . increases the industry of the common people," wrote Adam Smith in *The Wealth of Nations*. "The wages of labor are the encouragement of industry, which, like every other human quality, improves in proportion to the encouragement it receives."[8]

While Smith relied only on his own keen powers of observation, modern management research confirms that, at the company level, raising pay creates a stronger sense of reciprocal obligation in the minds of workers that leads them to work harder and smarter, with a greater sense of optimism and purpose.[9]

But it is not only the level of pay that affects worker performance; it is also the equality or inequality of that pay. Economist Matt Bloom came to that conclusion after studying data from Major League Baseball, where the pay of the sport's superstars has been pulling away from the rank-and-file players for years. Comparing win–loss statistics to the level of pay inequality of each team, Bloom found that the teams with the most unequal pay tended to finish farther down in the standings. He also found that the superstars on the teams with the widest pay gaps performed less well than the superstars on teams with more equal pay.[10] A separate study of the National Football League found similar results.[11]

In his recent book *Broken Ladder*, Keith Payne, a professor of psychology at the University of North Carolina, concludes from these and other studies that inequality creates resentments among players that weakens cooperation and teamwork.[12] And what's true in sports, he writes, is true in business as well. One large study found that a wider gap in pay between top executives and frontline workers was associated with a lower quality of product produced by those workers.[13]

Consider the implication of these insights for an economy in which the pay of those frontline workers has not only fallen behind those at the top, but failed to keep up with the increase in how much they were producing.

The next graph captures the shop-floor reality.[14] For many years, average labor productivity and the hourly compensation of non-supervisory workers tracked each other so closely that a generation of economists had come to believe they were inextricably linked. But beginning in the mid-1970s, the two lines began to diverge. Since that time, worker productivity has climbed 65 percent, while hourly compensation of the average non-supervisory worker has risen by just over 8 percent.[15]

You might also notice one other thing from the graph.

Figure 4.3 Pay for Performance?

Output per hour worked and average hourly earnings, 1948–2016

In the past, the pay of American workers rose in line with increased productivity. But beginning in 1979, that connection was broken, with most of the benefits of productivity gains going to investors and consumers.

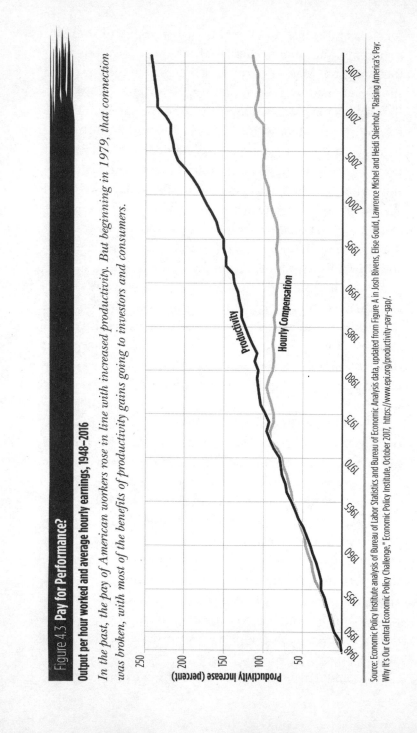

Source: Economic Policy Institute analysis of Bureau of Labor Statistics and Bureau of Economic Analysis data, updated from Figure A in Josh Bivens, Elise Gould, Lawrence Mishel and Heidi Shierholz, "Raising America's Pay: Why It's Our Central Economic Policy Challenge," Economic Policy Institute, October 2017, https://www.epi.org/productivity-pay-gap/.

Since about 2006, growth in productivity has also begun to slow. This slowdown, dubbed "secular stagnation," has now become something of an obsession among economists, and there are a lot of theories about what factors are driving it.[16] I can't prove for certain that rising inequality is one of those factors. At the same time, I have yet to hear a plausible story explaining how the productivity of frontline workers has *not* been hurt by a prevailing business ethic that explicitly seeks to keep their wages as low as possible so that shareholders and top executives can capture an ever-increasing share of the increased profits.

In the United States, worker resentment over lagging pay no longer manifests itself in picket lines and walkouts. But you hear it regularly over the office coffeepot, read it on employee message boards and see it in the strong political support for increases in the minimum wage and higher taxes on corporations.[17] You see it reflected in the increase in the number of working-age males who have dropped out of the workforce rather than take the low-wage jobs that are on offer.[18] Nor is it mere coincidence that the level of engagement of American workers, as measured through regular employee surveys, has remained at a dismal 30 percent or less for the last decade.[19] When Gallup recently polled American workers, it found that roughly half feel they are now underpaid.[20]

At the same time, business publications such as *Fast Company*, *Inc.* and the *Harvard Business Review* regularly run compelling stories from business owners who have tried various ways of sharing gains with employees and found it can yield the same or even better results in terms of employee engagement, productivity, product quality and profits.[21]

The point of all this is a simple one: if it is true, as defenders of market justice insist, that making market incomes more equal would *discourage* work effort at the top, then the same logic should dictate that more equality would *encourage* work effort at the bottom. Surely the incentive sword cuts both ways. And if so, then there is an argument that a modest equalization of market incomes—predistribution—might increase productivity and output overall, not reduce it.

Indeed, one of the fallacies at the heart of most arguments for market justice is a presumption that frontline employees are interchangeable and easily replaceable cogs in the economy, while those at the top—those who design, manage and finance the economic machinery—are the only ones who matter in terms of innovation and increased productivity. The justification for the extraordinary levels of pay for executives and financiers rests on this false and self-serving presumption.

Can the same be said for redistribution of income through progressive taxes and transfers after the market has rendered its judgment? Doesn't redistribution, as defenders of market justice reflexively argue, discourage work and breed dependency among those who are at the receiving end? The answer is that it depends on what form the redistribution takes.

In general, giving people cash assistance untethered to work has a negative effect on work effort. The cash welfare program known as Aid to Families with Dependent Children, for example, was found to have reduced employment for welfare mothers by anywhere from 10 to 50 percent when it was introduced. Food stamps, housing vouchers and Medicaid have also been found to have a negative effect on work, although a more modest one.[22] On the other hand, some forms of assistance—the wage supplement known as "earned income tax credit" and childcare subsidies are two big ones—are unambiguously pro-work.[23]

The form and structure of any redistribution also

matters in another way—politically. People are much more willing to help the poor if the help is conditioned on work. While our moral instincts lead us to feel good about helping those who are suffering or in need, those same instincts lead us to be outraged whenever we hear of those who take advantage of our sympathy and generosity by not making enough effort to help themselves. That is particularly true of Americans, who in surveys are more than twice as likely as Europeans to say they believe that poverty is due to laziness rather than bad luck. Our altruism, it turns out, tends to be highly conditional, based on expectations of reciprocity.[24]

Indeed, one of the great puzzles in American politics is that even those who are most likely to benefit from safety-net programs are skeptical of them and vote for politicians who want to cut or eliminate them. Scratch the surface, and what you find is that their thinking is colored by examples, real or imagined, of people abusing those programs. Their moral outrage overrides any rational calculation of self-interest.[25]

So where does all of this leave us in terms of the trade-off between equalizing incomes and work effort?

In the United States, it is fair to say that we are well past that point in the inequality curve where we have to worry that a more equal distribution of income would significantly reduce the work effort of high-income earners and cause them to withhold their excellence. That didn't happen when top tax rates were raised during the Clinton administration, or the Obama administration, or twice during the Reagan administration. The reason successful people continue to work as hard and productively as they do has more to do with psychic than financial rewards. They will grumble. They will lobby politicians to lower their taxes and try to punish politicians who raise them. They will surely look for creative new ways to reduce their taxes. But retire? Not so much.

On the other hand, there is good reason to think that the rise in inequality of market incomes has had a deleterious effect on the engagement and productivity of frontline workers who actually make products and deliver services to customers, and that well-structured predistribution and redistribution could help reverse that and actually make the pie bigger.

Poverty and Growth

Defenders of market justice frequently complain that concern about income inequality is overblown, and that from a moral standpoint, our focus should be on alleviating poverty. It is possible, of course, for overall income inequality to rise while poverty falls—think of China over the last two decades. And even in the United States, poverty rates have remained relatively steady at around 15 percent during a period in which market incomes have become increasingly unequal, thanks largely to government safety-net programs.

But for Americans, the more relevant question is why the poverty rate hasn't *declined* as our rich country has become even richer. Why hasn't a rising tide lifted all boats?

By one calculation, if the distribution of income had remained the same in the decades after 1980 as it had in the decades before, rising wages would have virtually eliminated poverty, which in the United States is defined as the amount of money needed to buy the bare essentials of life.[26] Slower growth, immigration and changes in family structure have also been factors in keeping the poverty rate as high as it is, after falling dramatically during the 1960s and '70s. But by far the biggest factor in the persistence of poverty has been the declining share of market income going to the working poor.

Moreover, there is reason to believe that the persistence of high rates of poverty has contributed to slower economic growth. For if an increasingly unequal distribution of income prevents poverty rates from falling, and if childhood poverty is likely to reduce economic output later in life, then we can be fairly certain that the poverty caused by higher inequality in one generation will lead to lower output in the next. We may never know exactly how much economic growth has been lost because of talent that is not developed, ambition that is not fulfilled, ingenuity that is not tapped among those unlucky enough to be born into poverty. But we should have no doubt about its economic significance.

There is also reason to believe that in the poorest households, where there is little or no income from working, a bit of old-fashioned welfare might also be beneficial to the economy as a whole, even if such assistance is undeserved.

Several years ago, philosopher Charles Karelis published *The Persistence of Poverty*, which questioned the widely held view that giving money to people who are very poor reduces their incentive to discipline themselves in ways that might improve their economic prospects—finishing school, getting a job, not having children, avoiding alcohol and drugs. Living in deep poverty, Karelis reasoned, is like living with a dozen bee stings all at once: life is so miserable for so many different reasons that it hardly makes sense to make the sacrifices necessary to fix any one of them. From that perspective, what looks like irrational, self-destructive behavior to the rest of society might actually be quite rational.

But that rational calculus would change, Karelis reasoned, if the very poor were given enough money to lift them out of their wretched, hopeless state. At that point, with only a few bee stings left to deal with, a poor person might have a shot at escaping from their miserable existence and begin to make the same choices about work and lifestyle as the rest of us.

The policy implication Karelis drew from this insight was that even if cash assistance reduces the work effort of those at or above the poverty line, it could actually increase work incentives for those who are stuck well below it.

Inequality and Investment

The more credible argument for why more inequality might lead to more growth focuses not on work effort but on savings and investment.

We know that the higher people's income, the more likely they are to save. In the United States, the top 1 percent of households, for example, saves about half of its income, compared to 10 percent among the middle class and close to zero among the working class.[27] What that means is that as more of the nation's income is shifted to those at the top, a smaller percentage of it will be used to buy goods and services in the here and now, while more will be saved and invested. To the extent that this increased pool of savings lowers the cost of capital for businesses and leads to increased investment in research and development, new machinery, worker training and other things that boost productivity and productive capacity, a more unequal economy is likely to grow faster over the long term. Or so goes the standard economic theory.

Recent developments, however, offer some reasons to doubt the links between any one country's savings, its level of business investment and how fast its economy grows.

For starters, as economies are globalized and capital

flows more freely across borders, it becomes harder to draw the connection between the savings and the investment that goes on within any one country. A growing portion of the money saved by Americans, for example, is invested in other countries, just as a growing share of foreign savings is invested in American businesses or lent to American households, businesses and governments. Because of our large and persistent trade deficit, the United States, in fact, has become the world's biggest importer of capital, and the world's biggest debtor. And yet our recent experience is that investors and central banks around the world are only too eager to lend us the money we need to live beyond our means, at interest rates that, by historical standards, are quite low. Given those realities, it is hard to justify giving ever-larger shares of national income to high-income Americans because of the extra domestic investment that might come from it.

Indeed, in recent decades, despite the plentiful supply of cheap capital, the long-term trend of business investment as a share of the economy is down, not up.[28] Instead, companies have increasingly been using their profits, or money borrowed from capital markets, to return cash to shareholders, either in the form of dividends or stock buybacks.[29] It is unclear whether lagging business investment is due to lack of good investment opportunities in the United States, or to better opportunities outside the country, or to increased pressure from Wall Street to increase returns for investors. It is likely some combination of all three. But whatever the cause, there is no evidence that, in an open and advanced economy such as ours, making rich people a bit less rich will lead to a significant decrease in productive business investment.

Moreover, there is evidence that, to the extent that rising

inequality has reduced the incomes of middle- and working-class households, it has reduced the financial capacity of those households to invest in developing their own skills. Such investments in human capital, as economists call it, have historically had high rates of return not only for the individuals who make them, but also for society at large.[30] The inability of low-income parents to invest in higher education for their children is surely one reason why less than half of Americans earn a college degree by the time they turn 35. Whereas the United States was once the world's leader in terms of educational attainment, we now lag behind Japan, Korea and Canada.[31] In an era when globalization and technological change have increased the demand for high-skilled workers, that forgone investment in human capital can hardly have been a plus for economic growth.

Of course, if households don't earn enough money to pay college tuitions, they can always borrow it—and every year, more and more do. The amount of outstanding college loans, in fact, has increased 450 percent since 2003.[32] And there is the irony. For in effect, what we have done by allowing the rich to capture a larger share of national income is make it possible for them to lend a portion of it back to the working class so they can send their kids to colleges that they can no longer afford. Wouldn't it be fairer and economically more efficient if the distribution of market income had remained more like it used to be, so that working households could earn and save enough to finance their children's college tuitions without going into debt? Or, alternatively, wouldn't it be fairer and more economically efficient to raise taxes on upper-income households in order to restore state support for public universities, so they could once again be affordable to the working class?

More Finance, Less Growth

What's true of college loans, in fact, has been true of consumer borrowing generally. In response to stagnant or declining incomes, many households have not chosen to go without the accouterments of middle-class life, but rather to borrow the money to pay for them from richer households whose share of the national income is increasing.

In his book *Fault Lines*, University of Chicago economist Raghuram Rajan argued that rising income inequality has contributed to both the supply and the demand for this surge in household debt, setting the stage for the boom and bust cycles of the past 30 years.[33] The increased savings of those in the top 5 percent of households are the mirror image of sharp increases in borrowing in the bottom 95 percent. This borrowing binge caused household debt to rise to dangerous and unprecedented levels.[34]

In other words, the big problem with the rapid growth in incomes at the top is not that it has dampened overall demand for goods and services, as some liberal economists have suggested. Rather, the problem is that it has led to the overexpansion of a financial sector, one that routinely misallocates both capital and talent and foments financial instability.[35]

Consider that back in the 1950s, the financial sector accounted for about 3 percent of the U.S. economy; today, it's more than double that, at 6.5 percent. Back then, financial-sector profits were about 8 percent of all business profits; just before the 2008 crash, they grew to 40 percent before dropping back to 25 percent today.[36]

Despite its rapid growth in profits, the financial sector still employs fewer than 5 percent of all workers, which explains why banks and investment funds can afford those seven-figure bonuses. It's hard to believe that, until 1990, people who worked in finance earned about the same as workers in other industries with the same skills and levels of education. By 2006, financial firms were paying their workers a premium of 50 percent.[37]

Every economy, of course, needs an efficient financial sector that serves the role of intermediary, pooling the savings of millions of households and then channeling it to businesses and consumers who need it most, either in the form of loans or investment. That role, however, could be served by a financial sector that is much smaller and less profitable than the one we have today. As demonstrated repeatedly—from the savings and loan crisis of the 1980s to the Asian financial crisis of the 1990s, from the tech and telecom bubble in 2000 to the financial meltdown of 2008— the only way the financial sector could get this big and this profitable is by transforming itself from an efficient intermediary for the nation's savings into a giant casino where the primary purpose is gambling and the house takes an ever increasing share of the pot.

In 1990, three of America's best young economists— Kevin Murphy, Andrei Shleifer and Robert Vishny—wrote a prescient paper in which they argued that much of the trading they observed in financial markets was not about efficiently allocating capital to the real economy. Rather, they argued, much of what happens on Wall Street is merely the "transfer of wealth to the smart traders from the less astute who trade with them out of institutional needs or outright stupidity."

The problem for the economy, as they saw it, was that the outsized rewards offered by this activity siphoned too much of a country's best talent—talent that could have been used more productively to start new companies, invent new products, cure diseases and solve the world's most difficult problems. Just as people in some countries are attracted to government service because of the opportunity to enrich themselves with bribes and kickbacks, so many of today's best and brightest now flock to occupations such as finance and law where they can earn fabulous sums not by creating wealth but by redistributing it. Using the number of lawyers and engineers in different countries as proxies, the trio demonstrated that countries with more "rent seekers" than entrepreneurs had lower levels of economic growth—not because they hadn't developed enough human capital but because their human capital was directed toward unproductive ends.[38]

More recently, economists with the Bank for International Settlements, the central bank of central banks, looked at the experience of 21 advanced economies and concluded that growth of a financial sector is "good only up to a point, after which it becomes a drag on growth." The reason: the tendency to reallocate capital from low-collateral, high-productivity businesses such as technology and manufacturing to high-collateral, low-productivity sectors such as construction, finance and real estate. In other words, when a financial sector gets too big, its focus shifts from productively channeling savings into growing businesses to bidding up the price of real estate, stocks and other financial instruments. The damage is particularly significant, they found, in economies where financiers are able to command above-market compensation and divert skilled labor from other sectors—exactly what we've seen happen in the United States and Britain over the last 30 years.[39]

What all this calls into question is the macroeconomic assumption that economic growth is fostered when rich people get a bigger share of the pie because it increases investment. We now know that a significant share of that extra investment capital has been skimmed off the top by a Wall Street oligopoly whose lavish profits and compensation undermine any claim that it is an efficient intermediary for the nation's savings. And what we also know is that too much of that savings has been used to finance speculative trading, risky lending and unproductive mergers and acquisitions.

It can hardly be a coincidence that we've already had three unsustainable stock market bubbles since inequality began its upward march, one in each decade, with hints of a fourth one just over the horizon. The long-term increase in the ratio of share prices to expected profits, the explosive growth in split-second computerized trading, the tidal wave of share buybacks, the fantastic sums being paid for new public companies—all of these are signs of too much capital chasing too few good investment opportunities. Undoubtedly some of that reflects the inflow of foreign capital and the peak savings of baby boomers heading into retirement. But given that the top 10 percent of households now hold more than 80 percent of all financial assets, it is hard to escape the conclusion that the shift of wealth and income to those at the top has contributed to a boom-and-bust cycle in financial and real estate markets that, over the long term, has resulted in lower levels of economic growth.[40]

Public Investment

At the same time, there are lots of productive public investments that could have been made but haven't, in part because tax cuts benefiting the rich have reduced the financial capacity of government at every level. These include investments in physical infrastructure such as roads, bridges, rail and transit systems, ports and airports, along with computer systems and other equipment used by government agencies; investments in research and development; investments in technology infrastructure such as telecommunications systems, the electrical grid and the air-traffic control network; and investment in education and worker training. Government data shows that net public investment outside of defense—that is, spending minus depreciation of existing stock—has declined dramatically since 1970, from 2.5 percent of GDP to 0.5 percent.[41] The Congressional Budget Office estimates such public investments, on average, have an annual return, or payoff, of about 7.5 percent every year.[42]

How much more public investment could productively be made? The American Society of Civil Engineers estimates that, because of years of deferred maintenance and public investment, the expected shortfall of investment in physical infrastructure alone will reach $5 trillion over the next decade.[43] At a time when the government's long-term borrowing costs are running at less than 3 percent, even the deficit hawks at the Committee for a Responsible Federal Budget have concluded that failing to make those investments amounts to economic and fiscal malpractice.[44]

The Unproductive Arms Race for Status Goods

Robert Frank, the Cornell University economist, has written a lot about the link between rapidly rising incomes at the top and the amount of unproductive private investment and spending it has generated—in particular, the bidding war for the limited supply of what are often called "status goods." Think of brownstones in Brooklyn, ski condos in Aspen, beach houses on Martha's Vineyard. Think of Maseratis and Teslas. Think of professional sports teams and thoroughbred racehorses. Think of memberships in exclusive clubs, rooms at the most elite vacation resorts and places at the most sought after private schools and colleges.

Or think of great works of art. Increased demand for fine art has pushed the most coveted paintings to once unthinkable prices. The art world was stunned several years ago when Picasso's *Les Femmes d'Alger* was auctioned for $179 million at Christie's.[45] The same month, hedge fund billionaire Kenneth Griffin plunked down $500 million to buy a Jackson Pollock and a Willem de Kooning owned by the foundation of Hollywood mogul David Geffen. In short order, however, those records were shattered when Saudi Arabia's crown prince paid $450 million at auction to purchase a long-lost painting by Leonardo da Vinci. The supply of Picassos, de Koonings and da Vincis isn't increasing, but thanks to rising inequality of wealth and income, the number of people eager and able to bid on them certainly has.

"It's a spectacle of excess at the highest level," Abigail Asher, a leading art consultant, told the *New York Times*. "The last few years have been building up to this moment. A new class of buyer has entered the market and they're prepared to pay staggering sums for trophy pictures."[46]

This increased demand for a relatively fixed supply has meant that prices of status goods have been rising as fast as the incomes of rich households that covet them. For example, the average price of yearlings sold at the first session of the fall auction at Keeneland, where all the best thoroughbreds are traded, has doubled over the last 20 years.[47] Over the same time period, the annual all-in cost of tuition, room and board at an Ivy League college such as Dartmouth has shot up 130 percent. The average value of an NFL franchise has increased 236 percent.[48] On the East Side of Manhattan, where activist investor Bill Ackman recently paid $92 million for a 14,000-foot, six-bedroom penthouse atop a new 76-floor glass tower, the average price per square foot of apartments has climbed by more than 250 percent.[49]

It has got to the point that even the wealthy have been heard to complain and wonder how much higher the price of status goods can go. As Yogi Berra might have put it, the cost of being rich has gotten prohibitively expensive.

Obviously, these status goods and investments must give the wealthy enough pleasure that they are still willing to buy and invest in them at these astronomical prices. But what is equally certain is that this bidding war is economically and socially unproductive. Given all the other available investment opportunities, public and private, that might actually enhance economic growth and deliver significant returns to society as a whole, this multibillion-dollar arms race for status goods has made the American economy smaller, less productive and less competitive than it otherwise could have been.

Inequality and Political Dysfunction

And let's not forget that other unproductive arms race—the bidding war for political influence. Wealthy interests have always used some of their wealth to lobby legislators and regulators, influence the outcome of elections and vigorously pursue their economic interests through the courts, but never as much as they do today.

Nearly $7 billion was spent to influence the results of the 2016 presidential and congressional elections in the United States, up from $3 billion in the 2000 election cycle.[50] To that we must add another $3 billion a year that corporations and industry associations now spend on lobbying, double what it was 20 years ago.[51]

This escalation in spending is partly the result of court rulings that have chipped away at limits on what individuals and corporations can donate and spend to support policies and candidates they favor and oppose those they do not. But it is also the result of an upward shift in the distribution of income. When a small network of billionaires headed by brothers Charles and David Koch is both able and willing to spend $900 million in a single election cycle, it's not unreasonable to wonder if the United States has crossed the line into plutocracy.[52]

And what have the wealthy bought with their political investment?

Most obviously, they have bought a government that leaves them with more disposable income by lowering their effective tax rates, individually and through the businesses they own and control.[53] In the tax bill recently enacted by the Republican Congress, more than 80 percent of the tax cuts will go to the top 1 percent of households by 2027.[54]

Their political investments have bought a regulatory apparatus and a judiciary that have systematically undermined and weakened protections for workers, consumers and small investors.

Most significantly, they have brought to power politicians at all levels of government who have embraced globalization, weakened the social safety net, eroded the minimum wage and made it harder for workers to form unions, while reducing investment in public goods.

Because of political money, the country has doubled down on many of the policies that caused incomes to become more unequal in the first place, creating a self-reinforcing dynamic in which concentrations of economic and political power feed off each other.[55] A widely cited study by political scientists Ben Page, Larry Bartels and Martin Gilens confirms what most of us have long suspected and now observe almost daily—namely, that the preferences of wealthy individuals and business interests have far more impact on public policy than the preferences of the poor and middle class.[56]

These days, even conservatives regularly complain about the ways in which large swaths of the economy have been "captured" by insiders who manipulate the levers of government to restrict competition, hoard opportunity or benefit from insider dealing.

"The unique brand of American capitalism—which in the last 60 years has created tens of millions of jobs, lifted millions of immigrants out of poverty and inspired the world over—seems to be losing its luster, slowly degenerating into a form of crony capitalism that undermines both our prosperity and our democracy," writes Luigi Zingales in his book *A Capitalism for the People.* An unabashedly pro-market economist at the University of Chicago, Zingales warns that an unholy marriage between economic and political elites is slowly strangling the American economy, much as it did in his native Italy.[57]

Brink Lindsey of the libertarian Niskanen Center and Steven Teles, a political scientist at Johns Hopkins University, make a similar case in their book *The Captured Economy.* Lindsey and Teles identify several sectors of the economy that have become less competitive and innovative as a result of regulations bought and paid for by special interests. These include copyright and trademark laws that have become so restrictive they do as much to deter innovation and creativity as they do to promote it; occupational licensing that limits the supply of professionals and craftsmen in ways that protect incumbents and raise prices for medical care or getting your toilet fixed; and implicit government subsidies, like bank bailouts and home-mortgage guarantees, that have contributed to a bloated and inefficient financial sector.[58]

While both political parties have participated in, and been influenced by, the arms race in political spending, the impact has hardly been symmetric. The Republican Party has experienced an electoral resurgence in no small part because of a tsunami of funds from wealthy donors and business interests. It is this money that best explains why Republican officeholders have for the last 20 years been moving to the right on economic issues—not only to the right of where they had previously been, but also to the right of the voters who elect them. And it is this money that best explains why Republican officeholders have been increasingly unwilling and unable to compromise on issues of interest to major financial backers. As Democratic officeholders respond in kind with a similar intransigence, the policy-making process has become polarized. As a result, the comity, compromise and cooperative norms that once characterized much of American politics have been badly eroded.[59]

The accompanying graphic illustrates the close correlation between the rise in income inequality in the United States and the growing ideological divergence in policy positions between Republican and Democratic members of Congress.[60] But it's not just the politicians who have been affected. Rising income inequality has also changed the attitudes and behavior of American voters, sowing resentment, fanning prejudice and eroding the sense of shared values, shared purpose and shared destiny that once held the country together.[61] These resentments and prejudices have been stoked by politicians and interest groups looking for votes, and by media outlets looking to lure readers and viewers, breeding a we-versus-them mentality that lies at the heart of political polarization.[62]

What is clear to both the casual observer and the careful social scientist is that income inequality and political polarization have become mutually reinforcing, creating a

Figure 4.4 More Inequality, More Polarization

Index of Gini coefficient and index of ideological gap between Republican and Democratic members of the U.S. House, 1947–2000

As the level of income inequality began to rise in the late 1970s, so, too, did the ideological gap between the average Democrat and average Republican member of Congress. The two developments have tracked each other closely ever since.

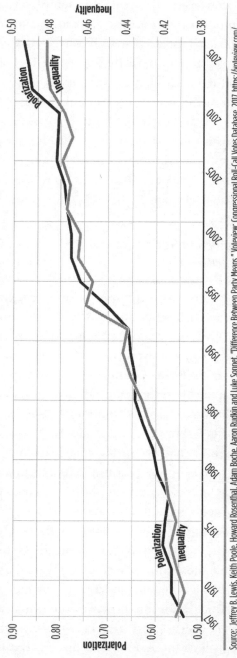

Source: Jeffrey B. Lewis, Keith Poole, Howard Rosenthal, Adam Boche, Aaron Rudkin and Luke Sonnet, "Difference Between Party Means," Voteview: Congressional Roll-Call Votes Database, 2017, https://voteview.com/articles/party_polarization; and U.S. Census Bureau, "Table: H-4. Gini Indexes for Households, by Race and Hispanic Origin of Householder: 1967–2016," August 10, 2017, https://www.census.gov/data/tables/time-series/demo/income-poverty/historical-income-households.html.

vicious downward spiral that now manifests itself daily in the erosion of norms around civility and truth telling, the declining trust in political institutions, legislative gridlock and political dysfunction.[63] The negative effect on the economy is unambiguous and, over time, likely to be substantial. We know from the sweep of economic history that economies do not grow and thrive without inclusive economic and political institutions that can respond quickly and effectively to changing circumstances and challenges.[64] Countries do not grow rich or poor in spite of their government policies but because of them.

Inequality and Social Capital

Perhaps the most overlooked channel by which inequality affects the economy is the impact on social capital, the trust we have in each other and in social, economic and government institutions that foster mutual cooperation. In 1995, Robert Solow, who won the Nobel Prize in economics for modeling the determinants of economic growth, dismissed social capital as nothing more than a "buzzword," a notion so vague, he argued, that it could not be sufficiently quantified to be included in economic models.[65] Since then, however, as economists have begun to recognize the impact of institutions and norms on economic performance, social capital has assumed its rightful place in the economic debate.[66]

As a general matter, countries with less income inequality also have higher levels of trust (as measured by the "most people can be trusted" question on the General Social Survey), while those with more inequality tend to have lower levels of trust. It is equally possible to conclude from such data that distrust causes inequality as the other way around—or that both distrust and inequality spring from some third factor, such as the level of corruption. But those who have

studied the relationship have generally concluded, as economists at the International Monetary Fund recently put it,
that there is "robust evidence that overall inequality lowers
an individual's sense of trust in others in the United States
[and] other advanced economies."[67]

There are various theories about why this is so. Those
whose relative incomes are declining may view the success
of others as unmerited, due mostly to luck, connections, discrimination or other unfair advantages. Inequality could
exacerbate disagreements between haves and have-nots
about what public goods should be provided, how they
should be paid for and how they should be distributed. Perhaps most significantly, high levels of inequality may lead to
the kind of sorting where the rich increasingly segregate
themselves from the rest of society, aggravating the natural
distrust we have for those with whom we have little social
interaction and whom we view as unlike ourselves. Americans
have recently seen evidence of all of these dynamics at work.

The level of social capital also closely tracks our sense
of happiness and well-being, for which the determinants go
beyond income to things such as our physical and mental
health, the strength of our families, how safe we feel and the
level of social mobility. Richard Wilkinson and Kate Pickett,
two British researchers, used these and other factors to
compile an index of social health for the world's richest
countries, and then compared each country's index score
with two other measures—its level of income per person
and its level of income inequality. The results were surprising. Among rich countries, they found virtually no correlation between social health and the level of income—how
rich a country was. At the same time, they found a strong
relationship between social health and the level of income
inequality.

"The evidence merely confirms the common intuition

that inequality is divisive and socially corrosive," they write in *The Spirit Level*.[68]

Whatever the reasons, it is pretty clear that inequality erodes our trust in society and in each other. One study estimates that, in advanced countries, a 1 percentage point increase in measures of income inequality leads to a 2 percentage point decrease in measures of trust. This effect is mostly driven by a concentration of income at the top of the income scale.[69] In another study, IMF researchers estimate that rising inequality was responsible for nearly half of the decline in trust in the United States between 1980 and 2000.[70]

Just as rising inequality leads to less trust, the data is unambiguous that less trust leads to slower economic growth. French economists Yann Algan and Pierre Cahuc found that, during the period of 1981–2008, one-fifth of the variation in income per person among 106 countries could be explained by differences in generalized levels of trust. They found a similar correlation between trust and income among the 50 American states.[71]

Here, too, there are various theories about the ways in which trust influences economic performance. Levels of trust seem to have an impact on the efficiency of financial markets, which are an essential component of any modern economy.[72] Trust affects the appetite for risk-taking, entrepreneurship and innovation, which are highly correlated with measures of economic vitality and competitiveness.[73] Big, successful economies need big, successful companies that can grow to international scale only if owners and top executives have enough trust to delegate authority and responsibility to subordinates.[74] An environment of generalized trust also facilitates cooperation between labor and management, which is associated with higher levels of productivity and growth.[75]

Of course, economic growth fosters trust just as surely as trust fosters growth, creating a virtuous, self-reinforcing cycle that is present in virtually every successful economy. But as political scientists Edward Banfield and Robert Putnam observed in their separate studies of northern and southern Italy, a foundation of trust beyond the family is where that virtuous cycle begins.

"One of the most important lessons we can learn from an examination of economic life is that a nation's well-being, as well as its ability to compete, is conditioned by a single, pervasive cultural characteristic: the level of trust inherent in the society," wrote another political scientist, Francis Fukuyama, in his 1995 book *Trust*. "The greatest economic efficiency [is] not necessarily achieved by rational, self-interested individuals, but rather by groups of individuals who, because of a preexisting moral community, are able to work together effectively."[76]

As de Tocqueville first noted two centuries ago, such "moral communities" have dominated American life since the founding of the republic, but in the last 50 years, Fukuyama found that their influence has been eroded by a variety of factors. These include an increasing emphasis on individual rights, excessive demands for cultural diversity and inclusion, the breakdown of the family and the emergence of isolated, narrowly focused communities, both in the real world and in cyberspace.

Fukuyama meant to "sound the alarm" about what he saw back in the early 1990s as a dramatic and dangerous decline in social capital—and that was before the surge in income inequality, before the financial crisis and Great Recession, before the rise of cable news and social media, before the extreme political polarization and government dysfunction, before Donald Trump. It has taken more than two centuries to accumulate such capital, Fukuyama warned,

and history tells us that once it is spent, it can take generations to replace it.

Inequality and Growth, Reconsidered

So where does this leave us? Over the years, macroecono-
mists have tried to take in all of these factors and, by looking at growth and income data from many countries over
many years, determine if there is a causal link between the
level of income inequality and the pace of economic growth.
And as with almost all important questions, the answer to
this one is, it depends.

It depends if you look at developed countries or developing. It depends on whether a country's inequality is driven
by the gap between the rich and the middle class, or by a
gap between the middle class and the poor.

Nor are the results always linear. High concentrations
of income at the top, for example, seem to be associated with
faster growth in middle-class incomes but slower growth of
incomes of the poor. And while moderate amounts of redistribution appear to be benign or even helpful for growth,
high levels of redistribution have a negative effect.[77]

There are also questions about causality. We don't know
whether it's inequality that affects growth, or growth that affects inequality, although it is probably safe to assume that
causality flows in both directions.[78]

In short, the connection between inequality and growth
is something of a muddle, but not a hopeless one. It is fair
to conclude from all the evidence that at moderate levels—
in the middle ranges of the inequality–growth curve—there
is no systematic tradeoff between the level of inequality and
the level of economic growth. The curve in that range is
pretty flat. Countries with significantly different levels of inequality and redistribution have had similar levels of eco-

nomic success, while those with similar levels of inequality have had very different economic results. Much depends on the nature of the inequality and the mechanisms used to reduce it.[79]

At the same time, we have seen that there is good reason to suspect that high levels of inequality are incompatible with a vibrant and prosperous market economy. An advanced economy characterized by high levels of inequality provides inadequate incentives for loyalty and productivity from frontline workers. It suffers from insufficient levels of private investment in human capital and public investment in infrastructure and other public goods. It often results in the misallocation of capital and talent to an oversized and unproductive financial sector whose excesses spawn financial crises and recessions. Inequality encourages wasteful bidding wars among the rich for a limited supply of status goods. It erodes the trust and cooperation that lubricate markets and help assure the effectiveness of government. It increases the poverty that, over time, allows talent to go untapped. And it can lead to radical policies or populist revolutions that are almost always bad for economic growth.

Although I cannot precisely locate the point along the curve at which inequality goes from being economically useful or benign to economically harmful, there is mounting evidence that the United States and a number of other rich countries have gone past it.

"Growing inequality is harmful for long-term economic growth," concluded the Organisation for Economic Co-operation and Development, the economic research group of the world's richest countries. Its report, "In It Together: Why Less Inequality Benefits All," estimated that the significant rise in inequality had reduced economic growth by just under 5 percentage points, on average, in advanced economies.[80]

A similar conclusion was reached two years later by economists at the International Monetary Fund, based on a comprehensive review of the data and the economic literature.[81] Among their findings:

- In advanced countries, the recent rise in income inequality is associated with a slowdown in economic growth, not an increase.
- At the moderate levels of progressivity and redistribution now prevailing in advanced countries, there is no evidence that policies to reduce income inequality have a negative effect on economic growth.
- Among advanced countries, only Mexico has after-tax incomes more unequal than the United States and only Israel does less than the United States to use its tax and transfer system to reduce the inequality of market incomes.
- If Americans would prefer less inequality, there is significant scope to adopt well-designed policies that make incomes more equal without risk of hurting economic growth.

In short, for countries like the United States there is no "big tradeoff" between fairness and growth, between equality and efficiency. We don't have to tolerate levels of inequality that offend our moral instincts for our economy to remain prosperous and competitive. If we want to have a bigger pie, it won't hurt to divide the slices more evenly. In fact, it is likely to make the pie even bigger.

5

A Better Capitalism

Not many people have heard of Edward W. Conard, but anyone who has been involved in the debate about economic policy over the last 40 years would surely recognize the way he thinks about how wealth is created and how it ought to be distributed.

Conard is a successful private equity investor, a former partner and protégé of Mitt Romney at Bain Capital. Responding to the attacks on American capitalism in the wake of the 2008 financial crisis and the Occupy Wall Street movement, Conard wrote *Unintended Consequences*, which offered what may be the most uncompromising and unapologetic defense of market justice since the fictional Gordon Gekko gave his "greed is good" speech in the movie *Wall Street*. When Romney, as the Republican presidential candidate, displayed his disdain for "the 47 percent" of Americans he views as moochers, when Republican House Speaker Paul Ryan reflexively refers to all high-income earners as "job creators," when Steve Schwarzman, the billionaire financier, likened President Obama's proposal to raise taxes on private equity managers to Hitler's invasion of Poland, they are all singing from the same hymnal as Ed Conard.

To Conard's way of thinking, the last 40 years have been a golden age for American capitalism. Corporations, money managers and wealthy investors have poured massive amounts of capital into new ideas and technologies, triggering a productivity boom so strong that it not only created greater wealth and higher living standards for all Americans, but also for hundreds of millions of foreigners who were newly employed in factories and offices in Asia or came to work in the United States.[1]

Conard calculated that while some Americans got very rich in the process, 95 percent of the economic benefit from this surge in innovation was actually captured by workers and consumers in the form of cheaper goods and higher wages—much more than is reflected in the official economic statistics, he claimed. And he's quite sure the best way to sustain that virtuous cycle is to eliminate all taxes on the rich, and all regulation of the companies they control, so they can make even more investments that result in even more innovation and create even more wealth for themselves and everyone else.

Conard's book is a masterpiece of faulty logic, selective data, historical amnesia and moral vacuity. Like all briefs in defense of market justice, it is based on false presumptions about just deserts, equality of opportunity and the unavoidable tradeoff between fairness and growth. It demands that we ignore our instinctive distaste for much of what we see going on around us, and what we experience in our everyday lives, and rely instead on highly stylized calculations and convoluted logic that just happen to justify a massive transfer of wealth and power to people like him.

It's hardly surprising that there are people who think

this way. What is surprising is that this kind of market adulation continues to exercise a stranglehold over American politics and economic policy. How many scandals and financial crises, how much scummy and manipulative behavior on Wall Street, how much inequality of wealth, income and opportunity will it take before the business lobby, the free market mythmakers and the Republican Party will finally be forced to acknowledge that they have pushed their free market ideology too far?

Responsibility for the unsatisfactory nature of our debate on these issues, however, does not rest solely with the pro-market right. Some also lies with those on the anti-market left who are still unwilling to admit that too much regulation, overly generous union contracts and excessive government spending had, by 1980, made the American economy uncompetitive. Although liberals rail against the current level of income inequality, they have never been able to say how much or what kinds of inequality they would find morally acceptable. Many of their solutions for taming American capitalism are too bureaucratic and paternalistic, focusing too much on individual rights and too little on individual responsibility, too much on government regulation and not enough on changing business and social norms.

As an experiment, I recently asked a number of liberal critics of American capitalism to indicate how much inequality of income they would be prepared to accept.

Some of the answers were narrowly economic and statistical. A number of respondents agreed with Berkeley economist Emmanuel Saez, one of the creators of an international database on income inequality, who said he would be satisfied if the level of income inequality were rolled back to where it was in the golden years of the 1950s and '60s. Journalist Tim Noah, who wrote a book on the subject, would be satisfied when incomes at the top were rising no faster than they were for everyone else. Jared Bernstein, of the liberal Center on Budget and Policy Priorities, said there is too much inequality whenever worker pay fails to keep up with worker productivity.

Others were more utilitarian and practical. Lane Kenworthy, a University of Arizona sociologist, said he'd be willing to accept almost any level of market income inequality as long as government had the resources to provide necessary public goods and guarantee everyone access to health care. Robert Frank, the Cornell economist who was the first to write about the winner-take-all economy, said he'd know when inequality had fallen to acceptable levels when the rich no longer had the money to compete with each other to build bigger homes and throw ever-more-lavish weddings for their children.

Harvard economist Richard Freeman probably got closer to the heart of the problem when he wrote that inequality stops being acceptable when it breeds even more inequality, creating a vicious cycle of rich getting richer and poor getting poorer that ends with economic feudalism and social unrest.

My own preferences, however, run to more communitarian criteria, like those offered by Robert Reich, the former labor secretary and Berkeley professor, who said he'd dial back inequality until economic mobility was no longer slowing, politics was no longer polarized and faith in public institutions was restored. I also liked the reply from Harvard philosopher Michael Sandel, who wrote that inequality becomes unacceptable when rich and poor share so few common experiences together that it undermines the sense of community and solidarity a successful democracy requires.

What follows are some policy prescriptions that would

help address all of these concerns, restoring the moral legitimacy of American capitalism while enhancing its wealth-producing vitality.

In outlining this agenda, I am guided by three observations.

First, as Sandel and Reich have written, the biggest problem with ruthless business behavior and unequal economic outcomes is that they have eroded trust, undermined civic virtue and diminished our sense of common purpose.[2] In a democratic society, it becomes impossible to fix things when everything is viewed as a zero-sum contest and everyone we disagree with is thought to be dangerous and evil. Our first challenge is to reverse those trends, restore the balance between the personal and the communal and replenish our stock of social capital.

Second, there is no way to significantly advance equal opportunity, particularly for the poor, without more equality of income. There's not much we can do about the unequal distribution of natural talent and ambition, but there is a lot more we can do to get everyone closer to the same starting line. One of those things is to eliminate childhood poverty in the most direct way possible—by bolstering incomes at the bottom. We owe at least that to poor children, whether or not their parents "deserve" it.

Third, there are political and economic limits to how much income can be redistributed using taxes and transfers. The marginal tax rates that would be required on high-earning households to counteract the full effect of the increased inequality of market income would exceed 60 percent, the level now in place in Sweden, which years ago discovered that even higher tax rates were a significant check on long-term economic growth. Moreover, in a country as large and diverse as the United States, voters simply won't accept Scandinavian levels of explicit redistribution of income to people who are so different and geographically distant. Ours is a country in which "welfare" is viewed negatively even by people who might be eligible for it. "Predistribution"—altering how incomes are set in the market, before taxes and transfers—is politically more palatable and should continue to be the dominant strategy of delivering more equality of income and opportunity in the United States.

I do not pretend that the handful of ideas that follow constitutes a comprehensive agenda, or that I am the first to propose them, but I am confident that they would make a better capitalism, and better America, than we have today.

Limiting Special Interest Money in Politics

All you need to know about the American political system can be summed up in this simple calculation made by *Politico* in the midst of the 2016 presidential campaign: the 100 largest political donors in America contributed more than the 2 million smallest ones.[3]

As anyone familiar with political science literature knows—or anyone who simply follows the news understands—businesses and wealthy individuals have elected and captured a Republican majority in Congress that is committed to protecting their interests and pushing through their agenda, even if much of that agenda is opposed by a majority of voters.[4]

The only thing that stands in the way of an unchecked plutocracy in America is that liberal special interests also make use of the same corrupt system for financing elections. Indeed, the only difference between the current campaign finance system and a governing system based on bribery is merely one of semantics. Those with money can—and routinely do—buy votes, buy politicians, buy legislation and buy regulations. In some states, they can even buy judges. Even those who hate the system most—the politicians who have to spend inordinate amounts of their waking hours raising the money that robs them of their dignity and their freedom to do what they think is right—feel powerless to change it. It is impossible to overstate how corrosive this arms race in political money has been to American politics, American capitalism and American society.

None of this would have happened but for activist judges on the Supreme Court who have gradually chipped away at limits on political money enacted by the elected branches of government. Under the guise of protecting free speech, the Court has now created a constitutional right to bribe elected officials, with the prize going to the highest bidder. Supreme Court Justice Anthony Kennedy penned what could well be the most naïve, ill-informed and foolish sentence in American jurisprudence when he declared in his majority opinion in *Citizens United v. Federal Elections Commission*, "This Court now concludes that independent [political] expenditures, including those made by corporations, do not give rise to corruption or the appearance of corruption."

At this point, the only way to overturn such idiocy and put an end to this runaway, legalized corruption is through an amendment to the Constitution, one that will give Congress and the states the power "to protect the integrity of government and the electoral process by setting reasonable limits on the raising and spending of money by candidates and others to influence elections." Public opinion polls show a majority of Americans support such an initiative, but at this point it will take nothing short of a revolution, or a wave election, to turn that support into constitutional action.

This item tops the agenda for one simple reason: without it, the others are unlikely to happen.

Universal Service + Universal Basic Income

People everywhere agree that, in a country as rich as ours, no citizen should be allowed to suffer deep poverty and deprivation.[5] The moral instinct toward generosity and empathy is part of human nature. It is rooted, in part, in an expectation of reciprocity—that if we were ever in the same situation, we would want and expect others to act generously toward us. But it is also rooted in a more communal kind of self-interest. We have learned as a species that generosity helps to create an environment of trust and cooperation that makes us all safer, wealthier and happier.

In wealthy societies, there is another important rationale for a more egalitarian distribution of income. Consider an American worker and an Indian worker performing roughly the same tasks. Only a small portion of the enormous difference in their wages can be explained by differences in the time and effort they put in, the technology they work with or the skill with which they do the job. The rest—maybe as much as 90 percent, according to Herbert Simon, an intellectual polymath who won the Nobel Prize in economics—reflects the different context in which the American and the Indian work: the natural resources with which the country has been endowed, the physical infrastructure that has been created over the years, the collective know-how of fellow citizens, the quality of the public and private institutions and degree of trust that greases the wheels of commerce, politics and everyday life.[6] The value of this collective inheritance is considerably greater in the United States than in India and, by Simon's reckoning, now provides an ongoing dividend that should rightly be shared equally among all citizens, since none can claim credit for having created it.

It is for these two reasons—reciprocity and common inheritance—that we feel a moral obligation to protect each other from deprivation, however and whenever that may arise. In the United States, this economic safety net takes various forms.

Some of the assistance is conditioned on being poor— food stamps, housing subsidies, child tax credits, free school breakfast and lunch, Pell grants, Medicaid and Obamacare subsidies. Other forms of assistance are contingent on physical or mental disability, or involuntary unemployment. And there is assistance given only to the poor who are working, most notably the earned income tax credit.

There are drawbacks to these conditional programs. Some deserving people don't apply or don't qualify, while expensive bureaucracies are needed to administer these programs and make sure assistance goes only to those who meet the criteria. Those who are working may be discouraged from working more hours, or going for a higher-paying job, lest it make them ineligible for government support. A social stigma also attaches to those who rely on government assistance.

In addition to these conditional programs, there are Social Security and Medicare, the most successful and popular of our safety-net programs. It is no coincidence that they are also the only programs that are offered to almost all Americans once they reach a certain age, irrespective of income. This universality reflects not only our commitment to provide every citizen with economic security, but also our expectation that every citizen will have contributed to these programs during their working lives through the payroll tax.

Given the success and popularity of the more universal programs, and given the shortcomings of the more conditional ones, a fairly simple, straightforward strategy suggests itself. What I have in mind is a new compact between citizens and their government, one that commits all Americans to provide two or three years of national service in exchange for a commitment from the government to provide them with an annual "citizenship dividend" that guarantees they will be protected from deprivation and eases life's inevitable transitions.

I won't elaborate too much on the national service aspect—there have been a variety of different proposals over the years—other than to say we should be very flexible and not afraid to experiment.[7] To date, most of the discussion has focused on young people doing their national service after graduating from high school or college, but don't discount the possibility of people taking a year or two off midcareer, or doing some of their service after retirement. I imagine most service would be for modest pay, but not all. And while some government spending and bureaucracy will inevitably be required, I imagine that most citizens will choose to offer service through private organizations like Teach for America or local soup kitchens rather than through government programs.

National service would also help address another big problem: the resegregation of American society by race, class, educational achievement, political ideology and social values. This "big sort," as it has been called, is both a consequence and cause of rising inequality and the declining sense of trust and community.[8] National service could help mitigate those effects. With it, more Americans would spend more time with people who are not like themselves. It would also be one of the few experiences shared by all Americans, irrespective of background. The military has already demonstrated success in fostering social bonds and common purpose among a diverse set of participants, and this sense of civic responsibility and engagement extends long after their service has ended.[9] I've also observed the same holds true for Peace Corps veterans.

National service also offers a flexible way for Americans

to make individual decisions about the best ways to try to smooth the rough edges of American capitalism. Some will want to staff pre-K centers for poor children, while others might prefer running afterschool and summer recreation programs or mentoring high school dropouts. Some may think the highest priority is building low-income housing, others blazing hiking trails in national forests. In competing for volunteers, the most effective and impactful nonprofits are likely to grow while the least effective wither away.

Most significantly, national service would replenish social capital and reinforce not only our commitment to political and social equality but also our commitment to each other. A country that requires service from all citizens would have a political, economic and moral rationale for guaranteeing those citizens a basic income should they fall on hard times.

Over the years, the idea of a guaranteed minimum income has attracted support from an ideologically heterogeneous group that includes John Stuart Mill, Thomas Paine, Bertrand Russell, Friedrich Hayek, Huey Long, Milton Friedman, John Kenneth Galbraith, James Tobin, Paul Samuelson, Richard Nixon, George McGovern, Martin Luther King Jr., Charles Murray and Robert Reich. In various incarnations it has been called a negative income tax, a demogrant or universal basic income. Those on the left see it as a way to eliminate poverty and redistribute income, while those on the right would use it to replace the current hodgepodge of welfare programs. They have recently been joined by prominent members of the high-tech elite, who worry that all those robots and self-driving cars and artificial intelligence they are creating will lead to widespread unemployment.

Finland, Kenya and the city of Stockton, California, are now experimenting with forms of universal basic income.[10] Voters in Switzerland recently rejected the idea, largely out of fear that the high taxes required would jeopardize the success of their kinder and gentler form of capitalism.[11] Several books have recently been written outlining the history and the rationale for such a program, including those by Facebook cofounder Chris Hughes, the *Atlantic*'s Annie Lowery, labor leader Andy Stern and two Belgian academics, Philippe Van Parijs and Yannick Vanderborght, who have been beating the drum now for more than 30 years.[12] It has also drawn considerable interest from young economics writers.[13]

It was Thomas Paine who first came up with the idea of a national trust fund that would award every American a dividend of 15 pounds upon reaching the age of 18. "It is not charity but a right, not bounty but justice, that I am pleading for," he declared. Not long after, British philosopher John Stuart Mill advocated "a legal guarantee of subsistence for all the destitute . . . whether deserving or not."

A citizen's dividend would serve multiple purposes, starting with relieving the suffering and degradation of extreme poverty. The income floor that it would provide could also serve as an antidote to the anxiety, despair and helplessness that lead many who are desperately poor to not even try to discipline their wants and get their lives in order—that was Charles Karelis's point.

Cutting all Americans a check would also allow us to eliminate a number of existing welfare programs that not only have high bureaucratic costs but, because of all the checking up that is involved, have a tendency to rob the poor of their dignity and self-respect. The poor certainly won't miss the paternalism behind programs that rest on the implicit assumption that they cannot be trusted to spend cash in a responsible manner.

For the middle class, the citizen's dividend would provide a small measure of economic security against the possibility of job loss, serious illness and the natural or other disasters that life throws up. It could also provide extra confidence to strike out on a new career or a new business venture or the wherewithal to return to school. It could allow more people to stay home with young children or elderly parents.

A universal guaranteed income would also come with political benefits. It would reinforce our commitment to economic equality and the sense that we are all entitled to share in the nation's bounty and the fruits of investments made by generations before us. It would foster political unity and social harmony in the way Social Security and Medicare already do, while reducing the resentment that some feel against those now receiving various forms of assistance, since everyone would be getting it.

Critics of a guaranteed income have long questioned whether it would undermine the incentive to work—whether "by making the poor rich, we would wind up making the rich and everyone else poor," to use David Ricardo's classical formulation. The sharp-tongued John Kenneth Galbraith would remark centuries later how curious it is that those concerned about the economic and moral harm that might be inflicted on society by the idle poor do not share the same concern about the idle rich. In the end, how much and what kind of idleness would be induced will depend on the size and structure of the annual grants and what other programs are eliminated to help pay for it.

Let me sketch briefly what I have in mind.

Imagine that every American receives a check or direct deposit each quarter that, in a year, add up to $3,000, regardless of age or income or working status. Then imagine an additional $3,000 for everyone who works full time, similar to the earned income tax credit, or an additional $3,000

tuition tax credit for everyone attending college or partici-
pating in an approved training program full time.

Three thousand dollars per person would not be enough
to lift the unemployed and their families out of poverty, so
some other assistance programs may still be required. But
$6,000 per person would be more than enough to eliminate
poverty among full-time workers. A single person with a
full-time job at the federal minimum wage would have an
income of nearly $21,000, well above the government's offi-
cial poverty line of $12,000. A single mom with one child
working full time at the minimum wage would have an income of about $24,000, $8,000 over the poverty line. A
married couple with two children, one parent working full
time and the other half time at minimum-wage jobs, would
have an income of $39,000, well above the poverty thresh-
old of just over $25,000. That looks to me like a significant
safety net for households that otherwise would be in or
near poverty.

So where would all that money come from?

A portion would come from eliminating or curtailing a
number of current income-tested programs (food stamps,
temporary assistance to needy families, the child tax
credit, housing subsidies and the current earned income tax
credit). There could also be some offsetting reductions in
Social Security and disability checks and Pell grants that
still leave beneficiaries better off than they are under the
current system.

The biggest chunk of the money, however, would come
from raising income taxes in a way that would begin to claw
back some of the dividend when a household's income
reaches 50 percent of the country's median income, with tax
rates gradually increasing so that the dividend is completely
recaptured after the median is reached (today, that's roughly
$36,000 for a single-earner family and $87,000 for a two-

earner family).[14] For those in the top half of the income scale, the government would giveth with one hand and taketh away with the other. For those in the bottom half, some or all of the dividend would be retained.

To complete the financing, several other changes in the tax code would be required.

We might begin with a small tax on every financial transaction, which would fall heavily on the wealthy and Wall Street traders and hedge fund managers who have benefited so handsomely in recent decades.

And given the increasing role that inherited wealth plays in reducing equality of income and opportunity, there is good reason to raise additional revenue by restructuring the estate tax and extending it to more heirs. All estates would be required to pay the tax on any profits above $1 million from stock, real estate or other investments that are still in the deceased's portfolio and haven't been sold. (Under current law, the tax liability on those "unrealized capital gains" magically disappears at death.) And instead of imposing a tax on the estate, I would tax the individual heirs for any inheritance over $1 million at the 20 percent capital gains rate.

Anyone who has tried to cost out a guaranteed income scheme knows it first requires working out a huge number of details that I have neither the expertise nor the inclination to address. However, a rough back-of-the-envelope calculation suggests that with 325 million Americans, the equivalent of 140 million full-time workers and 15 million full-time college students, the sum of all those dividends would be $1.5 trillion a year. As much as $100 billion a year could be recouped through a restructuring of estate and inheritance taxes, with another $50 billion a year from a financial transactions tax.[15] The rest would come from higher income tax rates, starting at 1 percentage point for households just below the median, and rising to 5 or 6 percentage points for those in the highest bracket.

The overall effect would be an explicit redistribution of income from households in the top 40 percent of the income scale—whose incomes have been rising steadily in recent decades and who just received a significant cut in their taxes—to those in the bottom 40 percent, whose incomes have risen slowly, if at all, and who received little benefit from recent income tax cuts. It would make our system of taxes and transfers bigger and more progressive than it is now—not exactly Denmark or Sweden, but certainly moving in that direction. Numerous experiments—including an unscientific one I do every year with my own students—suggest that most Americans would prefer this more egalitarian distribution of income over the one we have now.[16]

From a political perspective, it would be important for every citizen to receive a dividend check (or direct deposit), whether or not it is eventually taxed away. Obviously, it would be simpler to run the dividends through the tax system by making it a refundable tax credit, along the lines of a negative income tax. But having every American receive a check or bank deposit from the Treasury on the same days each year would help ensure widespread political support while serving as a visible symbol that, as citizens, we all share equally in our collective inheritance.

It is also important that half of the dividend be conditioned on work or attending school. Guaranteed income purists will hate this idea because it undermines the philosophy of every citizen having a "right" to live in decency, reflecting the rights-based approach the left instinctively prefers. But the reality is that Americans at all income levels are so outraged by the prospect of their hard-earned dollars going to people unwilling to work that making half of the dividend conditioned on work is a political necessity.

The citizen's dividend program would be a big step toward eliminating poverty, would help to allay some of the economic anxieties of the working class and begin to reverse the widening gap between the rich and everyone else. It would make our income support programs fairer, more efficient and less demeaning and paternalistic, with less distortion of economic behavior. And by pairing it with universal national service, the dividend would remind us that just as we are each entitled to an equal share of the national bounty, we are equally responsible for the nation's well-being.

Sharing Profits with Employees

Part of the income inequality story is the increased share of national income going to owners of capital rather than workers. And a big reason for the increase in capital's share has been the deliberate strategy of those running businesses to focus aggressively on maximizing profits and shareholder returns.

Because this misconceived corporate purpose is now hardwired into American business culture, there is little prospect it will change quickly (more on that later). So one strategy for boosting market wages and salaries would be to nudge companies to share some of their "maximized" profits with the workers who produced them.

This nudge could come in the form of a new provision to the corporate tax code preventing a company from deducting the cost of any performance-based compensation for executives as a business expense unless an equal amount has also been set aside in a profit-sharing scheme for frontline employees.[17]

A second nudge could also come in a modest change in the tax treatment of stock buybacks—when companies buy back their own shares on the open market as a way of

boosting the stock price. Running at the rate of $600 bil-
lion a year, share buybacks have become the favored
method for channeling corporate profits back to shareholders. The economic logic of buybacks is that a company that spends $1 billion to buy back its own shares
effectively raises the value of the shares that remain outstanding by about $1 billion. From the perspective of share-
holders, then, the effect is similar to receiving a special $1
billion dividend, with one big difference: with the dividend,
shareholders would immediately have to pay a 20 percent
tax, whereas with a buyback, investors can put off paying
the equivalent 20 percent capital gains tax until they sell
their shares.

The second idea, borrowed from two Yale professors,
would be to allow shareholders to continue to enjoy the deferred tax treatment of share buybacks, but only if the company adopts a profit-sharing plan for all employees.[18] At
companies that failed to adopt such plans, the money spent
on the buyback would be treated, for tax purposes, as a dividend subject to an immediate tax. This may sound like a
small, technical modification, but I can assure you it would
put employee profit sharing at the top of the agenda in corporate boardrooms.

One reason for pushing profit sharing is that it is fair.
Another is that it is likely to boost worker productivity and
lead to even higher profits. We know that the executive class
has prospered handsomely from having salaries supple-
mented with large wads of performance pay—an arrangement, companies argue, that gives executives the incentive
to make the hard choices that improve sales and profits. A
recent review of more than 100 management studies found
that employee ownership and profit sharing is also likely to
have a small but positive effect on company performance.[19]

Certainly that has been the case at the "Big Three" auto

companies, which as recently as 2009 were either in or on the brink of bankruptcy. As part of the federal bailout of the industry in 2009, the United Automobile Workers union agreed to accept cuts to wages and benefits and changes in work rules in exchange for a share of any future profits, which at the time were anything but a sure bet. In 2017, as a result of record profits for those companies' North American operations, production workers at Chrysler received profit-sharing checks that averaged $5,000, at Ford $9,000 and at General Motors $12,000.[20] Company profits that year were at record levels.

Equalizing Educational Opportunity

The U.S. education system is no longer serving its historical role of equalizing economic opportunity and increasing social mobility. Rather, as we've seen, it has become an instrument by which children lucky enough to be born into favorable circumstances increase their economic advantage over those who were not.

It was 64 years ago that the Supreme Court, relying largely on evidence and expert opinion from social scientists, ruled in *Brown v. Board of Education* that sending black children to separate schools was inherently unequal. Now it is time to extend that constitutional principle and declare that it is no longer acceptable to organize and finance public education in a way that segregates poor children in separate schools.

Because of our reliance on local property taxes to fund public schools, and public school systems that organize schools around residential neighborhoods, we have a system that in many places provides less funding, less effective teachers and worse facilities to poor students who require more resources and better teachers to reach comparable educational goals. Moreover, there is clear evidence from social science research that segregating poor children in the same schools deepens their disadvantage. The only practical way to end this class segregation in education is the same way racial segregation was ended—with a Supreme Court finding that segregating poor students in the same schools denies them the equal protection of the law guaranteed by the Constitution.

As it happens, the Supreme Court explicitly rejected that view in 1973 in a case that few remember today, *San Antonio Independent School District v. Rodriguez*. In a 5–4 ruling, the Court—which only two decades before, in *Brown*, had recognized the importance of public education to a democratic society and a child's success in later life—reversed course and declared that public education was *not* a fundamental right under the Constitution. It also found that discrimination on the basis of class did not warrant the same strict scrutiny as discrimination on the basis of race. Writing for the majority, Justice Lewis Powell worried that if public education were to be treated as a fundamental right, the Court would find itself on a slippery slope that would also require it to give similar status to housing and medical care. Powell also questioned the link between per pupil funding and educational outcomes.[21]

Forty-five years later, it is time to revisit those issues. One reason, discussed in an earlier chapter, is new evidence from social science studies showing that the socioeconomic characteristics of a child's classmates are a better predictor of educational achievement than a child's own socioeconomic background. Another is the change in case law. In the intervening years, there has been a long line of Court decisions striking down affirmative action plans at universities or guaranteeing parents control over their children's schooling, in which the Court's conservative majority recognized something that sounds very much like a constitutional right to education. With a series of education reform bills, Congress has also established a strong federal interest in insuring that all students attain minimal levels of educational achievement, with a particular emphasis on low-performing students and school districts. All of these developments provide a solid legal basis to ask the Court to reconsider the issue and declare that *Rodriguez* was wrongly decided.[22]

There is nothing sacred about the idea that municipalities and school districts have to have the same boundaries, or that public education needs to be funded primarily through property taxes. To assure equal access to an adequate education, the federal courts could require states to redraw school district boundaries in ways that would end desegregation by class and put rich and poor students in the same school systems. Courts could order states to devise statewide funding formulas that would begin to break the pernicious link between local property values, per pupil spending and educational achievement. And judges could even insist that the newly redrawn school districts rely on student choice for school assignments and make extensive use of magnet schools.

I don't underestimate the political and legal difficulties in bringing about such a radical restructuring of public education. I am old enough to remember the bruising battles over busing, and I am aware that the process of bringing racial integration to public schools has hardly been a smashing success. Class integration would be no less challenging, but it is also no less of a moral imperative.

It is worth recalling that the campaign to overturn the separate but equal doctrine in *Plessy v. Ferguson* energized a generation of Americans in the 1960s. The campaign to overturn the legalization of abortion in *Roe v. Wade* energized a generation of conservatives beginning in the 1980s.

Overturning *Rodriguez* and establishing the fundamental right of all children to a decent education could be the legal issue that energizes a new generation eager to ensure that history continues to bend toward justice. It will take patience, persistence and political courage, but this is the kind of defining moral issue that is worth the effort.

Reducing Concentration, Restoring Competition

As in the Agatha Christie mystery *Murder on the Orient Express,* our earlier investigation into who is responsible for rising income inequality revealed that, in the end, "they all did it." Unfortunately, there is not much we can, or should, do about increased trade and immigration or technological advances that improve productivity and lower prices. And it's probably too late to hold out much hope of restoring the power of the labor movement in a postindustrial economy.

But there are a few inequality culprits that call for some attention from policy-makers, starting with the increased domination of a handful of firms in too many industries. Because of dramatically reduced competition, some of the country's biggest and most successful companies now are able to earn outsized profits and share those "rents" with executives and employees, who have pulled ahead of other workers with similar skills and experience. Some studies now blame undue industry concentration for the bulk of the increase in measured income inequality in the last decade. There is also a growing economics literature demonstrating that the dominance of superstar companies in many industries has contributed to a reduction in business investment, a decline in the rate of entrepreneurial startups and an overall loss of dynamism in what was once one of the world's most dynamic economies.[23]

I propose a three-prong strategy for reducing concentration and restoring a healthier level of competition in industries where rents are highest and the income gains have been greatest. The first involves creating an economic and legal foundation for a more aggressive approach to antitrust enforcement in industries that are already highly concentrated. The second harkens back to an old, Progressive Era idea of creating financial institutions that are owned by their customers. And the third proposes a reform of patent and copyright law so that it better serves its original purpose of promoting innovation and creativity rather than stifling it.

* * *

There is not much government can or should do to prevent a handful of companies from dominating industries in which there are strong network effects and economies of scale. Companies like Google, Facebook and Amazon are some of our most dynamic, most innovative and most productive enterprises, which is why they came out on top in the winner-take-all competition. But even as we celebrate their success, we should not allow them to leverage their dominance in one market to capture a dominant share in other markets. Nor should we allow them to gobble up young firms with technologies that could one day threaten their dominance.

A company like Facebook, for example, gained its quasi-monopoly fair and square, but once it gained such a dominant position, the government was foolish in allowing it to buy Instagram, an upstart that had the kind of platforms and technology that might one day have mounted a successful challenge to Facebook's dominance in social networking. For the same reason, Google should not have been allowed to buy YouTube or Waze. As innovative as these firms may be, they might have been forced to be even more innovative if they were unable to use their formidable profits to buy up any upstart with a product or technology or business model that might someday disrupt the market.[24]

The antitrust law has also failed to restrain dominant firms from becoming even more dominant by buying up their suppliers or their customers. With the rise of "Chicago school" economics in the 1970s, federal courts came to view such "vertical" mergers as benign, reasoning that robust competition in the adjacent markets would effectively prevent the newly merged firm from raising prices or placing competitors at a disadvantage.

That theory, however, only applies when those adjacent markets are highly competitive, and in today's economy, that is not always the case.[25] Yet the antitrust case law assumes it is. That is why regulators allowed one of the world's biggest pharmaceutical companies to buy the largest U.S. pharmacy benefit manager (Merck–Medco), and allowed the largest concert promoter to merge with the largest ticketing company (Ticketmaster–Live Nation). It is why the government allowed the world's largest brewer (AB InBev, owner of Budweiser, Beck's and Stella Artois) to go around the country buying up some of the country's biggest regional beer distributors, and allowed the world's dominant eyeglass maker (Luxottica) to take control of the top eyeglass chains (LensCrafters and Pearle Vision). It is why the largest cable provider was allowed to take over a major television network and movie studio (Cablevision–NBCUniversal).

In November 2017, faced with mounting evidence that vertical mergers had resulted in higher prices and less competition, the Justice Department finally stepped in to block AT&T, one of the country's largest phone and internet service providers, from purchasing Time Warner, which—with its Warner Brothers studio, Turner Broadcasting network and HBO—is the leading producer of the video content distributed by its cable service. Seven months later, a federal judge rejected the government's arguments and allowed the merger to proceed. At this writing, the government is also considering whether to block CVS—already the product of a combination between the largest drugstore chain and one of the largest pharmacy benefit managers—from merging with Aetna, its biggest customer and one of the largest health insurance companies, and a similar hookup between insurer Cigna and pharmacy benefit manager Express Scripts. These cases present the first tests of whether the courts are willing to return to a pre-Chicago view of how dominant firms can use vertical mergers to extend their market power.

And then there is Amazon, a company that leveraged its position as the nation's largest online bookseller to become the largest online retailer, selling not only consumer goods made by other companies, but increasingly its own line of products in dozens of high-volume categories. Along the way, Amazon also managed to create the country's largest online sales platform, used by millions of smaller retailers. Amazon also recently purchased Whole Foods and combined it with its own nascent online grocery business, with only a cursory review from government antitrust regulators.

Amazon is a truly amazing, fiercely customer-focused company that has revolutionized online retailing by lowering prices and setting new standards for customer service—in the process making itself one of the most valuable companies on the planet.[26] Yet within the next decade, it is possible that this amazing company could use its market position to achieve a 40 percent or more share of the total U.S. retail market in books, groceries, clothing, hardware, electronics, home furnishings and any other category it chooses to enter, even as it grows to rival UPS in shipping, Oracle in computing and Comcast in media content.

Antitrust law is ill-equipped to deal with a company of

this scale and scope.[27] Antitrust analysis generally assumes dominant firms exercise their market power by raising prices in clearly defined markets. But in this new era, what if the way a company like Amazon increases its profits is not by raising prices but by squeezing the profit margins of suppliers, or using its dominant position in one market to quickly and easily achieve a dominant share in another, and then another, and then another? What if Amazon's efficiencies allow it to offer prices so low that it is virtually impossible for a small, disruptive rival ever to get a foothold in the marketplace? How can antitrust regulators analyze a company's power in any particular market when its competitors are also its customers and suppliers?

The antitrust case law as it has developed is simply too narrow and shortsighted to deal with the competitive dynamics of today's winner-take-all markets. In the case of dominant firms like Amazon or Google or Facebook, the focus of antitrust enforcement must not be on prices but on profits, not on consumers so much as on competition. The test should not be whether a merger or a business practice of a dominant firm might immediately decrease competition in some precisely defined market segment—the current standard—but whether, in the long run, it could foreclose potential competition that could serve as a check on the market power it has already accumulated.

Given the simple, sweeping language of current antitrust laws, there is no need to seek legislative changes to accommodate a different approach. Antitrust law, for the most part, has evolved through the actions and guidelines issued by regulators, and by court rulings in cases brought by regulators, competitors and customers. It is those guidelines and those precedents that now need changing.

For starters, the legal burden of proof should be shifted from the government to prove a merger or business practice is harmful, and placed instead on the dominant firm to prove that it will not reduce competition, stifle innovation or foreclose entry into the market by a rival firm. That may sound like a small change, but any antitrust lawyer will tell you it is not.

Antitrust law should also require judges to apply stricter scrutiny to business practices and acquisitions in industries that are characterized by network efficiencies and winner-take-all competition. That would include social networks such as Twitter and Facebook, telecommunications companies like AT&T and Verizon, and makers of operating software such as Microsoft and Apple. This stricter scrutiny should also be applied to "double-sided markets"—markets in which firms sell to two sets of customers at the same time. Think of credit card companies that court both consumers who use their cards and merchants who accept them, ride-sharing services like Uber and Lyft that match up riders and drivers, or search engines such as Google that count both users and advertisers as their customers.

It may get to the point that, because of network and scale efficiencies, the winner-take-all tendency in some of these markets is so strong that they naturally become monopoly markets in which only one firm survives. In the past, the way we dealt with natural monopolies was to regulate them as public utilities, with the government designating one firm to be the sole supplier and determining what prices it can charge and how much profit it can make. That is what happened in the early years of railroads, telephones, electricity, airlines and cable television, and the same approach might be required in some of today's high-tech industries.

* * *

A more aggressive and updated antitrust policy won't help much in banking and finance, where for the last 40 years, consolidation was allowed to run amok. No objective observer now thinks the mergers that eliminated most community and regional banks and led to the creation of Citigroup or Bank of America or JPMorgan Chase were a good idea, or that it makes sense for half a dozen institutions to control half of all of the country's bank assets, credit card transactions or derivatives trading. We learned from the 2008 financial crisis that these institutions are not just too big to fail—they are also too big to manage or regulate.

While some still hold out hope that the big banks can be broken up, I fear it is too late to unscramble those eggs. Instead, I propose we take a page from the Progressive Era by nudging consumers to take back their savings from giant financial institutions and put them in the hands of smaller, local institutions owned by, and run for the benefit of, their customers.

It was Supreme Court Justice Louis Brandeis, while still a crusading lawyer in Boston, who championed the chartering of mutual savings banks, mutual insurance companies and mutual investment funds as a way of breaking the financial oligarchy that he felt had a chokehold on the American economy in those days.[28] Most of these mutual institutions would later be sold off to big stockholder-owned rivals during the 1970s and '80s based on the false promises of greater efficiency and lower prices, but the few mutuals that survive continue to offer honest products and superior service at lower prices.[29] The federal government could rekindle interest in mutual institutions by offering federal charters that come with lighter regulation, more favorable tax treatment and the power to operate across state lines.

On the investment side of finance, there is probably nothing the government can do to break up the oligopoly among the Wall Street investment banks that dominate trading in stocks, bonds, derivatives and other securities and serve as gatekeepers to the issuance of those securities.

People looking to buy or sell securities naturally want to go to a market where they can find the most people wanting to sell or buy securities, which is why the world wants a limited number of exchanges and trading desks—enough to provide some choice and competition, but not so many that it becomes difficult or time consuming to execute a mutually agreeable transaction. To use the language of finance, there is a benefit to having deep, liquid markets with narrow bid-ask spreads, and that often requires a limited number of large exchanges and market makers.

At the same time, while some financial market liquidity and efficiency is a good thing, more of it is not always better. As with many good things, there is a point of diminishing return where getting the next increment of improvement often comes at too great a cost.

Much of the profit earned on Wall Street today by the big investment banks and hedge funds has nothing to do with allocating scarce capital to individuals and businesses that can put it to the most productive use—the traditional rationale for a financial system. Rather, it comes as a result of rapid and incessant trading in financial instruments, buying and selling in a matter of hours, minutes and seconds, based on preprogrammed computer algorithms. This is nothing more than a sophisticated form of gambling or speculation whose only economic benefit is to modestly increase the liquidity and efficiency of already liquid and efficient markets. We also know that sometimes speculative profit is made on the basis of inside information—the coin of the realm in the hedge fund world—or unfair advantages gained from locating high-speed trading computers one millisecond closer to an automated exchange, as Michael Lewis described in his book *Flash Boys*.

One way to reduce that speculation is to impose a small tax on every trade of a financial instrument—stock, bond, derivative—which I proposed earlier as a way to finance the citizen dividend. Another is to restructure the tax on capital gains—the tax on investment profits—so that the tax rate is raised for short-term profits but declines gradually for longer-term investments (investments held for less than a year are already taxed as ordinary income). The likely effect of a steeply tiered capital gains tax would not be to raise additional revenue for the Treasury, but to nudge activity on Wall Street back in the direction of old-fashioned, long-term investing.

As a result of these two tax changes, a lot of trading would disappear, along with many of the fortunes now earned by the big investment banks, hedge funds and other Wall Street wise guys. One additional benefit is that all of those highly trained rocket scientists who now spend their days writing clever trading algorithms could go back to being real rocket scientists again.

* * *

Outside of finance, the biggest concentrations of new wealth are to be found in industries that are driven by the extraordinary talent and creativity of artists, scientists and inventors, but also derive great benefit from lucrative government-granted monopolies in the form of copyrights and patents.[30]

The Constitution gives Congress the power to establish an intellectual property regime to promote the creative arts and technological innovation "by securing for limited times to authors and inventors the exclusive right to their respective writings and discoveries." In recent years, however, those "limited times" have been so often extended—to 75 years in the case of copyrights—and the definition of what can be patented and copyrighted has been stretched so far that intellectual property law is doing as much to discourage innovation and creativity as to foster it.

American companies now spend tens of billions of dollars each year defending themselves against patent suits filed by competitors and patent trolls whose only business is to buy up patents and use them to extract quick ransoms from companies that may or may not be violating them. And they spend billions more using the patent courts to prevent anyone from entering the market with a competitive product.

As Brink Lindsey and Steven Teles demonstrate in their book *The Captured Economy*, what started out as a law to protect intellectual property has now morphed into a law that creates intellectual monopolies—monopolies that generate huge profits for a handful of giant entertainment, technology and drug companies and deliver capacious salaries for their executives and professional employees.[31] The result is an economically toxic combination of lost vibrancy for American business and a widening gap between pay in those industries and every other.

Reforming patent and copyright law is a subject so arcane that it is guaranteed to make eyes glaze over, so I won't try to outline it here. Because of the enormous amounts of money that are at stake, changing the laws has proven politically difficult and often results in an unsatisfactory compromise. A better approach would be for state attorney generals or public-interest lawyers to bring some well-chosen cases to the Supreme Court that would give the justices the opportunity to set more stringent limits on what can be patented, as they did recently with a ruling overturning a patent on human genes.[32] An interesting constitutional challenge could also be brought asking the Court to rule that the periods of exclusive use now authorized in patent and copyright law are so long as to violate the framers' intent that they be only for "a limited time." Like antitrust, intellectual property law is largely judge-made, so it is the courts that we must rely on to ensure that the law keeps up with the constant changes in technology and the dynamics of market competition.

Minimizing the Maximizing of Shareholder Value

Allow me to close where I began, with the misguided notion that the sole purpose of business is to maximize value for owners and shareholders. Any search for the reason why American capitalism lost its way must begin there.

Although there is nothing in law that requires directors and executives to run corporations solely to maximize profits and share prices, a generation of corporate executives, directors, shareholders, stock analysts and lawyers has come to believe that it does—and behave accordingly.[33]

But imagine what might happen if the Securities and Exchange Commission (SEC), which regulates companies with publicly traded stock, were to require those companies to provide a succinct statement of corporate purpose at the beginning of each year's annual report—a statement giving investors a sense of the company's business objectives, priorities, values, and the time horizon it uses to set its strategic goals.

I have no doubt that some companies would declare themselves ruthless maximizers of shareholder value over the short term, and continue to attract investment from many hedge fund traders and Wall Street money managers. And that's okay. One of the retorts you commonly hear is that critics of maximizing shareholder value just want to impose their own liberal, anti-market, worker-coddling, Earth Day–celebrating, social responsibility ethic and values on every business. In fact, it is the shareholder-value crowd that wants to impose its own one-size-fits-all value system on the entire corporate sector, while it is we critics who want to encourage diversity, experimentation and competition in the corporate ecosystem. My proposal is simply to require that every company tell the world what kind of company it aspires to be.

Any company that chooses shareholders over everyone else, however, would run the risk of offending an important and growing segment of consumers—particularly younger consumers—who want the brands they support with their purchases to reflect their social values, and are willing to pay higher prices, if necessary, to achieve such alignment.[34]

Any company that advertises itself as a profit maximizer would find it more difficult to recruit young employees to the hardest-to-fill positions. Many millennials simply won't work for a company whose values and practices and products they do not respect.[35]

And any company that promises to maximize returns for investors might be viewed as untrustworthy partners by cities and states that are frequently asked to offer businesses subsidies and tax breaks to locate within their borders.

Because of these conflicting pressures, requiring companies to issue and regularly update a statement of purpose would force a much-needed conversation within firms, and within the business community, about the role of business in a capitalist society. My guess is that, before long, most companies would settle on a much broader statement of purpose that touched on satisfying the needs of all stakeholders in a way that maximizes the interests of none of them.

The dirty little secret is that nobody dislikes the move to shareholder capitalism more than corporate executives and directors, who, in the process, lost the freedom and discretion they once had to balance the competing interests of corporate stakeholders. For years many have chafed at being dictated to by number-crunching stock analysts and

cocky hedge fund managers who understand little of what
it takes to produce great products and services, manage a
large organization and still feel good about what you do at
the end of the day. They resent having to deliver double-
digit earnings growth each quarter, perfectly in line with
analyst expectations, or face the wrath of activist investors
and the near-certain prospect of being fired. They hate
having their motives questioned by employees, customers
and even their own family members any time a tough decision had to be made.

Because they founded their own companies and owned
large chunks of the stock, successful entrepreneurs like Apple's Steve Jobs and Amazon's Jeff Bezos could get away with
telling Wall Street to piss off. By requiring every corporation
to articulate its own corporate purpose, values and investment time horizons, the SEC could encourage and empower
other executives to demonstrate similar courage, indepen-
dence and leadership.

Some have already done so. More than 2,000 companies
around the world, including Etsy, Patagonia, Ben & Jerry's
and Warby Parker here in the United States, have set themselves up as something known as a "B Corp," or benefit
corporation, as distinguished from the more common C
Corporation. B Corps are required to establish in their corporate charters a fiduciary duty to consider a range of interests that include employees, suppliers, the environment
and society at large. An independent nonprofit known as the
B Lab must regularly certify that B Corps meet minimum
criteria for transparency, accountability and social and environmental responsibility.

One challenge to B Corps is that the major stock exchanges, which are controlled by the big Wall Street firms,
have their own rules about corporate governance for compa-

nies whose stocks are listed. The major exchanges have not
exactly welcomed listings by B Corps. Another challenge
comes from the state of Delaware, where a majority of big
corporations are chartered. While Delaware's Court of Chancery has given corporate directors and executives wide lati-
tude in decision-making under its "business judgment" rule,
its focus continues to be protecting the rights and interests of
shareholders. A statement of purpose requirement from the
SEC would nudge the exchanges and the Delaware chancel-
lors to recognize that considering the needs of customers,
employees and society is not merely a means to maximizing
shareholder value, but a legitimate end in and of itself.

A New Political Vocabulary

A constitutional amendment putting limits on special interest money. A guaranteed minimum income in exchange for
national service. Profit sharing for all employees. Ending
class segregation in public schools. Restoring competition
to overly consolidated markets through more aggressive antitrust enforcement, reform of copyright and patent law and
greater reliance on customer-owned financial institutions.
Requiring public companies to be transparent about their
purposes and priorities. That these sound like radical and
politically unachievable ideas speaks to the paucity of our
political imagination and the lack of faith in our institutions
to adapt to new circumstances.

    We need a new framework and a new vocabulary for
talking about economic justice. Too much of the academic
debate has been dominated by technical squabbles over
data, philosophic hairsplitting and outdated economic ide-
ologies. Too much of the popular debate is framed in terms
of greed and envy or what will create the most jobs.

More satisfying would be a conversation that starts from a set of morally intuitive first principles about what kind of society we want to live in and what kind of social contract should govern our relationships with each other. It is only by judging economic institutions and outcomes against a broader set of criteria that it is possible to free ourselves from the natural tendency to think of things in terms of where things are, and instead begin to think of things in terms of where we want them to be. An economic system is a means to an end, not an end in itself, and if it is not serving those ends, we ought to change it.

One of my favorite political speeches—and one I play each year in my introductory economics class—was given by Robert Kennedy while he was running for president in that tragic spring of 1968. It was a speech about the gross national product, which measures the economy's output and is often used as a proxy for a nation's well-being. Kennedy's point was that maybe it shouldn't be.

> Our Gross National Product, now, is over $800 billion a year, but that Gross National Product—if we judge the United States of America by that—that Gross National Product counts air pollution and cigarette advertising, and ambulances to clear our highways of carnage. It counts special locks for our doors and the jails for the people who break them. It counts the destruction of the redwood and the loss of our natural wonder in chaotic sprawl. It counts napalm and counts nuclear warheads and armored cars for the police to fight the riots in our cities. It counts [the assassin's] rifle and [the murderer's] knife and the television programs which glorify violence in order to sell toys to our children.

And then he turned to the things it leaves out:

Yet the gross national product does not allow for the health of our children, the quality of their education or the joy of their play. It does not include the beauty of our poetry or the strength of our marriages, the intelligence of our public debate or the integrity of our public officials. It measures neither our wit nor our courage, neither our wisdom nor our learning, neither our compassion nor our devotion to our country. It measures everything in short, except that which makes life worthwhile. And it can tell us everything about America except why we are proud that we are Americans.

What seems so striking about this speech today is not only its eloquence—when was the last time you heard a politician give a stump speech like that—but also the clarity of its *moral* vision.

What we need in our economic conversation today is more in the way of thoughtful moralizing, not less. As Adam Smith understood, the wealth of nations depends on the vigorous pursuit of self-interest by individuals whose natural and productive selfishness is tempered by moral sentiments such as compassion, generosity and a sense of fair play. An economic system that regularly ignores those sentiments forfeits its moral legitimacy. And, in time, it will forfeit its prosperity as well.

Acknowledgments

In a very real sense, I've been working on this book for 40 years, ever since I wrangled a job in 1979 as a business reporter for the nightly news show on Boston's public television station. I had never taken any courses in business or economics, so I had to pick things up as I went along, reading and talking to the best people I could. And that's been pretty much the strategy ever since—as a founding editor and publisher of the monthly *Boston Observer*, as a senior editor at *Inc.* magazine, and then for 30 years at the *Washington Post*, where I have been an editor, a reporter and an opinion columnist. My tutors have been many of the world's best economists, business executives, policy-makers and management experts, who explained things, shared their insights and experiences and helped me correct and refine my own ideas. That they number too many to be named individually does not diminish the gratitude and admiration I have for all of them.

I have also learned much from many generous colleagues over the years, benefiting from their knowledge and experience as well as their understanding, loyalty and friendship. It was the late, great editor Ben Bradlee who took a chance and hired me to be a business editor at the *Post*, and over the years some of the best in the business have shared their ideas, improved my copy and offered support. Although it would take a small book to name them all, I would be remiss not to mention David Ignatius, first and foremost, as well as Don Graham, Chris Ma, Bo Jones, Leonard Downie, Bob Kaiser, Steve Coll, Tom Wilkinson, Phil Bennet, Marcus Brauchli, Liz Spayd, Marty Baron, Pete Behr, Jill Dutt, Sandy Sugawara, Greg Schneider, David Cho, Nell Henderson, Marilee Schwartz, Claudia Townsend, Carlos Lozada, Steven Levingston, Tracy Grant, Vince Rinehart, Mike Shepard, Scott Patton, Doug Feaver, Paul Blustein, Steve Mufson, Mike Getler and Ezra Klein. For the last decade, Kelly Johnson has been a careful editor of my copy, a gentle minister to my psyche and a loyal friend.

Much of this book is taken from three public lectures I delivered in the spring of 2017 at George Mason University in Fairfax, Virginia, where I have a wonderful perch from which to teach economics, politics, public policy and anything else that interests me to a remarkably diverse and engaged set of undergraduates. I am indebted to former Mason president Alan Merten and former provost Peter Stearns for offering a professorship to a journalist with no advanced degree, and to Angel Cabrera and David Wu, their successors, for their continuing support.

Portions of the book first appeared in columns and articles I have written for the *Washington Post*, which graciously allowed me to reuse the material and gave me a sabbatical to incorporate it into a book. That includes the passages about the history of Xerox Corp. It also includes much of the discussion of maximizing shareholder value, which I later expanded into a monograph for the Brookings Institution, with the support of Elaine Kamark of Brookings and Judy Samuelson of the Aspen Institute.

I make no claim that any of the ideas in this book are original with me, or that I conducted any of the research behind them. I have tried to credit the work of others whenever I was aware of it, either in the text or in the notes, and apologize to any whose contributions I may have inadvertently overlooked. Many thanks to researcher Fredrick Toohey for his fact checking and the careful and efficient way he went about pulling together the notes and the data for the charts and graphs.

Evan Thomas, an insightful journalist and historian, pushed me to write this book and he and his wife, Oscie, have provided invaluable guidance and friendship ever since. I am particularly grateful to my friends Belle Sawhill, Neil Irwin, Steve Weisman, Robin Hanson, Tom Edsall and Jim Millstein, who read drafts and provided insightful guidance. Richard Reeves and Jerry Muller have generously shared their deep knowledge. When this project hit some bumps a few years back, Rafe Sagalyn, a most capable agent and friend, was instrumental in getting me back on track, as were Peter and Amy Bernstein, Linc Caplan, Gerald and Linda Stern, Michael Wheeler, Jamie Gorelick, Candy Lee, Peter Hart, Arthur Segel, Patti Saris and Eric Rayman.

At St. Martin's Press, I am indebted to Tim Bartlett, a patient and gifted editor who signed on not once but twice to this project, and his assistant, Alice Pfeifer, who never drops a ball. Diana Walker is as good a friend as she is a photographer, which is why I look better than I deserve to on the jacket cover.

My wife, Wendy Gray, not only provided the inspiration and encouragement to write the book and get over the rough spots, but was patient and understanding during all those nights, weekends and forgone vacations when her husband, or his mind, was somewhere else. She has been a steadfast friend, a wise and wonderful mom to two fabulous children and loving partner in everything for 35 years. I would be lost without her.

Washington, DC
September 2018

Notes

Introduction

1   Harvard University Institute of Politics, "Spring 2016 Youth Poll," April 25, 2016, http://iop.harvard.edu/youth-poll/past/harvard-iop -spring-2016-poll.

2   YouGov, "Annual Report on US Attitudes Toward Socialism," October 2017, http://victimsofcommunism.org/wp-content/uploads/2017 /11/YouGov-VOC-2017-for-Media-Release-November-2-2017-final.pdf.

3   Max Ehrenfreund, "A Majority of Millennials Now Reject Capitalism, Poll Shows," Wonkblog, *Washington Post*, April 26, 2016.

4   Bruce Stokes, "Public Divided on Prospects for the Next Generation," Pew Research Center, June 5, 2017, http://www.pewglobal.org/2017/06 /05/2-public-divided-on-prospects-for-the-next-generation/.

5   Rick Wartzman, *The End of Loyalty: The Rise and Fall of Good Jobs in America* (New York: PublicAffairs, 2017).

6   Joseph Nocera, *A Piece of the Action: How the Middle Class Joined the Money Class* (New York: Simon & Schuster, 1994).

7   Steven Pearlstein, "Reinventing Xerox Corp," *Washington Post*, June 29, 1998.

8   Malcolm Gladwell, "Creation Myth, Xerox PARC, Apple and the Truth About Innovation," *New Yorker*, May 16, 2011.

9   Steven Pearlstein, "How Big Business Lost Washington," *Washington Post*, September 2, 2016.

10   Icahn contested the sale in court, arguing a better sales price could have been had.

11   Steve Lohn and Carlos Tejada, "After Era That Made It a Verb, Xerox, in a Sale, Is Past Tense," *New York Times*, January 31, 2018.

12 Martin Wolf, "Reforming Western Capitalism," in *The Occupy Handbook*, ed. Janet Bryne (New York: Back Bay Books, 2012).

13 Laurence Fink, "A Sense of Purpose," BlackRock, Annual Letter to CEOs, December 2017, https://www.blackrock.com/corporate/investor-relations/larry-fink-ceo-letter.

14 Jerry Z. Muller, "Capitalism and Inequality, What the Left and the Right Get Wrong," *Foreign Affairs*, March/April 2013.

1: Is Greed Good?

1 Rana Foroohar, "The Original Wolf of Wall Street, Carl Icahn, Returns," *Time*, December 16, 2013.

2 Charles Karelis, conversation with author.

3 SEC v. Goldman Sachs & Co. and Fabrice Tourre, complaint, April 16, 2010, 7 (U.S. S. Dist. NY, 2010), https://www.sec.gov/litigation/complaints/2010/comp-pr2010-59.pdf.

4 *Wall Street and the Financial Crisis: The Role of Investment Banks: Hearing Before the Permanent Subcommittee on Investigations of the Committee on Homeland Security and Governmental Affairs*, 111 Cong., 2nd Sess. (April 27, 2010), 7 and 135.

5 Steve Eder and Karey Wutkowski, "Goldman's 'Fabulous' Fab's Conflicted Love Letters," Reuters, April 25, 2010.

6 Jerry Z. Muller, *The Mind and the Market: Capitalism in Western Thought* (New York: Anchor Books, 2003), 51.

7 Voltaire, *On the Pensees of Pascal* (1728), quoted in Muller, *The Mind and the Market*, 36.

8 David Hume, *On Luxury* (1742).

9 Adam Smith, *The Theory of Moral Sentiments* (London: Penguin Books, 2009; reprint of 1759 ed.), pt. 3, ch. 2.

10 Smith, *Moral Sentiments*, pt. 1, sect. 3, ch. 2.

11 Smith, *Moral Sentiments*, pt. 1, sect. 1, ch. 5.

12 Smith, *Moral Sentiments*, pt. 2, sect. 2, ch. 2.

13 Smith, *Moral Sentiments*, pt. 4, ch. 1.

14 Adam Smith, *The Wealth of Nations* (New York: Barnes and Noble, 2004; reprint of 1776 ed.), vol. 1, ch. 8.

15 See Edward D. Kleinbard, *We Are Better Than This: How Government Should Spend Our Money* (Oxford: Oxford University Press, 2014); Muller, *The Mind and the Market*; Russ Roberts, *How Adam Smith Can Change Your Life: An Unexpected Guide to Human Nature and Happiness* (New York: Portfolio/Penguin, 2014); Amartya Sen, Introduction to Smith, *Moral Sentiments*; Vernon L. Smith, "The Two Faces of Adam Smith," *Southern Economic Journal* 65, no. 1 (July 1998): 1–19; and Dennis C. Rasmussen, "The Problem with Inequality, According to Adam Smith," *The Atlantic*, June 9, 2016.

16 Smith, *Moral Sentiments*, pt. 3, sect. 2, ch. 2.

17 See Mark Ridley, *The Cooperative Gene: How Mendel's Demon Explains the Evolution of Complex Beings* (New York: Free Press, 2001).

18 Charles Darwin, *The Descent of Man, and Selection in Relation to Sex* (1871).

19 Darwin, *Descent of Man*, quoted in Jonathan Haidt, *The Righteous Mind: Why Good People Are Divided by Politics and Religion* (New York: Vintage Books, 2012), 226.
20 David DeSteno, "How to Keep Your Resolutions," *New York Times Sunday Review*, December 31, 2017.
21 Paul J. Zak, *The Moral Molecule: The New Science of What Makes Us Good or Evil* (London: Bantam Press, 2012), 168.
22 Haidt, *The Righteous Mind*, 249.
23 Zak, *The Moral Molecule*, 14–15.
24 Zak, *The Moral Molecule*, xviii.
25 James Q. Wilson, *The Moral Sense* (New York: Free Press, 1993), 23.
26 Joshua Greene, *Moral Tribes: Emotion, Reason, and the Gap Between Us and Them* (New York: Penguin Press, 2013), 24–25.
27 Geoffrey Hodgson, *From Pleasure Machines to Moral Communities: An Evolutionary Economics Without Homo Economicus* (Chicago: University of Chicago Press, 2013). See also Herbert Gintis and Samuel Bowles, *A Cooperative Species: Human Reciprocity and Its Evolution* (Oxford: Oxford University Press, 2011); and David Sloan Wilson, *Does Altruism Exist: Culture, Genes, and the Welfare of Others* (New Haven, CT: Yale University Press, 2015).
28 Yuval Noah Harari, *Sapiens: A Brief History of Humankind* (New York: Harper, 2015). See also Peter Turchin, *Ultra Society: How 10,000 Years of War Made Humans the Greatest Cooperators on Earth* (Chaplin, CT: Beresta Books, 2015); and Walter Scheidel, *The Great Leveler: Violence and the History of Inequality from the Stone Age to the Twenty-First Century* (Princeton, NJ: Princeton University Press, 2017).
29 Much of this section is taken from an earlier essay by Pearlstein: Steven Pearlstein, "Social Capital, Corporate Purpose and the Revival of American Capital," Brookings Institution, January 2014.
30 Robert Reich, *The Common Good* (New York: Knopf, 2018). Shkreli quoted in Dan Munro, "Top Ten Healthcare Quotes for 2015," *Forbes*, December 6, 2015, https://www.forbes.com/sites/danmunro/2015/12/06/top-10-healthcare-quotes-for-2015/#467024da7957.
31 Lynn Stout, *The Shareholder Value Myth* (San Francisco: Berrett-Koehler, 2012). Additional support for this legal interpretation can be found in Henry Hansmann and Mariana Pargendler, "The Evolution of Shareholder Voting Rights: Separation of Ownership and Consumption," *Yale Law Journal* 123 (February 17, 2013): 100–165.
32 Ibid.
33 Milton Friedman, "The Social Responsibility of a Business Is to Increase Its Profits," *New York Times Magazine*, September 13, 1970, http://www.colorado.edu/studentgroups/libertarians/issues/friedman-soc-resp-business.html.
34 Ralph Gomory and Richard Sylla, "The American Corporation," *Daedalus* 142, no. 2 (Spring 2013).
35 Ibid.
36 The S&P 500 Index, a commonly used measure of the performance of U.S. equity markets, hit a high of 118 at the end of 1972 that it did not see again until July 1980.

37 Robert Shiller, *Irrational Exuberance*, 2nd ed. (New York: Crown Business, 2006).

38 The Aspen Institute Center for Business Education, "Where Will They Lead?: MBA Student Attitudes about Business and Society," 2008, http://www.aspeninstitute.org/sites/default/files/content/docs/bsp/SAS_PRINT_FINAL.PDF.

39 Lynn Stout, "The Problem of Corporate Purpose," *Issues in Governance Studies* 48 (June 2012), https://www.brookings.edu/research/the-problem-of-corporate-purpose/.

40 A study by McKinsey & Company cites several examples of publicly traded companies that have either stopped producing quarterly earnings reports or diminished their focus on short-term financial measurements, including Google, Citigroup, Motorola and Intel. The report attributes a 7 percent decline in Google's value in February 2006 to exuberant expectations influenced by Google's lack of earnings guidance for investors. Peggy Hsieh, Timothy Koller and S. R. Rajan, "The Misguided Practice of Earnings Guidance," *McKinsey on Finance* (March 2006), http://www.mckinsey.com/insights/corporate_finance/the_misguided_practice_of_earnings_guidance.

41 Michiyo Nakamoto and David Wighton, "Citigroup Chief Stays Bullish on Buyouts," *Financial Times*, July 9, 2007, http://www.ft.com/cms/s/0/80e2987a-2e50-11dc-821c-0000779fd2ac.html#axzz2mSZC3Swy.

42 Michael C. Jensen and William H. Meckling, "Theory of the Firm: Managerial Behavior, Agency Costs and Ownership Structure," *Journal of Financial Economics* 3, no. 4 (October 1976): 305–360.

43 Michael C. Jensen and Kevin J. Murphy, "CEO Incentives: It's Not How Much You Pay, But How," *Harvard Business Review* (May/June 1990): 138–153.

44 Lawrence Mishel and Jessica Schneider, "CEO Pay Remains High Relative to the Pay of Typical Workers and High Wage Earners," Economic Policy Institute, July 20, 2017, http://www.epi.org/files/pdf/130354.pdf.

45 Roger L. Martin, *Fixing the Game: Bubbles, Crashes, and What Capitalism Can Learn from the NFL* (Boston: Harvard Business Review Press, 2011).

46 Rakesh Khurana, *From Higher Aims to Hired Hands: The Social Transformation of American Business Schools and the Unfulfilled Promise of Management as a Profession* (Princeton, NJ: Princeton University Press, 2007), 364.

47 William Lazonick, "Stock Buybacks: From Retain-and-Reinvest to Downsize-and-Distribute," Initiative on Twenty-First Century Capitalism, Brookings Institution, April 2015, https://www.brookings.edu/research/stock-buybacks-from-retain-and-reinvest-to-downsize-and-distribute/.

48 Sam Ro, "Stock Market Investors Have Become Absurdly Impatient," *Business Insider*, August 7, 2012, http://www.businessinsider.com/stock-investor-holding-period-2012-8.

49 Jeffrey Sonnenfeld, "CEO Exit Schedules: A Season to Stay, a Season to Go," *Fortune*, May 6, 2015.

50 "CPP Investment Board and McKinsey & Company: Global Survey Signals Short-Term Pressures on Business Leaders Are Mounting," Mar-

ketWired, May 22, 2013, http://www.marketwired.com/press-release/cpp-investment-board-mckinsey-company-global-survey-signals-short-term-pressures-on-1793872.htm.

51 Dominic Barton, Joseph Manyika, Timothy Koller, Robert Palter, Jonathan Goodsell and Joshua Zoffer, "Measuring the Economic Impact of Short-Termism," McKinsey Global Institute, February 2017; see also Dominic Barton, Jonathan Bailey and Joshua Zoffer, "Rising to the Challenge of Short-Termism," FCLT Global, September 2016.

52 David Langstaff, "Rethinking 'Shareholder Value' and the Purpose of the Corporation" (speech, Aspen Institute Business and Society Program, March 7–8, 2013).

53 Lawrence H. Summers, "U.S. Economic Prospects: Secular Stagnation, Hysteresis, and the Zero Lower Bound," *Business Economics* 49, no. 2 (2014): 65–73, doi:10.1057/be.2014.13; see also Robert J. Gordon, *The Rise and Fall of American Growth: The U.S. Standard of Living Since the Civil War* (Princeton, NJ: Princeton University Press, 2016).

54 Associated Press, "American Airlines Announced Pay Raises, and Investors Balk," April 27, 2017, http://www.latimes.com/business/la-fi-american-airlines-raises-20170427-story.html.

55 Michael Wheeler, "Three Years Ago, This Boss Set a $70,000 Minimum Wage for His Employees—and the Move Is Still Paying Off," personal blog, https://www.linkedin.com/pulse/best-boss-america-year-3-michael-wheeler. See also Paul Keegan, "Here's What Really Happened at That Company That Set a $70,000 Minimum Wage," *Inc.*, November 2015, https://www.inc.com/magazine/201511/paul-keegan/does-more-pay-mean-more-growth.html.

56 *Offshore Profit Shifting and the US Tax Code—Part 2 (Apple Inc.): Hearing Before the Permanent Subcommittee on Investigations of the Committee on Homeland Security and Governmental Affairs*, 113 Cong., 1 Sess. (May 21, 2013), https://www.gpo.gov/fdsys/pkg/CHRG-113shrg81657/pdf/CHRG-113shrg81657.pdf.

57 Ibid., 37.

58 Gwyn Topham, "Google's Eric Schmidt: Change British Law and We'd Pay More Tax," *Guardian*, May 26, 2013.

59 Jeremy Kahn, "Google's 'Dutch Sandwich' Shielded 16 Billion Euros from Taxes," *Bloomberg*, January 2, 2018.

60 Khurana, *From Higher Aims to Hired Hands*, 379.

61 Gallup, "Confidence in Institutions," 2016, http://news.gallup.com/poll/1597/confidence-institutions.aspx.

62 Peter F. Drucker, *The Practice of Management*, 2nd ed. (New York: Harper Business, 2006), 37.

63 Roger Martin, *Fixing the Game, Bubbles, Crashes and What Capitalism Can Learn from the NFL* (Cambridge, MA: Harvard Business Review Press, 2011).

64 Watermark Consulting, "2013 Customer Experience ROI Study," Water-Remarks (blog), April 2, 2013, https://www.watermarkconsult.net/blog/2013/04/02/the-watermark-consulting-2013-customer-experience-roi-study/.

65 Joseph L. Bower and Lynn S. Paine, "The Error at the Heart of Corporate Leadership," *Harvard Business Review*, May-June, 2017.

66 Patrick Radden Keefe, "Carl Icahn's Raid on Washington: Was President Trump's Richest Adviser Focused on Helping the Country—Or Helping His Bottom Line?" *New Yorker*, August 29, 2017.

67 Lynn Stout, "Taking Conscience Seriously," in *Moral Markets: The Critical Role of Values in the Economy*, ed. Paul Zak (Princeton, NJ: Princeton University Press, 2008), 157–158.

68 Uri Gneezy and Aldo Rustichini, "A Fine Is a Price," *Journal of Legal Studies* 29, no. 1 (2000): 1–17. The results of the original study were replicated in a second study in 2005: Uri Gneezy and Aldo Rustichini, "The Second Day-Care Study," September 2005, http://arielrubinstein .tau.ac.il/papers/WC05/GR1.pdf.

69 See Steven Pearlstein, "Italy's Culture Threatens Its Economic Future," *Washington Post*, June 29, 2012.

70 James S. Coleman, "Social Capital in the Creation of Human Capital," *American Journal of Sociology* 94 (1988): S95-S120.

71 Ibid., S99.

72 Alexis de Tocqueville, *Democracy in America* (1835), 515, cited in David Halpern, *Social Capital* (Cambridge: Polity, 2004), 5.

73 See Halpern, *Social Capital*, ch. 7 and 199–244.

74 "U.S. General Social Survey," as reported in Esteban Ortiz-Ospina and Max Roser, "Trust," Our World in Data, 2016, ourworldindata.org/trust.

75 Bureau of Justice Statistics, "Prisoners in 2016," January 2018, https:// www.bjs.gov/content/pub/pdf/p16_sum.pdf; Bureau of Justice Statistics, "National Sources of Law Enforcement Employment Data," October 4, 2016, https://www.bjs.gov/content/pub/pdf/nsleed.pdf; and Samuel Bowles and Arjun Jayadev, "One Nation Under Guard," *New York Times*, February 15, 2014, https://opinionator.blogs.nytimes.com/2014/02/15 /one-nation-under-guard/.

76 Federal Judicial Center, "Caseloads: Civil Cases, Private, 1873–2016," https://www.fjc.gov/history/courts/caseloads-civil-cases-private-1873 -2016; Keith Lee, "Historical Growth Rate of Lawyers in USA—Chart," *Associate's Mind*, https://associatesmind.com/2013/08/19/historical-growth -rate-of-lawyers-in-usa-chart/; and National Association for Law Placement, "What Do New Lawyers Earn?: A 15-Year Retrospective, 1994– 2008," *NALP Bulletin*, August 2009, https://www.nalp.org/aug09 newlawyersal.

77 Thom File, "Who Votes? Congressional Elections and the American Electorate: 1978–2014," U.S. Census Bureau, July 2015, https://www .census.gov/content/dam/Census/library/publications/2015/demo /p20-577.pdf; and Pew Research Center, "Trust in Government: 1958– 2015," November 23, 2015, http://www.people-press.org/2015/11/23/1 -trust-in-government-1958-2015/.

78 Gallup, "Confidence in Institutions," 2016, http://news.gallup.com /poll/1597/confidence-institutions.aspx; and Clare Malone, "Americans Don't Trust Their Institutions Anymore," *FiveThirtyEight*, November 16, 2016, https://fivethirtyeight.com/features/americans-dont-trust -their-institutions-anymore/.

79 Robert Putnam, *Our Kids: The American Dream in Crisis* (New York: Simon & Schuster, 2015.

2: Not-So-Just Deserts

1 John Locke, *Second Treatise on Civil Government* (1689).

2 Robert Nozick, *Anarchy, State and Utopia* (New York: Basic Books, 1974).

3 This is Rawls's famous "difference principle," spelled out in his *A Theory of Justice* (Belknap Press, 1999; revision of 1971 ed.).

4 Lawrence Summers, "40 Years Later—The Relevance of Okun's Equality and Efficiency: The Big Tradeoff" (speech, Brookings Institution, Washington, DC, May 4, 2015).

5 Congressional Budget Office, "The Distribution of Household Income and Federal Taxes, 2013," June 2016, https://www.cbo.gov/sites/default/files/114th-congress-2015-2016/reports/51361-householdincomefedtaxes.pdf.

6 Meeting of the OECD Council at Ministerial Level, "Update Report 2017—Inclusive Growth," Organisation for Economic Co-operation and Development, Paris, June 7–8, 2017, http://www.oecd.org/mcm/documents/C-MIN-2017-3-EN.pdf.

7 Department of the Treasury, "Income Mobility in the U.S. from 1996 to 2005," November 13, 2007, https://www.treasury.gov/resource-center/tax-policy/Documents/Report-Income-Mobility-2008.pdf.

8 Stephen J. Rose, "Was JFK Wrong? Does Rising Productivity No Longer Lead to Substantial Middle Class Income Gains?" Information Technology and Innovation Foundation, December 2014, http://www2.itif.org/2014-rising-productivity-middle-class.pdf.

9 Jonathan Fisher, David Johnson and Timothy Smeeding, "Measuring the Trends in Inequality of Individuals and Families: Income and Consumption" (draft, American Economics Association session "Perspectives on Inequality and Mobility in the US," December 28, 2012).

10 For a longer discussion, see John Nye, "Real Inequality: Why Things Are Better Than They Seem and Will Almost Surely Get Worse," Mercatus Center, George Mason University, July 17, 2014, https://www.mercatus.org/expert_commentary/real-inequality-why-things-are-better-they-seem-and-will-almost-surely-get-worse.

11 Pew Research Center, "Inside the Middle Class: Bad Times Hit the Good Life," April 9, 2008, http://www.pewsocialtrends.org/2008/04/09/inside-the-middle-class-bad-times-hit-the-good-life/; Pew Research Center, "Fewer, Poorer, Gloomier: The Lost Decade of the Middle Class," August 22, 2012, http://www.pewsocialtrends.org/2012/08/22/the-lost-decade-of-the-middle-class/; and Alan B. Krueger, "The Rise and Consequences of Inequality in the United States" (speech, Center for American Progress, Washington, DC, January 12, 2012).

12 Edward N. Wolff, "Household Wealth Trends in the United States, 1962–2016: Has Middle Class Wealth Recovered?" NBER Working Paper 24085, National Bureau of Economic Research, November 2017.

13 Thomas Piketty, *Capital in the Twenty-First Century* (Cambridge, MA: Harvard University Press, 2014), 300.

14 Jaison R. Abel and Richard Deitz, "Do the Benefits of College Still Outweigh the Costs?" *Current Issues in Economics and Finance* 20, no. 3 (2014).

15 George Borjas, "Immigration and the American Worker: A Review of the Academic Literature," Center for Immigration Studies, April 2013; see also Adam Looney and Michael Greenstone, "What Immigration Means for U.S. Unemployment and Wages," Brookings Institution, May 4, 2012, https://www.brookings.edu/blog/jobs/2012/05/04/what -immigration-means-for-u-s-employment-and-wages/.

16 David R. Howell, "The Great Laissez-Faire Experiment: American Inequality and Growth from an International Perspective," Center for American Progress, December 2013.

17 Michael Greenstone and Adam Looney, "The Marriage Gap: The Impact of Economic and Technological Change on Marriage Rates," Hamilton Project, February 3, 2012, https://www.brookings.edu/blog /jobs/2012/02/03/the-marriage-gap-the-impact-of-economic-and -technological-change-on-marriage-rates/; and W. Bradford Wilcox and Robert I. Lerman, "For Richer, for Poorer: How Family Structures Economic Success in America," American Enterprise Institute, October 28, 2014, http://www.aei.org/publication/for-richer-for-poorer-how -family-structures-economic-success-in-america/.

18 Robert D. Mare, "Educational Homogamy from Two Gilded Ages, Evidence from Intergenerational Mobility Studies," *Annals of the American Academy of Political and Social Science* 663, no. 1 (2015): 117–139. For a more skeptical view, see Lasse Eika, Magne Mogstag and Basit Zafar, "Educational Assortative Mating and Household Income Inequality," Staff Report No. 682, Federal Reserve Bank of New York, August 2014 (rev. March 2017).

19 Sandra E. Black, Diane Whitmore Schanzenbach and Audrey Breitwieser, "The Recent Decline in Women's Labor Force Participation," Hamilton Project, October 2017, https://www.brookings.edu/wp-content /uploads/2017/10/es_10192017_decline_womens_labor_force _participation_blackschanzenbach.pdf.

20 Abel and Deitz, "Do the Benefits of College Still Outweigh the Costs?"

21 Derek Thompson, "How America's Marriage Crisis Makes Income Inequality So Much Worse," *The Atlantic*, October 1, 2013. Note that the data refers to "family" income, a data set produced by the Census Bureau for households with two or more people related by birth or marriage. By that definition, many households are not families.

22 Jeremy Greenwood, Nezih Guner, Georgi Kocharakov and Cezar Santos, "US Income Inequality and Assortative Marriages," *VOX EU*, February 22, 2014, https://voxeu.org/article/us-income-inequality-and-assortative -marriages; and "Sex, Brains and Inequality: How Sexual Equality Increases the Gap Between Rich and Poor Households," *Economist*, February 8, 2014.

23 Bureau of Labor Statistics, "Union Membership 10.7 Percent in 2016," *Economics Daily*, February 9, 2017, https://www.bls.gov/opub/ted/2017 /union-membership-rate-10-point-7-percent-in-2016.htm.

24 Keith Bender and John Heywood, "Out of Balance, Comparing Public and Private Sector Compensation over 20 Years," National Institute on Retirement Security, April 2010.

25 Craig K. Elwell, "Inflation and the Real Minimum Wage: A Fact Sheet," Congressional Research Service, January 8, 2014.

26 The superstar effect was first identified by economist Sherman Rosen in "The Economics of Superstars," *American Economic Review*, December 1981, but was popularized by Robert Frank and Philip Cook, *The Winner-Take-All Society: Why the Few at the Top Get So Much More Than the Rest of Us* (London: Penguin, 1996).

27 Jon Bakija, Adam Cole and Bradley T. Heim, "Jobs and Income Growth of Top Earners and the Causes of Changing Income Inequality: Evidence from U.S. Tax Return Data," working paper, April 2012, https://web.williams.edu/Economics/wp/BakijaColeHeimJobsIncomeGrowthTopEarners.pdf.

28 Lucien Bebchuk and Yaniv Grinstein, "The Growth of Executive Pay," NBER Working Paper 11443, National Bureau of Economic Research, June 2005.

29 Nuno Fernandes, Miguel A. Ferreira, Pedro Matos and Kevin J. Murphy, "Are US CEOs Paid More? New International Evidence," *Review of Financial Studies* 26, no. 2 (2012).

30 Francesco Guerrera, "We Are Overpaid, Say US Executives," *Financial Times*, October 14, 2007.

31 Josh Bivens, "The Decline in Labor's Share of Corporate Income Since 2000 Means $535 Billion Less for Workers," Economic Policy Institute, September 10, 2015, https://www.epi.org/publication/the-decline-in-labors-share-of-corporate-income-since-2000-means-535-billion-less-for-workers/.

32 For the economy as a whole, labor share has fallen 5 percentage points, to 59 percent, which in an $18.5 trillion economy represents a shift in annual income of more than $900 billion. Much of that shift, however, reflects the increase in real estate values. See Timothy Taylor, "Digging into Capital and Labor Shares," Conversable Economist (blog), March 20, 2015, http://conversableeconomist.blogspot.com/2015/03/digging-into-capital-and-labor-income.html. Other explanations focus on the substitution of technology for labor and the increased use of outsourcing in the manufacturing sector. See Michael W. L. Elsby, Bart Hobijn and Ayşegül Şahin, "The Decline of the U.S. Labor Share," *Brookings Papers on Economic Activity*, Fall 2013, https://www.brookings.edu/wp-content/uploads/2016/07/2013b_elsby_labor_share.pdf.

33 Bakija, Cole and Heim, "Jobs and Income Growth of Top Earners." See also Thomas Philippon and Ariell Reshef, "Wages and Human Capital in the U.S. Financial Industry: 1909–2006," NBER Working Paper 14644, National Bureau of Economic Research, January 2009, http://www.nber.org/papers/w14644.

34 Thomas Philippon, "Finance vs. Wal-Mart: Why Are Financial Services So Expensive?" in *Rethinking the Financial Crisis*, eds. Alan Blinder, Andrew Lo and Robert Solow (New York: Russell Sage Foundation, 2012), 235–246.

35 White House Council of Economic Advisers, "Benefits of Competition and Indications of Market Power," Council of Economic Advisers Issue Brief, April 2016.

36 David Autor, David Dorn, Lawrence F. Katz, Christina Patterson and John Van Reenen, "Concentrating on the Fall of the Labor Share," NBER Working Paper 23108, National Bureau of Economic Research, January 2017, http://www.nber/org/papers/w23108; and Jason Furman and Peter Orszag, "A Firm-Level Perspective on the Role of Rents in the Rise in Inequality" (presentation, A Just Society Centennial Event: In Honor of Joseph Stiglitz, Columbia University, New York, NY, October 16, 2015).

37 See Frank Levy and Peter Temin, "Inequality and Institutions in 20th Century America," NBER Working Paper 13106, National Bureau of Economic Research, May 2007, http://www.nber.org/papers/w13106.

38 Amartya Sen, "Just Deserts," *New York Review of Books*, March 4, 1982. See also Liam Murphy and Thomas Nagel, *The Myth of Ownership: Taxes and Justice* (Oxford: Oxford University Press, 2004).

39 Piketty, *Capital in the Twenty-First Century*, 311.

40 Ibid., 331.

41 Greg Bouchard, "What NBA Salaries Would These Superstar Players Make Today?" *Deal Room*, May 20, 2016, https://www.firmex.com/thedealroom/what-nba-salaries-would-these-superstar-players-make-today/.

3: Is Equality of Opportunity Possible or Even Desirable?

1 Theodore Roosevelt, "The Radical Movement Under Conservative Direction" (speech, New Haven Chamber of Commerce, December 13, 1910), http://www.theodore-roosevelt.com/images/research/txtspeeches/792.pdf.

2 Matt Ridley, "Heritable IQ Is a Sign of Social Mobility," Rational Optimist (blog), December 15, 2013, http://www.rationaloptimist.com/blog/heritable-iq-is-a-sign-of-social-mobility/.

3 Tarmo Strenze, "Intelligence and Socioeconomic Success: A Meta-Analytic Review of Longitudinal Research," *Intelligence* 35 (2007): 401–426.

4 Jay Zagorsky, "Do You Have to Be Smart to Be Rich? The Impact of IQ on Wealth, Income and Financial Distress," *Intelligence* 35 (2007): 489–501.

5 Stephen Ceci and Wendy Williams, "Schooling, Intelligence and Income," *American Psychologist* 52, no. 10 (1997): 1051–1058.

6 Chao-Qiang Lai, "How Much of Human Height Is Genetic and How Much Is Due to Nutrition?" *Scientific American*, December 11, 2006, https://www.scientificamerican.com/article/how-much-of-human-height/; and Timothy Judge and Daniel Cable, "The Effect of Physical Height on Workplace Success and Income," *Journal of Applied Psychology* 89, no. 3 (2004): 428–441.

7 David C. Rowe, Mary Clapp and Janette Wallis, "Physical Attractiveness and the Personality Resemblance of Identical Twins," *Behavior Genetics* 17, no. 2 (1987): 191–201, cited in Satoshi Kanazawa and Jody L. Kovar, "Why Beautiful People Are More Intelligent," *Intelligence* 32, no. 3 (2004): 227–243.

8 Timothy Judge, Charlice Hurst and Lauren Simon, "Does It Pay to Be Smart, Attractive, or Confident (or All Three)? Relationships Among General Mental Ability, Physical Attractiveness, Core Self-Evaluations and Income," *Journal of Applied Psychology* 94, no. 3 (2009): 742–755.
9 P. Roszell, D. Kennedy and E. Grabb, "Physical Attractiveness and Income Attainment Among Canadians," *Journal of Psychology* 124, no. 6 (1989): 547–559.
10 Melissa Groves, "Personality and the Intergenerational Transmission of Economic Status," in *Unequal Chances: Family Background and Economic Success*, eds. Samuel Bowles, Herbert Gintis and Melissa Osborne Groves (Princeton, NJ: Princeton University Press, 2005).
11 Jack Shonkoff and Deborah Phillips, eds, *From Neurons to Neighborhoods: The Science of Early Childhood Development* (Washington, DC: National Academies Press, 2000), http://www.nap.edu/catalog/9824.html.
12 Robert Putnam, *Our Kids: The American Dream in Crisis* (New York: Simon & Schuster, 2015), ch. 3; Paul Touch, *How Children Succeed: Grit, Curiosity, and the Hidden Power of Character* (Boston: Houghton Mifflin, 2012); and James J. Heckman, Jora Stixrud and Sergio Urzua, "The Effects of Cognitive and Noncognitive Abilities on Labor Market Outcomes and Social Behavior," NBER Working Paper 12006, National Bureau of Economic Research, 2006.
13 West Virginia Early Childhood Training Connections and Resources, "The Thirty Million Word Gap," excerpted from Betty Hart and Todd Risley, "The Early Catastrophe: The 30 Million Word Gap by Age 3," *American Educator* 4, no. 9 (Spring 2003), http://www.wvearlychildhood.org/resources/C-13_Handout_1.pdf; and Michael Balter, "Poverty May Affect the Growth of Children's Brains," *Science Magazine*, March 30, 2015, http://www.sciencemag.org/news/2015/03/poverty-may-affect-growth-children-s-brains.
14 Putnam, *Our Kids*; on kindergarteners and the alphabet, he cites Greg J. Duncan and Richard J. Murnane, *Restoring Opportunity: The Crisis of Inequality and the Challenge for American Education* (New York: Russell Sage Foundation, 2014), 32.
15 Putnam, *Our Kids*; Amedeo D'Angiulli, Anthony Herdman, David Stapells and Clyde Hertzman, "Children's Event-Related Potentials of Auditory Selective Attention Vary with Their Socioeconomic Status," *Neuropsychology* 22, no. 3 (2008): 293–300; Pilyoung Kim, Gary W. Evans, Michael Angstadt, S. Shaun Ho, Chandra S. Sripada, James E. Swain, Israel Liberzon and K. Luan Phan, "Effects of Childhood Poverty and Chronic Stress on Emotion Regulatory Brain Function in Adulthood," *Proceedings of the National Academy of Sciences* 110, no. 46 (2013): 18442–18447; and National Scientific Council on the Developing Child, "Excessive Stress Disrupts the Architecture of the Developing Brain," Working Paper 3, 2014, http://developingchild.harvard.edu/wp-content/uploads/2005/05/Stress_Disrupts_Architecture_Developing_Brain-1.pdf.
16 Kimberly G. Noble, Suzanne M. Houston, Natalie H. Brito, Hauke Bartsch, Eric Kan, Joshua M. Kuperman, Natacha Akshoomoff, David G.

Amaral, Cinnamon S. Bloss, Ondrej Libiger, Nicholas J. Schork, Sarah S. Murray, B. J. Casey, Linda Chang, Thomas M. Ernst, Jean A. Frazier, Jeffrey R. Gruen, David N. Kennedy, Peter Van Zijl, Stewart Mostofsky, Walter E. Kaufmann, Tal Kenet, Anders M. Dale, Terry L. Jernigan and Elizabeth R. Sowell, "Family Income, Parental Education and Brain Structure in Children and Adolescents," *Nature Neuroscience* 18, no. 5 (2015): 773–778.

17 Putnam, *Our Kids*, 117–124.

18 Richard V. Reeves and Kimberly Howard, "The Parenting Gap," Center on Children and Families, Brookings Institution, September 8, 2013.

19 Sendhil Mullainathan and Eldar Shafir, *Scarcity: The True Cost of Not Having Enough* (London: Penguin Books, 2013).

20 James Heckman, Rodrigo Pinto and Peter Savelyev, "Understanding the Mechanisms Through Which an Influential Early Childhood Program Boosted Adult Outcomes," *American Economic Review* 103, no. 6 (2013): 2052–2086.

21 Sean F. Reardon, "The Widening Academic Achievement Gap Between the Rich and the Poor: New Evidence and Possible Explanations," in *Whither Opportunity? Rising Inequality, Schools, and Children's Life Chances*, eds. Greg J. Duncan and Richard J. Marnat (New York: Russell Sage Foundation, 2011).

22 Bruce D. Baker, David G. Sciarra and Danielle Farrie, "Is School Funding Fair? A National Report Card, Third Edition," Education Law Center, January 2014.

23 Eduardo Porter, "In Public Education, Edge Still Goes to the Rich," *New York Times*, November 5, 2013.

24 See Eric Hanushek and Alfred A. Lindseth, *Schoolhouses, Courthouses and Statehouses: Solving the Funding-Achievement Puzzle in America's Public Schools* (Princeton, NJ: Princeton University Press, 2009); and Rob Greenwald, Larry V. Hedges and Richard Laine, "The Effect of School Resources on Student Achievement," *Review of Educational Research* 66, no. 3 (1996): 361–396, cited in Putnam, *Our Kids*.

25 Greg Duncan and Katherine Magnuson, "The Nature and Impact of Early Achievement Skills, Attention Skills, and Behavior Problems," in *Whither Opportunity?*, eds. Duncan and Marnat.

26 Gregory J. Palardy, "High School Socioeconomic Segregation and Student Attainment," *American Educational Research Journal* 50, no. 4 (2013), cited in Putnam, *Our Kids*.

27 Reyn van Ewijk and Peter Sleegers, "The Effects of Peer Socioeconomic Status on Student Achievement: A Meta-Analysis," *Educational Research Review* 5, no. 2 (2010): 134–150; as cited in Putnam, *Our Kids*.

28 Richard Fry and Paul Taylor, "The Rise of Residential Segregation by Income," Social and Demographic Trends, Pew Research Center, August 1, 2012, http://www.pewsocialtrends.org/2012/08/01/the-rise-of-residential-segregation-by-income/.

29 Stacy Teicher Khadaroo, "Economic Segregation Rising in Public Schools," *Christian Science Monitor*, May 27, 2010.

30 Edward D. Kleinbard, *We Are Better Than This: How Government Should Spend Our Money* (Oxford: Oxford University Press, 2014), 197.

31 Greg J. Duncan and Richard J. Murnane, *Restoring Opportunity: The Crisis of Inequality and the Challenge for American Education* (Cambridge, MA, and New York: Harvard Education Press and Russell Sage Foundation, 2014), 26–28.
32 College Board, "Trends in Higher Education: Average Net Price over Time for Full-Time Students, by Sector," 2017, https://trends.collegeboard.org/college-pricing/figures-tables/average-net-price-over-time-full-time-students-sector.
33 Caroline Hoxby and Christopher Avery, "The Missing 'One-Offs': The Hidden Supply of High-Achieving, Low Income Students," Brookings Papers on Economic Activity, Brookings Institution, Spring 2013.
34 Putnam, *Our Kids*, 187, 189.
35 Susan Goldberger, "Doing the Math, What It Means to Double the Number of Low-Income College Graduates," in *Minding the Gap: Why Integrating High School with College Makes Sense and How to Do It*, eds. Nancy Hoffman, Joel Vargas, Andrea Venezia and Marc. S. Miller (Cambridge, MA: Harvard Education Press, 2007). See also Robin Chait and Andrea Venezia, "Improving Academic Preparation for College," Center for American Progress, January 2009.
36 Michael N. Bastedo and Ozan Jaquette, "Running in Place: Low-Income Students and the Dynamics of Higher Education Stratification," *Educational Evaluation and Policy Analysis* 33, no. 3 (2011): 318–339; Susan Dynarski, "Rising Inequality in Postsecondary Education," Brookings Social Mobility Memos, Brookings Institution, February 13, 2014; Sean Reardon, "Education," in *State of Union: The Poverty and Inequality Report*, Stanford Center on Poverty and Inequality, 2014, https://inequality.stanford.edu/sites/default/files/Pathways_SOTU_2014.pdf.
37 Raj Chetty, John N. Friedman, Emmanuel Saez, Nicholas Turner and Danny Yagan, "Mobility Report Cards: The Role of Colleges in Intergenerational Mobility," NBER Working Paper 23618, National Bureau of Economic Research, December 2016; and Lawrence H. Summers and Rachel Lipson, "Revisiting Harvard and the American Dream," *Washington Post*, November 8, 2017.
38 Karin Fisher, "Engine of Inequality," *Chronicle of Higher Education*, January 17, 2016. See also Richard V. Reeves, *Dream Hoarders: How the American Upper Middle Class Is Leaving Everyone Else in the Dust, Why That Is a Problem and What to Do About It* (Washington, DC: Brookings Institution Press, 2017).
39 Pew Charitable Trusts, "Pursuing the American Dream: Economic Mobility Across Generations," July 9, 2011, http://www.pewtrusts.org/en/research-and-analysis/reports/0001/01/01/pursuing-the-american-dream. Some researchers using different data and methodology get lower numbers. See Leila Bengali and Mary Daly, "U.S. Economic Mobility: The Dream and the Data." FRBSF Economic Letter 2013–06, Federal Reserve Bank of San Francisco, March 4, 2013.
40 Raj Chetty, David Grusky, Maximilian Hell, Nathaniel Hendren, Robert Manduca and Jimmy Narang, "The Fading American Dream: Trends in Absolute Income Mobility Since 1940," NBER Working Paper 22910, National Bureau of Economic Research, December 2016.

41 Miles Corak, "Income Inequality, Equality of Opportunity, and Inter-generational Mobility," IZA Discussion Paper No. 7520, Institute of Labor Economics, Bonn, Germany, July 2013. See also Miles Corak, Matthew J. Lindquist and Bhashkar Mazumder, "A Comparison of Upward and Downward Intergenerational Mobility in Canada, Sweden and the United States," *Labor Economics* 30 (2014): 185–200.

42 Daniel Aaronson and Bhashkar Mazumder, "Intergenerational Economic Mobility in the U.S., 1940 to 2000," Working Paper 2005–12, Federal Reserve Bank of Chicago, February 2007. See also Bhashkar Mazumder, "Upward Intergenerational Economic Mobility in the United States," Economic Mobility Project, Pew Charitable Trusts, August 7, 2008.

43 Richard V. Reeves and Isabel Sawhill, "Social Mobility: A Promise That Could Still Be Kept," *Milken Institute Review,* July 15, 2016.

44 Markus Jäntti, Bernt Bratsberg, Knut Röed, Oddbjørn Raaum, Robin Naylor, Eva Österbacka, Anders Bjørklund and Tor Eriksson, "American Exceptionalism in a New Light: A Comparison of Intergenerational Earnings Mobility in the Nordic Countries, the United Kingdom and the United States," IZA Discussion Paper No. 1938, Institute for the Study of Labor, Bonn, Germany, January 2006; and Corak, "Income Inequality, Equality of Opportunity, and Intergenerational Mobility."

45 Miles Corak, "Do Poor Children Become Poor Adults? Lessons for Public Policy from a Cross Country Comparison of Generational Earnings Mobility," IZA Discussion Paper 1993, Institute for the Study of Labor, Bonn, Germany, March 2006.

46 Chetty et al., "The Fading American Dream."

47 Alan B. Krueger, "The Rise and Consequences of Inequality in the United States" (speech, Center for American Progress, July 12, 2012). See in particular the reference to the Great Gatsby curve.

48 Stuart Butler, "Social Norms and Cultural Mobility," Brookings Institution, February 24, 2014; see also J. D. Vance's best-selling book, *Hillbilly Elegy: A Memoir of a Family and Culture in Crisis* (New York: HarperCollins, 2016).

49 Bowles, Gintis and Groves, eds., *Unequal Chances.*

50 David J. Hardin, Christopher Jencks, Leonard M. Lopoo and Susan E. Mayer, "The Changing Effect of Family Background on the Incomes of American Adults," in *Unequal Chances,* Bowles, Gintis and Groves, eds.

51 Adam Swift, "Justice, Luck and the Family: The Intergenerational Transmission of Economic Advantage from a Normative Perspective," in *Unequal Chances,* Bowles, Gintis and Groves, eds.

52 See the writing of Ronald Dworkin and John Roemer.

53 Daniel Bell, "On Meritocracy and Equality," *Public Interest,* Fall 1972; James Coleman, "Equal Schools or Equal Students?" *Public Interest,* Summer 1966. See also Dylan Matthews, "The Case Against Equality of Opportunity," *VOX,* September 21, 2015, https://www.vox.com/2015/9 /21/9334215/equality-of-opportunity.

4: Fairness and Growth—A False Choice

1 Gary Becker, "The Transformation of the Kibbutz and the Rejection of Socialism," Becker-Posner Blog, August 2, 2007, http://www.becker -posner-blog.com/2007/09/the-transformation-of-the-kibbutz-and-the -rejection-of-socialism-becker.html.

2 Arthur M. Okun, *Equality and Efficiency: The Big Tradeoff* (Washington, DC: Brookings Institution Press, 1975).

3 Arthur Laffer, *The Laffer Curve: Past, Present and Future*, Heritage Foundation, June 1, 2004, https://www.heritage.org/taxes/report/the-laffer -curve-past-present-and-future.

4 Richard Freeman and Alex Gelber, "Prize Structure and Information in Tournaments: Experimental Evidence," *American Economic Journal: Applied Economics* 2, no. 1 (2010): 149–164.

5 Jacob Hacker, "The Institutional Foundations of Middle Class Democracy," *Policy Network*, May 2011, http://www.policy-network.net/pno _detail.aspx?ID=3998.

6 For reviews of the literature, see Robert McClelland and Shannon Mok, "A Review of Recent Research on Labor Supply Elasticities," Working Paper 2012-12, Congressional Budget Office, October 2012; and Emmanuel Saez, Joel Slemrod and Seth Giertz, "The Elasticity of Taxable Income with Respect to Marginal Tax Rates: A Critical Review," *Journal of Economic Literature* 50, no. 1 (2012): 3–50.

7 Adam Smith, *The Theory of Moral Sentiments* (London: Penguin Books, 2009; reprint of 1759 ed.), pt. 1, sect. 3, ch. 1.

8 Adam Smith, *The Wealth of Nations* (New York: Barnes and Noble, 2004; reprint of 1776 edition), vol. 1, ch. 8.

9 Alain Cohn, Ernst Fehr and Lorenz Goette, "Fair Wages and Effort Provision: Combining Evidence from the Lab and the Field," working paper, University of Zurich Department of Economics, January 2013, http:// ssrn.com/abstract=2201602; George A. Akerlof and Janet L. Yellen, "The Fair Wage-Effort Hypothesis and Unemployment," *Quarterly Journal of Economics* 105, no. 2 (1990): 255–283; Zeynep Ton, *The Good Jobs Strategy: How the Smartest Companies Invest in Employees to Lower Costs and Boost Profits* (Seattle: New Harvest, 2014); James W. Hesford, "Do Higher Wages Pay for Themselves? An Intra-Firm Test of the Effect of Wages on Employee Performance," December 2014, http://hdl.handle.net /10945/46668.

10 Matt Bloom, "The Performance Effects of Pay Dispersion on Individuals and Organizations," *Academy of Management Journal* 42, no. 1 (1999): 25–40.

11 Mike Mondello and Joel Maxcy, "The Impact of Salary Dispersion and Performance Bonuses in NFL Organizations," *Management Decision* 47, no. 1 (2009): 110–123.

12 Keith Payne, *The Broken Ladder: How Inequality Affects the Way We Think, Live, and Die* (New York: Viking Press, 2017).

13 Douglas M. Cowherd and David I. Levin, "Product Quality and Pay Equity Between Lower-Level Employees and Top Management: An Investigation of Distributive Justice Theory," *Administrative Science Quarterly* 37, no. 2 (1992): 302–320.

14 Economic Policy Institute, "The Productivity-Pay Gap," October 2017, https://www.epi.org/productivity-pay-gap/. See also Josh Bivens and Lawrence Mishel, "Understanding the Historic Divergence Between Productivity and a Typical Worker's Paw," Economic Policy Institute, September 2, 2015, https://www.epi.org/publication/understanding -the-historic-divergence-between-productivity-and-a-typical-workers -pay-why-it-matters-and-why-its-real/.

15 Elise Gould, "Why America's Workers Need Faster Wage Growth—and What We Can Do About It," EPI Briefing Paper 382, Economic Policy Institute, August 27, 2014, https://www.epi.org/publication/why-americas -workers-need-faster-wage-growth/.

16 Lawrence Summers, "The Age of Secular Stagnation: What It Is and What to Do About It," *Foreign Affairs*, February 15, 2016.

17 Pew Research Center, "Top Frustrations with Tax System: Sense That Corporations, Wealthy Don't Pay Fair Share," April 14, 2017, http:// www.people-press.org/2017/04/14/top-frustrations-with-tax-system -sense-that-corporations-wealthy-dont-pay-fair-share/.

18 Eleanor Krause and Isabel Sawhill, "What We Know and Don't Know About Declining Labor Force Participation: A Review," Brookings Institution, May 2017, https://www.brookings.edu/wp-content/uploads /2017/05/ccf_20170517_declining_labor_force_participation_sawhill1 .pdf.

19 John Mackey and Raj Sisodia, *Conscious Capitalism: Liberating the Heroic Spirit of Business* (Cambridge, MA: Harvard Business Review Press, 2014).

20 Gallup Consulting, "State of the American Workplace: 2008–2010," September 22, 2012, http://www.gallup.com/services/177077/state -american-workplace-2008-2010-pdf.aspx.

21 See Michael Porter and Mark Kramer, "Creating Shared Value," *Harvard Business Review*, January/February 2011; and Alex Bryson and Richard Freeman, "Profit Sharing Boosts Employee Productivity and Satisfaction," *Harvard Business Review*, December 13, 2016.

22 Hilary Williamson Hoynes and Diane Whitmore Schanzenbach, "Work Incentives and the Food Stamp Program," NBER Working Paper 16198, National Bureau of Economic Research, July 2010; Brian A. Jacob and Jens Ludwig, "The Effects of Housing Assistance on Labor Supply: Evidence from a Voucher Lottery," *American Economic Review* 102, no. 1 (2012): 272–304; and Katherine Baicker, Amy Finkelstein, Jae Song and Sarah Taubman, "The Impact of Medicaid on Labor Force Activity and Program Participation: Evidence from the Oregon Health Insurance Experiment," NBER Working Paper 19547, National Bureau of Economic Research, October 2013.

23 For a review of the literature, see Robert Moffitt, "Welfare Programs and Labor Supply," NBER Working Paper 9168, National Bureau of Economic Research, September 2002; Nada Eissa and Hilary Hoynes, "Behavioral Responses to Taxes: Lessons from the EITC and Labor Supply," NBER Working Paper 11729, National Bureau of Economic Research, November 2005; and McClelland and Mok, "A Review of Recent Research on Labor Supply Elasticities."

24 Christina Fong, Samuel Bowles and Herbert Gintis, "Reciprocity and the Welfare State," in *Handbook of the Economics of Giving, Altruism and Reciprocity*, eds. Jean Mercier-Ythier and Serge Kolm (Amsterdam: Elsevier, 2006), https://ssrn.com/abstract=565801; Christina M. Fong, "Evidence from an Experiment on Charity to Welfare Recipients: Reciprocity, Altruism and the Empathetic Responsiveness Hypothesis," *Economic Journal* 117, no. 522 (2007): 1008–1024; and Hugh Heclo, "The Political Foundations of Antipoverty Policy," in *Fighting Poverty: What Works and What Doesn't*, eds. Sheldon H. Danziger and Daniel H. Weinberg (Cambridge, MA: Harvard University Press, 1986).

25 Alec MacGillis, "Who Turned My Blue State Red?" *New York Times*, November 20, 2015, https://www.nytimes.com/2015/11/22/opinion/sunday/who-turned-my-blue-state-red.html?_r=0. See also J. D. Vance, *Hillbilly Elegy: A Memoir of a Family and Culture in Crisis* (New York: HarperCollins, 2016); and Justin Gest, *The New Minority: Working Class Whites in an Era of Immigration and Inequality* (Oxford: Oxford University Press, 2016).

26 Elise Gould, Alyssa Davis and Will Kimble, "Broad-Based Wage Growth Is the Key Tool in the Fight to Reduce Poverty," EPI Briefing Paper 399, Economic Policy Institute, Washington, DC, May 20, 2015, https://www.epi.org/publication/broad-based-wage-growth-is-a-key-tool-in-the-fight-against-poverty/. See also Jared Bernstein, "Poverty and Inequality, in Charts," *New York Times*, January 13, 2014; and Sheldon H. Danziger, "Fighting Poverty Revisited: What Did Researchers Know 40 Years Ago? What Do We Know Today?" *Focus* 25, no. 1 (2007).

27 Karen Dynan, Jonathan Skinner and Stephen Zeldes, "Do the Rich Save More?" *Journal of Political Economy* 112, no. 2 (2004).

28 Federal Reserve Bank of St. Louis, "Shares of Gross Domestic Product: Gross Private Domestic Investment: Fixed Investment: Nonresidential," July 28, 2017, https://fred.stlouisfed.org/series/A008RE1Q156NBEA.

29 Joseph W. Gruber and Steven B. Kamin, "Corporate Buybacks and Capital Investment: An International Perspective," International Finance Discussion Paper Note, Board of Governors of the Federal Reserve System, April 2017. See also William Lazonick, "Stock Buybacks: From Retain-and-Reinvest to Downsize-and-Distribute," Brookings Institution, April 2015; and William Lazonick, "Profits Without Prosperity," *Harvard Business Review*, September 2014.

30 George Psacharopoulos and Harry Anthony Patrinos, "Returns to Investment in Education: A Further Update," *Education Economics* 12, no. 2 (2004); also George Psacharopoulos, "The Value of Investment in Education: Theory, Evidence and Policy," *Journal of Education Finance* 32, no. 2 (2006): 113–136. For a more critical view, see Bryan Caplan, *The Case Against Education: Why the Education System Is a Waste of Time and Money* (Princeton, NJ: Princeton University Press, 2017).

31 Organisation for Economic Co-operation and Development, "Population with Tertiary Education," doi: 10.1787/0b8f90e9-en.

32 Federal Reserve Bank of New York, "Quarterly Report on Household Debt and Credit," May 2017, https://www.newyorkfed.org/medialibrary/interactives/householdcredit/data/pdf/HHDC_2017Q1.pdf.

33 Raghuram Rajan, *Fault Lines: How Hidden Fractures Still Threaten the World Economy* (Princeton, NJ: Princeton University Press, 2010), 9.

34 Barry Cynamon and Steven Fazzari, "Inequality and Household Finance During the Consumer Age," Working Paper No. 752, Levy Economics Institute of Bard College, February 2013. See also Michael Kumhof and Romain Rancière, "Inequality, Leverage and Crises," IMF Working Paper 10/268, International Monetary Fund, November 2010; and Branko Milanovic, *The Haves and the Have-Nots: A Brief and Idiosyncratic History of Global Inequality* (New York: Basic Books, 2011).

35 Luigi Zingales, "Does Finance Benefit Society?" NBER Working Paper 20894, National Bureau of Economic Research, January 2015. See also Kumhof and Rancière, "Inequality, Leverage and Crises."

36 Michael Konczal, "Frenzied Financialization," *Washington Monthly*, November/December 2014.

37 Thomas Philippon and Ariell Reshef, "Wages and Human Capital in the U.S. Finance Industry: 1909–2006," *Quarterly Journal of Economics* 127, no. 4 (2012): 1551–1609.

38 Kevin Murphy, Andrei Shleifer and Robert Vishny, "The Allocation of Talent: Implications for Growth," *Quarterly Journal of Economics* 106, no. 2 (1991): 503–530.

39 Stephen Cecchetti and Enisse Kharroubi, "Reassessing the Impact of Finance on Growth," BIS Working Paper No. 381, Bank of International Settlements, Basel, Switzerland, July 2012.

40 William Domhoff, "Wealth, Income and Power," Who Rules America? (blog), September 2005 (updated April 2017), https://www2.ucsc.edu/whorulesamerica/power/wealth.html; Jonathan D. Ostry, Andrew Berg and Charalambos G. Tsangarides, "Redistribution, Inequality and Growth," IMF Discussion Note 14/02, International Monetary Fund, February 2014; Andrew G. Berg and Jonathan D. Ostry, "Inequality and Unsustainable Growth: Two Sides of the Same Coin," IMF Staff Discussion Note 11/08, International Monetary Fund, April 8, 2011.

41 Anna Malinovskaya and David Wessel, "The Hutchins Center Explains: Public Investment," Brookings Institution, January 3, 2017, https://www.brookings.edu/blog/up-front/2017/01/03/the-hutchins-center-explains-public-investment/.

42 Congressional Budget Office, "The Macroeconomic and Budgetary Effects of Federal Investment," June 2016, https://www.cbo.gov/sites/default/files/114th-congress-2015-2016/reports/51628-Federal_Investment.pdf.

43 American Society of Civil Engineers, "2017 Infrastructure Scorecard," 2017, https://www.infrastructurereportcard.org.

44 Committee for a Responsible Federal Budget, "How Fast Can the Economy Grow?" May 18, 2017, http://www.crfb.org/papers/how-fast-can-america-grow.

45 Wan Jie and Thierry Ehrmann, "The Art Market in 2014," artprice.com, 2015.

46 Scott Reyburn, "Christie's Has Art World's First $1 Billion Week," *New York Times*, May 14, 2015.

47 Keeneland, "Keeneland Sales Summaries," http://flex.keeneland.com/summaries/summaries.html.

48 Statista, "National Football League Average Franchise Value from 2000 to 2017," 2018, https://www.statista.com/statistics/193435/average -franchise-value-in-the-nfl-since-2000.

49 *New York Times*, "A Duplex at One57 for $91.5 Million," April 17, 2015; see also Trulia Market Trends, "Real Estate Data for New York," https:// www.trulia.com/real_estate/New_York-New_York/market-trends/.

50 Center for Responsive Politics, "Cost of Election," https://www.opensecrets .org/overview/cost.php?display=T&infl=N.

51 Center for Responsive Politics, "Lobbying Database," https://www .opensecrets.org/lobby/.

52 Jane Mayer, *Dark Money: The Hidden History of the Billionaires Behind the Rise of the Radical Right* (New York: Doubleday, 2016).

53 Congressional Budget Office, "The Distribution of Household Income and Federal Taxes, 2013," June 2016, https://www.cbo.gov/sites/default/files /114th-congress-2015-2016/reports/51361-householdincomefedtaxes.pdf.

54 Tax Policy Center, "Distributional Analysis of the Conference Agreement for the Tax Cut and Jobs Act," December 18, 2017, http://www .taxpolicycenter.org/publications/distributional-analysis-conference -agreement-tax-cuts-and-jobs-act/full.

55 See Jacob S. Hacker and Paul Pierson, *Winner-Take-All Politics: Public Policy, Political Organization, and the Precipitous Rise of Top Incomes in the United States* (New Haven, CT: Yale University Press, 2010).

56 Martin Gilens and Benjamin I. Page, "Testing Theories of American Politics: Elites, Interest Groups, and Average Citizens," *Perspectives on Politics* 12, no. 3 (2014): 564–581; and Benjamin I. Page, Lawrence Bartels and Jason Seawright, "Democracy and the Policy Preferences of Wealthy Americans," *Perspectives on Politics* 11, no. 1 (2013): 51–73.

57 Luigi Zingales, foreword to the 2014 edition of *A Capitalism for the People: Recapturing the Lost Genius of American Prosperity* (New York: Basic Books, 2012).

58 Brink Lindsey and Steven Teles, *The Captured Economy: How the Powerful Become Richer, Slow Down Growth and Increase Inequality* (Oxford: Oxford University Press, 2017).

59 Thomas Mann and Norman Ornstein, *It's Even Worse Than It Looks: How the American Constitutional System Collided with the New Politics of Extremism* (New York: Basic Books, 2012).

60 Nolan McCarty, Keith T. Poole and Howard Rosenthal, "Political Polarization and Income Inequality," Princeton University and Russell Sage Foundation, January 27, 2003; Howard Rosenthal, Keith T. Poole and Nolan McCarty, *Polarized America: The Dance of Ideology and Unequal Riches* (Cambridge, MA: MIT Press, 2006).

61 Thomas B. Edsall, *The Age of Austerity: How Scarcity Will Remake American Politics* (New York: Anchor Books, 2012).

62 Paul Taylor, "The Demographic Trends Shaping American Politics in 2016 and Beyond," Pew Research Center, January 27, 2016, http://www .pewresearch.org/fact-tank/2016/01/27/the-demographic-trends -shaping-american-politics-in-2016-and-beyond/.

63 John Voorheis, Nolan McCarty and Boris Shor, "Unequal Incomes, Ideology and Gridlock: How Rising Inequality Increases Political Polarization,"

working paper, August 31, 2015; John V. Duca and Jason L. Saving, "Income Inequality and Political Polarization: Time Series Evidence over Nine Decades," Working Paper 1408, Federal Reserve Bank of Dallas, January 2014; Michael Barber and Nolan McCarty, "Causes and Consequences of Polarization," in *Solutions to Political Polarization in America*, ed. Nathaniel Persily (Cambridge: Cambridge University Press, 2015).

64 Daron Acemoglu and James A. Robinson, *Why Nations Fail: The Origins of Power, Prosperity, and Poverty* (New York: Crown Publishing Group, 2012); and Daron Acemoglu, Simon Johnson and James A. Robinson, "Institutions as the Fundamental Cause of Long-Run Growth," in *Handbook of Economic Growth*, vol. 1A, eds. Philippe Aghion and Steven N. Durlauf (Amsterdam: Elsevier, 2005).

65 Robert M. Solow, "But Verify," *New Republic*, September 11, 1995.

66 Emanuele Ferragina, "Social Capital and Equality: Tocqueville's Legacy: Rethinking Social Capital in Relation with Income Inequalities," *Tocqueville Review* 31, no. 1 (2010): 73–98.

67 Eric D. Gould and Alexander Hijzen, "Growing Apart, Losing Trust? The Impact of Inequality on Social Capital," IMF Working Paper 16/176, International Monetary Fund, August 2016; Guglielmo Barone and Sauro Mocetti, "Inequality and Trust: New Evidence from Panel Data," *Economic Inquiry* 52, no. 2 (2016): 794–809; Jean M. Twenge, W. Keith Campbell and Nathan T. Carter, "Declines in Trust in Others and Confidence in Institutions Among American Adults and Late Adolescents, 1972–2012," *Psychological Science* 25, no. 10 (2014); Magnus Gustavsson and Henrik Jordahl, "Inequality and Trust in Sweden: Some Inequalities Are More Harmful Than Others," *Journal of Public Economics* 92, no. 1–2 (February 2008): 348–365; Bo Rothstein and Eric M. Uslander, "All for All: Equality, Corruption and Social Trust," *World Politics* 58 (2005): 41–72; Alberto Alesina and Eliana La Ferrara, "Who Trusts Others?" *Journal of Public Economics* 85 (2002): 207–234.

68 Richard Wilkinson and Kate Pickett, *The Spirit Level: Why Greater Equality Makes Societies Stronger* (New York: Bloomsbury Press, 2010), 195.

69 Barone and Morcetti, "Inequality and Trust."

70 Gould and Hijzen, "Growing Apart, Losing Trust?"

71 Yann Algan and Pierre Cahuc, "Trust, Growth and Well-Being: New Evidence and Policy Implications," Discussion Paper No. 7464, Institute for the Study of Labor, Bonn, Germany, June 2013. See also Stephen Knack and Philip Keefer, "Does Social Capital Have an Economic Payoff? A Cross-Country Investigation," *Quarterly Journal of Economics* 112, no. 4 (1997): 1251–1288; Luigi Guiso, Paola Sapienza and Luigi Zingales, "Does Culture Affect Economic Outcomes?" NBER Working Paper 11999, National Bureau of Economic Research, January 2006; Guido Tabellini, "The Scope of Cooperation: Values and Incentives," CESIFO Working Paper No. 2236, Center for Economic Studies, Munich, Germany, February 2008.

72 Luigi Guiso, Paola Sapienza and Luigi Zingales, "The Role of Social Capital in Financial Development," *American Economic Review* 94, no. 3 (2004): 526–556.

73 Ron E. Hall and Charles I. Jones, "Why Do Some Countries Produce So Much More Output Per Worker Than Others?" *Quarterly Journal of Economics* 114, no. 1 (1999): 83–116.

74 Federico Cingano and Paolo Pinotti, "Trust, Firm Organization and the Structure of Production," Paolo Baffi Centre Research Paper No. 2012–133, Paolo Baffi Centre, Milan, Italy, December 1, 2012; and Nicholas Bloom, Raffaella Sadun and John Van Reenen, "Americans Do IT Better: US Multinationals and the Productivity Miracle," *American Economic Review* 102, no. 1 (2012): 167–201.

75 Sandra Black and Lisa Lynch, "How to Compete: The Impact of Workplace Practices and Information Technology on Productivity," *Review of Economics and Statistics* 83, no. 3 (2001): 434–445.

76 Francis Fukuyama, *Trust: Human Nature and the Reconstitution of Social Order* (New York: Free Press, 1996).

77 Ostry, Berg and Tsangarides, "Redistribution, Inequality and Growth"; Berg and Ostry, "Inequality and Unsustainable Growth"; Dan Andrews, Christopher Jencks and Andrew Leigh, "Do Rising Top Incomes Lift All Boats?" *B.E. Journal of Economic Analysis and Policy* 11, no. 1 (2011); and Scott Winship, "Inequality Does Not Reduce Prosperity: A Compilation of the Evidence Across Countries," Manhattan Institute, October 29, 2014, https://www.manhattan-institute.org/html/inequality -does-not-reduce-prosperity-compilation-evidence-across-countries -6032.html.

78 See Benjamin Friedman, *The Moral Consequences of Economic Growth* (New York: Vintage Books, 2006). Friedman demonstrates that the best antidote to rising income inequality is stronger growth.

79 Winship, "Inequality Does Not Reduce Prosperity."

80 Organisation for Economic Co-operation and Development, "In It Together: Why Less Inequality Benefits All," Paris, May 21, 2015, http:// www.oecd.org/social/in-it-together-why-less-inequality-benefits-all -9789264235120-en.htm.

81 International Monetary Fund, "Tackling Inequality," IMF Fiscal Monitor, October 2017, http://www.imf.org/en/Publications/FM/Issues /2017/10/05/fiscal-monitor-october-2017.

5: A Better Capitalism

1 Edward Conard, *Unintended Consequences: Why Everything You've Been Told About the Economy Is Wrong* (New York: Portfolio, 2012).

2 Michael J. Sandel, *What Money Can't Buy: The Moral Limits of Markets* (New York: Farrar, Straus and Giroux, 2012); and Robert Reich, *Saving Capitalism: For the Many, Not the Few* (New York: Knopf, 2015).

3 Kenneth P. Vogel and Isaac Arnsdorf, "The Politico 100: Billionaires Dominate 2016," *Politico*, February 8, 2016, https://www.politico.com /story/2016/02/100-billionaires-2016-campaign-finance-218862.

4 See Robert G. Kaiser, *So Damn Much Money: The Triumph of Lobbying and the Corrosion of American Government* (New York: Knopf, 2009); Jane Mayer, *Dark Money: The Hidden History of the Billionaires Behind the Rise of the Radical Right* (New York: Doubleday, 2016); Benjamin I. Page,

Larry M. Bartels and Jason Seawright, "Democracy and the Policy Preferences of Wealthy Americans," *Perspectives on Politics* 11, no. 1 (2013): 51–73; Thomas Mann and Norman Ornstein, *It's Even Worse Than It Looks: How the American Constitutional System Collided with the New Politics of Extremism* (New York: Basic Books, 2012); Mike Lofgren, *The Party Is Over: How Republicans Went Crazy, the Democrats Became Useless and the Middle Class Got Shafted* (New York: Penguin, 2012); and Mike Lofgren, *The Deep State: The Fall of the Constitution and the Rise of Shadow Government* (New York: Viking, 2016).

5 Gregory Mitchell, Philip E. Tetlock, Barbara A. Mellers and Lisa D. Ordonez, "Judgments of Social Justice: Compromises between Equality and Efficiency," *Journal of Personality and Social Psychology* 65, no. 4 (1993): 629–639.

6 Herbert A. Simon, "UBI and the Flat Tax," *Boston Review*, October/November 2000, http://bostonreview.net/archives/BR25.5/simon.html; response to a previous article by Philippe Van Parijs, "A Basic Income for All," *Boston Review*, October/November 2000, http://bostonreview .net/archives/BR25.5/vanparijs.html.

7 See E. J. Dionne and Kayla Meltzer Drogosz, "United We Serve? The Debate over National Service," Brookings Institution, September 1, 2002, https://www.brookings.edu/articles/united-we-serve-the-debate -over-national-service/.

8 Bill Bishop, *The Big Sort: Why the Clustering of Like-Minded America Is Tearing Us Apart* (Boston: Houghton Mifflin Harcourt, 2009).

9 Sven E. Wilson and William Ruger, "Warriors Don't Bowl Alone: Military Service and Civic Participation," working paper, August 27, 2008, https://fhss.byu.edu/polsci/SiteAssets/pages/wilson/papers/home /Civic%20Participation.doc.pdf.

10 Jon Henley, "Money for Nothing: Is Finland's Universal Basic Income Trial Too Good to Be True?" *Guardian*, January 12, 2018; Jon Henley, "Finland Trials Basic Income for Unemployed," *Guardian*, January 3, 2017; Dylan Matthews, "This Kenyan Village Is a Laboratory for the Biggest Basic Income Experiment Ever," *VOX*, March 6, 2017, https:// www.vox.com/policy-and-politics/2017/3/6/14007230/kenya-basic -income-givedirectly-experiment-village; and Chris Weller, "Thousands of People in Kenya Are Getting Basic Income for 12 Years in an Experiment That Could Redefine Social Welfare Around the World," *Business Insider*, January 29, 2018, http://www.businessinsider.com/basic -income-study-kenya-redefining-nature-of-work-2018-1.

11 Raphael Minder, "Guaranteed Income for All? Switzerland's Voters Say No Thanks," *New York Times*, June 5, 2016.

12 Philippe Van Parijs and Yannick Vanderborght, *Basic Income: A Radical Proposal for a Free Society and a Sane Economy* (Cambridge, MA: Harvard University Press, 2017); Andy Stern and Lee Kravitz, *Raising the Floor: How a Universal Basic Income Can Renew Our Economy and Rebuild Our American Dream* (New York: PublicAffairs, 2010); and Chris Hughes, *Fair Shot: Rethinking Inequality and How We Earn* (New York: St. Martin's Press, 2018).

13 Annie Lowrey, *Give People Money: How a Universal Basic Income Would End Poverty, Revolutionize Work, and Remake the World* (New York: Crown Publishing Group, 2018); Dylan Matthews, "A Guaranteed Income for Every American Would Eliminate Poverty—And It Wouldn't Destroy the Economy," *VOX*, July 23, 2014, https://www.vox.com/2014/7/23 /5925041/guaranteed-income-basic-poverty-gobry-labor-supply.

14 United States Census Bureau, "Income and Poverty in the United States: 2016," September 12, 2017, https://www.census.gov/library /publications/2017/demo/p60-259.html.

15 Office of Tax Analysis, "Tax Expenditure for Exclusion of Capital Gains at Death," U.S. Department of the Treasury, August 2014, https://www.treasury.gov/resource-center/tax-policy/tax-analysis /Documents/Step-Up-Basis-2014.pdf; and Josh Bivens and Hunter Blair, "A Financial Transaction Tax Would Help Ensure Wall Street Works for Main Street," Economic Policy Institute, July 28, 2016, http:// www.epi.org/publication/a-financial-transaction-tax-would-help -ensure-wall-street-works-for-main-street/.

16 Dan Ariely, "Americans Want to Live in a Much More Equal Country (They Just Don't Realize it)," *The Atlantic*, August 2, 2012.

17 Douglas Kruse, Richard Freeman and Joseph Blasi, "Do Workers Gain by Sharing? Employee Outcomes Under Employee Ownership, Profit Sharing, and Broad-Based Stock Options," NBER Working Paper 14233, National Bureau of Economic Research, August 2008; also Richard Freeman, Joseph Blasi and Douglas Kruse, "Inclusive Capitalism for the American Workforce: Reaping the Rewards of Economic Growth Through Broad-Based Employee Ownership and Profit Sharing," Center for American Progress, March 2016.

18 Wanling Su and Rahul K. Goravara, "What Is a Dividend?" Yale Law and Economics Research Paper No. 531, June 2, 2016, http://dx.doi.org /10.2139/ssrn.2637929.

19 Douglas Kruse, "Does Employee Ownership Improve Performance?" *IZA World of Labor*, IZA Institute of Labor Economics, Bonn, Germany, December 2016, http://dx.doi.org/10.15185/izawol.311.

20 Joann Muller, "A Big Pay Day for Auto Workers as Ford, Chrysler Share the Wealth," *Forbes*, January 26, 2017; Brent Snavely, "GM Earns $9.43 Billion in 2016; UAW Workers Get Record Profit Sharing," *Detroit Free Press*, February 7, 2017.

21 For a more detailed discussion, see Lee C. Bollinger, "Educational Equity and Quality: Brown and Rodriguez and Their Aftermath" (speech, College Board Forum, November 3, 2003), http://www.collegeboard .com/prod_downloads/email/educationalequity.pdf.

22 See Charles J. Ogletree Jr. and Kimberly Jenkins Robinson, "Inequitable Schools Demand a Federal Remedy," in "Rodriguez Reconsidered: Is There a Federal Constitutional Right to Education?" *Education Next*, Spring 2017.

23 Ryan A. Decker, John Haltiwanger, Ron S. Jarmin and Javier Miranda, "Declining Business Dynamism: Implications for Productivity," Hutchins Center Working Paper #23, Brookings Institution, September 19, 2016;

Ryan A. Decker, John Haltiwanger, Ron S. Jarmin and Javier Miranda, "Where Has All the Skewness Gone? The Decline in High-Growth Young Firms in the U.S.," NBER Working Paper 21776, National Bureau of Economic Research, December 2015/January 2016; and Germán Gutiérrez and Thomas Philippon, "Investment-Less Growth: An Empirical Investigation," NBER Working Paper 22897, National Bureau of Economic Research, December 2016.

24 Jonathan B. Baker, "Beyond *Schumpeter vs. Arrow*: How Antitrust Fosters Innovation," *Antitrust Law Journal* 74, no. 3 (2007); also Jonathan B. Baker, "Market Power in the U.S. Economy Today," Washington Center for Equitable Growth, March 2017, http://equitablegrowth.org/research -analysis/market-power-in-the-u-s-economy-today/.

25 Steven C. Salop, "Invigorating Vertical Merger Enforcement," *Yale Law Journal*, forthcoming 2018, https://papers.ssrn.com/sol3/papers.cfm ?abstract_id=3052332.

26 Amazon's founder, Jeff Bezos, owns the *Washington Post*, where I have been an economics writer and columnist for many years.

27 Lina M. Khan, "Amazon's Antitrust Paradox," *Yale Law Journal* 126, no. 3 (2017): 564–907. See also Franklin Foer, *World Without Mind: The Existential Threat of Big Tech* (New York: Penguin Press, 2017).

28 Louis D. Brandeis, *Other People's Money: And How Bankers Use It* (New York: Frederick A. Stokes, 1914), https://archive.org/stream/otherpeoples mone00bran#page/n5/mode/2up.

29 Steven Pearlstein, "Occupy Wall Street? Just Defund It," *Washington Post*, December 1, 2012.

30 Another form of government-granted monopoly is the antitrust exemption extended to professional sports. One reason that professional athletes are able to earn millions of dollars each year, and owners able to reap hundreds of millions when selling their franchises, is the implicit or explicit antitrust exemption granted to Major League Baseball, the National Football League, the National Hockey League and the National Basketball Association. This exemption allows the leagues to earn monopoly rents in a variety of ways: by limiting the number of franchises; by negotiating exclusive contracts on behalf of all teams for broadcast rights and sales of sports paraphernalia; by negotiating a single contract with players' unions, limiting the competition among the teams and the players in the market for talent; and, most perniciously, by requiring that franchises be located only in cities where taxpayers agree to subsidize teams by building expensive stadiums in prime locations to the teams' exacting standards, and then lease them on ridiculously favorable terms at below-market prices. Government also helps out by allowing companies to deduct the cost of buying season tickets and club suites for owners, executives and employees—oh, and yes, the occasional customer—as a legitimate business expense.

    Forbes magazine calculates that professional sports now generate $75 billion a year in revenue that is split among team owners, coaches and players, which doesn't include the billions more in profit earned by the media networks and sportscasters who broadcast the games.

31 Brink Lindsey and Steven M. Teles, *The Captured Economy: How the Powerful Enrich Themselves, Slow Down Growth, and Increase Inequality* (Oxford: Oxford University Press, 2017).

32 Adam Liptak, "Justices, 9–0, Bar Patenting Human Genes," *New York Times*, June 13, 2013.

33 Lynn Stout, *The Shareholder Value Myth: How Putting Shareholders First Harms Investors, Corporations and the Public* (Oakland, CA: Berrett-Koehler Publishers, 2012).

34 Patrick Coffee, "Study: 83 Percent of Consumers 'Unsatisfied' by Relationships with Brands," *AdWeek*, October 15, 2014, http://www.adweek.com/digital/study-83-percent-of-consumers-unsatisfied-by-relationships-with-brands/; also "Will Consumers Pay More for Products from Socially Responsible Companies?" *Marketing Charts*, October 15, 2015, https://www.marketingcharts.com/brand-related-60166.

35 Cone Communications, "2016 Cone Communications Millennial Employee Engagement Study," 2016, https://static1.squarespace.com/static/56b4a7472b8dde3df5b7013f/t/5819e8b303596e3016ca0d9c/1478092981243/2016+Cone+Communications+Millennial+Employee+Engagement+Study_Press+Release+and+Fact+Sheet.pdf.

Index